R Graphs Cookbook

Second Edition

Over 70 recipes for building and customizing publication-quality visualizations of powerful and stunning R graphs

Jaynal Abedin

Hrishi V. Mittal

[PACKT] PUBLISHING open source
community experience distilled

BIRMINGHAM - MUMBAI

R Graphs Cookbook *Second Edition*

First published: January 2011

Second edition: October 2014

Production reference: 1211014

Published by Packt Publishing Ltd.
Livery Place
35 Livery Street
Birmingham B3 2PB, UK.

ISBN 978-1-78398-878-5

www.packtpub.com

Credits

Authors
Jaynal Abedin
Hrishi V. Mittal

Reviewers
Devangana
Vibhav Kamath
Kent Russell
Joshua F. Wiley

Commissioning Editor
Ashwin Nair

Acquisition Editor
Richard Brookes-Bland

Content Development Editor
Parita Khedekar

Technical Editor
Faisal Siddiqui

Copy Editors
Deepa Nambiar
Stuti Srivastava

Project Coordinator
Kartik Vedam

Proofreaders
Simran Bhogal
Stephen Copestake
Ameesha Green

Indexers
Mariammal Chettiyar
Monica Ajmera Mehta
Rekha Nair

Graphics
Disha Haria

Production Coordinators
Adonia Jones
Saiprasad Kadam
Alwin Roy

Cover Work
Alwin Roy

About the Authors

Jaynal Abedin currently holds the position of Senior Statistician at the Centre for Communicable Diseases (CCD) at icddr, b (`www.icddrb.org`). He attained his Bachelor's and Master's degrees in Statistics from University of Rajshahi, Rajshahi, Bangladesh. He has vast experience in R programming and Stata and has efficient leadership qualities. He has written an R package named *edeR: Email Data Extraction Using R,* which is available at CRAN (`http://cran.r-project.org/web/packages/edeR/index.html`). He is currently leading a team of statisticians. He has hands-on experience in developing training material and facilitating training in R programming and Stata along with statistical aspects in public health research. He has authored *Data Manipulation with R, Packt Publishing,* which got good reviews. His primary area of interest in research includes causal inference and machine learning. He is currently involved in several ongoing public health research projects and is a co-author of seven peer-reviewed scientific papers. Moreover, he engages in several work-in-progress manuscripts. He is also one of the reviewers of the following two journals:

- *Journal of Applied Statistics* (*JAS*)
- *Journal of Health Population and Nutrition* (*JHPN*)

Hrishi V. Mittal has been working with R for a few years in different capacities. He was introduced to the exciting world of data analysis with R when he was working as a senior air quality scientist at King's College, London, where he used R extensively to analyze large amounts of air pollution and traffic data for London's Mayor's Air Quality Strategy. He has experience in various other programming languages but prefers R for data analysis and visualization. He is also actively involved in various R mailing lists, forums, and the development of some R packages.

About the Reviewers

Devangana is a consultant and application developer at ThoughtWorks Inc., working on a range of exciting projects, primarily in the data analytics domain. She has over 4 years of experience in data analytics, social network analysis, machine learning, and information retrieval. She is also the founder of Women Who Code, Bengaluru. She holds a Master's degree in Theoretical Computer Science with specialization in Social Networks Analysis from PSG College of Technology, Coimbatore. In her spare time, she loves cooking and reading books, mostly in the History, Economics, and Social Sciences genres.

Vibhav Kamath holds a Master's degree in Industrial Engineering and Operations Research from Indian Institute of Technology, Bombay, and a Bachelor's degree in Electronics Engineering from College of Engineering, Pune. During his post graduation, he was intrigued with algorithms and mathematical modeling and has been involved in analytics since then. He is currently based out of Bangalore and works for an IT services firm. As a part of his job, he has developed statistical/mathematical models based on techniques such as optimization and linear regression using the R programming language. In the past, he has also handled data visualization and dashboarding for a leading global bank using platforms such as SAS, SQL, and Excel/VBA.

In the past, he has also worked in areas such as discrete event simulation and speech processing (both on MATLAB) as part of his academics. He likes building hobby projects in Python—one such project involves him working as a stock screener for the Indian stock market. He has also worked in the field of robotics in the past and built an autonomous robot called micromouse, which navigates through a maze. Apart from analytics and programming, Vibhav takes interest in reading and likes both fiction and nonfiction books. He plays table tennis in his free time, follows cricket and tennis, and likes solving puzzles (Sudoku, Kakuro) when really bored. You can get in touch with him through e-mail at `vibhav.kamath@hotmail.com` and on LinkedIn at `in.linkedin.com/in/vibhavkamath`).

Kent Russell works in finance as a portfolio manager in Birmingham, Alabama, and codes in R.

Joshua F. Wiley is a health researcher and senior analyst at Elkhart Group Ltd. As an analyst and statistical consultant, Joshua focuses on biostatistics and is interested in reproducible research and graphical displays of data and statistical models. Through his work at Elkhart Group Ltd., he has supported a wide array of clients, ranging from graduate students to experienced researchers and biotechnology companies.

www.PacktPub.com

Support files, eBooks, discount offers, and more

You might want to visit www.PacktPub.com for support files and downloads related to your book.

Did you know that Packt offers eBook versions of every book published, with PDF and ePub files available? You can upgrade to the eBook version at www.PacktPub.com and, as a print book customer, you are entitled to a discount on the eBook copy. Get in touch with us at service@packtpub.com for more details.

At www.PacktPub.com, you can also read a collection of free technical articles, sign up for a range of free newsletters, and receive exclusive discounts and offers on Packt books and eBooks.

http://PacktLib.PacktPub.com

Do you need instant solutions to your IT questions? PacktLib is Packt's online digital book library. Here, you can access, read, and search across Packt's entire library of books.

Why subscribe?

- ▸ Fully searchable across every book published by Packt
- ▸ Copy-and-paste, print, and bookmark content
- ▸ On-demand and accessible via web browsers

Free access for Packt account holders

If you have an account with Packt at www.PacktPub.com, you can use this to access PacktLib today and view nine entirely free books. Simply use your login credentials for immediate access.

Table of Contents

Preface

The open source statistical software, R, is one of the most popular choices among researchers from various fields. This software has the capability to produce high-quality graphics, and data visualization is one of the most important tasks in data science tracks. Through effective visualization, we can easily uncover the underlying pattern among variables without doing any sophisticated statistical analysis. In this cookbook, we have focused on graphical analysis using R in a very simple way with each independent example. We have covered the default R functionality along with more advanced visualization techniques such as lattice, ggplot2, and three-dimensional plots. Readers will not only learn the code to produce the graph but also learn why certain code has been written with specific examples.

What this book covers

Chapter 1, R Graphics, introduces the reader to the R graphic system, how R graphs work with default libraries, and also to the very recent revolution of lattice and ggplot2. Here, readers will get a flavor of what is going to be discussed in the subsequent chapters.

Chapter 2, Basic Graph Functions, introduces recipes for some basic types of graphs, useful in almost any kind of data analysis. We will go through all the steps to get you going from reading your data into R, making a first graph, tweaking it to suit your needs, and then saving and exporting it for use in presentations and publications.

Chapter 3, Beyond the Basics – Adjusting Key Parameters, looks more closely at various arguments to graph functions and their values, highlighting common pitfalls and workarounds. The par() function is explained with some useful examples, showing how to adjust colors, sizes, margins, and the styles of various graph elements such as points, lines, bars, axes, and titles. The subsequent chapters 3 to 9 cover the graph types introduced in the first two chapters in more detail.

Chapter 4, Creating Scatter Plots, has over a dozen recipes that cover scatter plots, some of the simplest and most commonly used types of graphs in data analysis. We will see how we can make more enhanced plots by adjusting various arguments and using some new functions.

Chapter 5, Creating Line Graphs and Time Series Charts, discusses some more intermediate to advanced recipes on customizing line graphs, improving and speeding up line graphs with multiple lines, processing dates to make time series charts, sparklines, and stock charts.

Chapter 6, Creating Bar, Dot, and Pie Charts, will show you how you can create many useful variations of bar graphs and dot plots by using only the base library functions. We will also look at a few recipes that address common criticisms of pie charts with some ways to make them more readable.

Chapter 7, Creating Histograms, enhances the basic histogram in R by changing the plotting mode and bins, in addition to style adjustments. We will also look at some advanced recipes that combine histograms with other types of graphs.

Chapter 8, Box and Whisker Plots, looks into various stylistic and structural adjustments to box plots. We will start by looking at some basic arguments to change individual aspects of a box plot and slowly move to more advanced recipes that involve the use of multiple function calls.

Chapter 9, Creating Heat Maps and Contour Plots, discusses various types of heat maps to visualize correlations, trends and multivariate data, and contour plots to show topographical information in various two- and three-dimensional ways.

Chapter 10, Creating Maps, builds on the introduction to visualizing data on geographical maps in the first chapter and covers recipes on plotting data from the World Bank, World Health Organization (WHO), Google Maps API, and some Geographical Information Systems (GIS).

Chapter 11, Data Visualization Using Lattice, contains various recipes to create the most common graphs using the lattice library. Lattice is one of the most popular data visualization libraries in R. This chapter contains 9 different recipes ranging from bar charts to distributional plots and empirical cumulative distribution.

Chapter 12, Data Visualization Using ggplot2, contains how we can create very high-quality data visualization using the concept of Grammar of Graphics. There are 8 different recipes to create the most common graphics. This chapter contains 1 special recipe where we discuss how to annotate a graph. The annotated graph contains an enormous amount of information. The recipe ranges from very basic graphics to advanced ones, where we show how we can incorporate layered graphs, such as a scatter plot embedded with the lowest and least square-fitted lines.

Chapter 13, Inspecting Large Datasets, contains recipes related to one of the newest concepts of finding patterns in large data through visualization. The recipes of this chapter show how to create nice graphs that tell us a story about the pattern of relationship among variables.

Chapter 14, Three-dimensional Visualizations, has most of its recipes centered on creating three-dimensional graphics ranging from scatter plots to density estimations. In this chapter, we also include how to create three-dimensional scatter plots with an estimated linear plane.

Chapter 15, Finalizing Graphs for Publications and Presentations, discusses some tricks and tips to add some polish to our graphs so that they can be used for publication and presentation. We will cover many important practical topics such as exported graph file formats, high resolution formats, vector formats such as PDF, SVG, and PS, mathematical and scientific notations, text descriptions, fonts, graph templates, and themes.

What you need for this book

The readers of this book need to have some knowledge on basic R programming along with basic knowledge on statistical analysis and graphics. Though most of the graphs discussed in this book are very common and easy to understand, there are some recipes where readers need to have statistical knowledge. All of the examples in this book have been created with R Version 3.0.2, so readers can reproduce all of the examples with this version or higher. However, it's possible that, if a reader uses a lower version, most of the examples will still run but not all.

Who this book is for

This recipe book is targeted at those reader groups who are already exposed to R programming and want to learn effective graphics with the power of R and its various libraries.

Conventions

In this book, you will find a number of styles of text that distinguish between different kinds of information. Here are some examples of these styles, and an explanation of their meaning.

Code words in text, database table names, folder names, filenames, file extensions, pathnames, dummy URLs, user input, and Twitter handles are shown as follows: "We also set the plot title using the `main` argument."

A block of code is set as follows:

```
install.packages("openair")
library(openair)
```

New terms and **important words** are shown in bold. Words that you see on the screen, in menus or dialog boxes for example, appear in the text like this: "By default, the data is in ascending order of total points scored by each player (as can be seen from the light to dark blue progression in the **Total Points** column)."

Warnings or important notes appear in a box like this.

Tips and tricks appear like this.

Reader feedback

Feedback from our readers is always welcome. Let us know what you think about this book—what you liked or may have disliked. Reader feedback is important for us to develop titles that you really get the most out of.

To send us general feedback, simply send an e-mail to feedback@packtpub.com, and mention the book title via the subject of your message.

If there is a topic that you have expertise in and you are interested in either writing or contributing to a book, see our author guide on www.packtpub.com/authors.

Customer support

Now that you are the proud owner of a Packt book, we have a number of things to help you to get the most from your purchase.

Downloading the example code

You can download the example code files for all Packt books you have purchased from your account at http://www.packtpub.com. If you purchased this book elsewhere, you can visit http://www.packtpub.com/support and register to have the files e-mailed directly to you.

Errata

Although we have taken every care to ensure the accuracy of our content, mistakes do happen. If you find a mistake in one of our books—maybe a mistake in the text or the code—we would be grateful if you would report this to us. By doing so, you can save other readers from frustration and help us improve subsequent versions of this book. If you find any errata, please report them by visiting `http://www.packtpub.com/submit-errata`, selecting your book, clicking on the **errata submission form** link, and entering the details of your errata. Once your errata are verified, your submission will be accepted and the errata will be uploaded on our website, or added to any list of existing errata, under the Errata section of that title. Any existing errata can be viewed by selecting your title from `http://www.packtpub.com/support`.

Piracy

Piracy of copyright material on the Internet is an ongoing problem across all media. At Packt, we take the protection of our copyright and licenses very seriously. If you come across any illegal copies of our works, in any form, on the Internet, please provide us with the location address or website name immediately so that we can pursue a remedy.

Please contact us at `copyright@packtpub.com` with a link to the suspected pirated material.

We appreciate your help in protecting our authors, and our ability to bring you valuable content.

Questions

You can contact us at `questions@packtpub.com` if you are having a problem with any aspect of the book, and we will do our best to address it.

1
R Graphics

R provides a number of well-known facilities that produce a variety of graphs to meaningfully visualize data. It has low-level facilities where we deal with basic shapes to draw graphs and high-level facilities. There are functions available here to produce quality graphs; these functionalities are usually developed using certain combinations of basic shapes. Using R, we can produce traditional plots, the trellis plot, and very high-level graphs inspired by the Grammar of Graphics implemented in the ggplot2 package. The default graphics package is useful for traditional plots, lattice provides facilities to produce trellis graphs, and the ggplot2 package is the most powerful high-level graphical tool in R. Other than these, there are low-level facilities that draw basic shapes, and arranging the shapes in their relative position is an important step in order to create meaningful data visualization. In this chapter, we will introduce both low-level graphics (also known as base graphics) and high-level graphics using different packages. Particularly, the content of this chapter will be as follows:

- ▸ Base graphics using the default package
- ▸ Trellis graphs using lattice
- ▸ Graphs inspired by Grammar of Graphics

Base graphics using the default package

It is well known that R has very powerful data visualization capabilities. The primary reason behind the powerful graphical utility of R is the low-level graphical environment. The `grid` graphic system of R makes data visualization much more flexible and intuitive. With the help of the `grid` package, we can draw very basic shapes that can be arranged to produce interesting data visualizations. There are functions in the `grid` graphics system that draw very basic shapes of a high-level data visualization, including lines, rectangles, circles, and texts along with some other functions that specify where to put which part of the visualization. Through the use of the basic function, we can easily produce components of high-level graphs, such as a rectangle, rounded rectangle, circle, line, and arrow. We will now see how we can produce these basic shapes. In a single visualization, we will show you all the output from the following code snippet:

```
# Calling grid library
library(grid)

# Creating a rectangle
grid.rect(height=0.25,width=0.25)

# A rounded rectangle
grid.roundrect(height=0.2,width=0.2)

# A circle
grid.circle(r=0.1)

# Inserting text within the shape
grid.text("R Graphics")
# Drawing a polygon
grid.polygon()
```

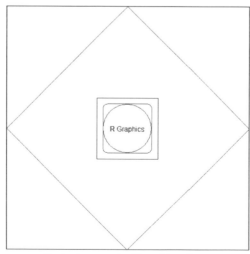

Basic shapes using the grid package

For any high-level visualization, we can use the basic shapes and arrange them as required. Now, we will list some of the functions for high-level data visualization where the basic shapes have been used:

- ▸ `plot`: This is a generic function that is used to plot any kind of objects. Most commonly, we use this function for x-y plotting

- ▸ `barplot`: This function is used to produce a horizontal or vertical bar plot

- ▸ `boxplot`: This is used to produce a box-whisker plot

- ▸ `pie`: This is used to produce a pie chart

- ▸ `hist`: This is used to produce a histogram

- ▸ `dotchart`: This is used to produce cleveland dot plots

- ▸ `image`, `heatmap`, `contour`, and `persp`: These functions are used to generate image-like plots

- ▸ `qqnorm`, `qqline`, and `qqplot`: These functions are used to produce plots in order to compare distributions

We will provide specific recipes for each of these functions in the subsequent chapters.

Trellis graphs using lattice

Though grid graphics have much more flexibility than trellis graphs, it is a bit difficult to use them from the point of view of general users. The `lattice` package enhances the data visualization capability of R through relatively easy code in order to produce much more complex graphs. This allows the user to produce multivariate visualization. The `lattice` package could be considered as a high-level data visualization tool that is able to produce structured graphics with the flexibility to adjust the graphs as required.

The traditional R graphics system has much more flexibility to produce any kind of data visualization with control over each and every component. However, it is still a difficult task for an inexperienced R programmer to produce efficient graphs. In other words, we can say that the traditional graphic system of R is not so user friendly. It would be good if the user could have complete high-level graphics with the use of minimal written code. To address this shortcoming, Trellis graphics have been implemented in S. The inspired `lattice` add-on package is the add-on package that provides similar capabilities for R users. One of the important features of the lattice graphics system is the formula interface. During data visualization, we can intuitively use the formula interface to produce conditional plots, which is difficult in a traditional graphics system.

For example, say we have a dataset with two variables, an incubation period, and the exposure category of a certain disease. This dataset contains one numeric variable, the incubation period itself, and another discrete variable with four possible values: 1, 2, 3, or 4. We want to produce a histogram for each exposure category. The following code snippet shows you the traditional code:

```
# data generation

# Set the seed to make the example reproducible
set.seed(1234)
incubation_period <- c(rnorm(100,mean=10),rnorm(100,mean=15),rnorm(100
,mean=5),rnorm(100,mean=20))
exposure_cat <- sort(rep(c(1:4),100))
dis_dat<-data.frame(incubation_period,exposure_cat)


# Producing histogram for each of the exposure category 1, 2, 3, and 4
# using traditional visualization code. The code below for
# panel histogram for different values of the variable
# exposure_cat. This code will produce a 2 x 2 matrix where
# we will have four different histograms.
op<-par(mfrow=c(2,2))
hist(dis_dat$incubation_period[dis_dat$exposure_cat==1])
hist(dis_dat$incubation_period[dis_dat$exposure_cat==2])
hist(dis_dat$incubation_period[dis_dat$exposure_cat==3])
hist(dis_dat$incubation_period[dis_dat$exposure_cat==4])
par(op)
```

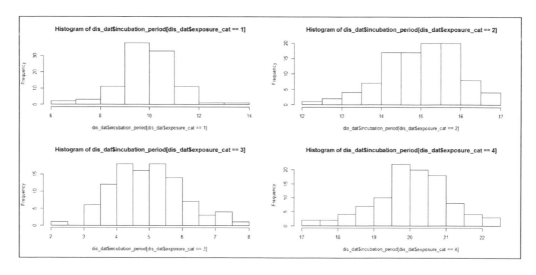

The following code snippet shows you the lattice implementation for the same histogram:

```
library(lattice)
histogram(~incubation_period | factor(exposure_cat), data=dis_dat)
```

In this lattice version of the code, it is much more intuitive to write the entire code to produce a histogram using the formula interface. The code that follows the ~ symbol contains the name of the variable that we are interested in to produce the histogram, and then we specify the grouping variable. The ~ symbol acts like the **of** preposition, for example, the histogram of the incubation period. The vertical bar is used to represent the panel variable over which we are going to repeat the histogram. Notice that we have used the factor command here to specify the grouping variable. If we do not specify the factor, then we will not be able to distinguish which plot corresponds to which category. The `factor()` command creates text labels. If the variable was left as a numeric value, it would show low to high values as though it were a continuous scale rather than discrete categories, as shown in the following figure:

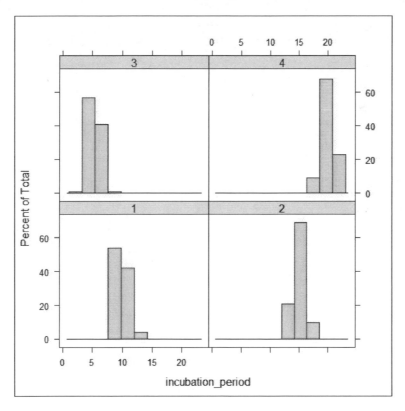

Now, if we change the code's formula part and use a plot generic function instead of the histogram, then the visualization will be changed as follows:

```
plot(incubation_period ~ factor(exposure_cat), data=dis_dat)
```

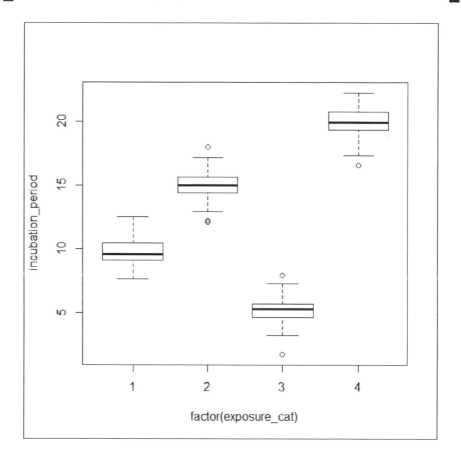

If we change the code further and just omit the factor function, then the same visualization will be turned into a scatter plot as follows:

```
plot(incubation_period ~ exposure_cat, data=dis_dat)
```

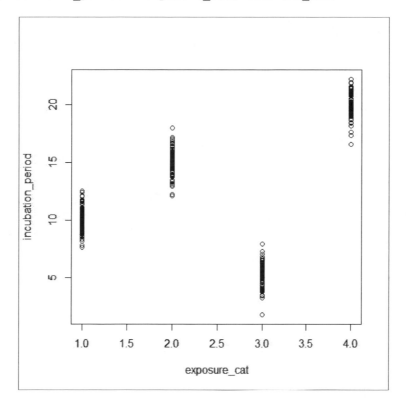

The `plot()` function is a generic function. If we put two numeric variables inside this function, it produces a scatter. On the other hand, if we use one numeric variable and another factor variable, then it produces a boxplot of the numeric variable for each unique value of the factor variable.

Graphs inspired by Grammar of Graphics

The `ggplot2` R package is based on *The Grammar of Graphics* by Leland Wilkinson, *Springer*). Using this package, we can produce a variety of traditional graphics, and the user can produce their customized graphs as well. The beauty of this package is in its layered graphics facilities; through the use of layered graphics utilities, we can produce almost any kind of data visualization. Recently, `ggplot2` has become the most searched keyword in the R community, including the most popular R blog (`www.r-bloggers.com`). The comprehensive theme system allows the user to produce publication quality graphs with a variety of themes of their choice. If we want to explain this package in a single sentence, then we can say that if whatever we can think about data visualization can be structured in a data frame, the visualization is a matter of few seconds.

In *Chapter 12, Data Visualization Using ggplot2*, on `ggplot2` , we will see different examples and use themes to produce publication quality graphs. However, in this introductory chapter, we will show you one of the important features of the `ggplot2` package that produces various types of graphs. The main function is `ggplot()`, but with the help of a different `geom` function, we can easily produce different types of graphs, such as the following:

- ▸ `geom_point()`: This will create a scatter plot
- ▸ `geom_line()`: This will create a line chart
- ▸ `geom_bar()`: This will create a bar chart
- ▸ `geom_boxplot()`: This will create a box plot
- ▸ `geom_text()`: This will write certain text inside the plot area

Now, we will see a simple example of the use of different `geom` functions with the default `mtcars` dataset in R:

```
# loading ggplot2 library
library(ggplot2)
# creating a basic ggplot object
p <- ggplot(data=mtcars)
# Creating scatter plot of mpg and disp variable
p1 <- p+geom_point(aes(x=disp,y=mpg))
# creating line chart from the same ggplot object but different
# geom function
p2 <- p+geom_line(aes(x=disp,y=mpg))
# creating bar chart of mpg variable
p3 <- p+geom_bar(aes(x=mpg))
# creating boxplot of mpg over gear
p4 <- p+geom_boxplot(aes(x=factor(gear),y=mpg))
# writing certain text into the scatter plot
p5 <- p1+geom_text(x=200,y=25,label="Scatter plot")
```

The visualization of the preceding five plots will look like the following figure:

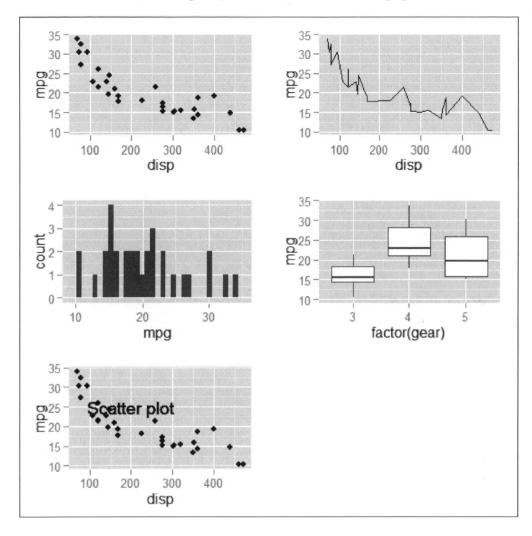

Basic Graph Functions

2

In this chapter, we will cover the following recipes:

- ► Creating scatter plots
- ► Creating line graphs
- ► Creating bar charts
- ► Creating histograms and density plots
- ► Creating box plots
- ► Adjusting *x* and *y* axes limits
- ► Creating heat maps
- ► Creating pairs plots
- ► Creating multiple plot matrix layouts
- ► Adding and formatting legends
- ► Creating graphs with maps
- ► Saving and exporting graphs

Introduction

In this chapter, we will see how to use R to make some very basic types of graphs, which can be used in almost any kind of analysis. The recipes in this chapter will give you a feel for how much can be accomplished with very little R code, which is one big reason why R is a good choice for an analysis platform.

Although the examples in this chapter are of a basic nature, we will go through all the steps to get you going from reading your data into R, making the first graph, tweaking it to suit your needs, and then saving and exporting it for use in presentations and publications.

First and foremost, you need to download and install R on your computer. All R packages are hosted on the **Comprehensive R Archive Network** or **CRAN** (`http://cran.r-project.org/`). R is available for all the three major operating systems at the following locations on the Web:

- ▶ Windows: `http://cran.r-project.org/bin/windows/base/`
- ▶ Linux: `http://cran.r-project.org/bin/linux/`
- ▶ Mac OS X: `http://cran.r-project.org/bin/macosx/`

 Read the FAQs (`http://cran.r-project.org/faqs.html`) and manuals (`http://cran.r-project.org/manuals.html`) on the CRAN website for detailed help on installation.

Just having the basic installation of R should set you up for all the recipes in this book.

Note that the R code in this book has some comments explaining the code. Any text on a line following the # symbol is treated by R as a comment. For example, you might see something like this:

```
col="yellow" #Setting the color to yellow
```

As you can see clearly, the text after the # explains what the code is doing, that is, setting the color to yellow in this case. Comments are a way of documenting code so that others reading your code can understand it better. It also serves to help you, and you can also understand your code better when you come back to it after a long period of time. Read each line of code carefully, and look out for any comments that will help you understand the code better.

Creating basic scatter plots

This recipe describes how to make scatter plots using some very simple commands. We'll go from a single line of code, which makes a scatter plot from preloaded data, to a script of few lines that produces a scatter plot customized with colors, titles, and axes limits specified by us.

Getting ready

All you need to do to get started is start R. You should have the R prompt on your screen as shown in the following screenshot:

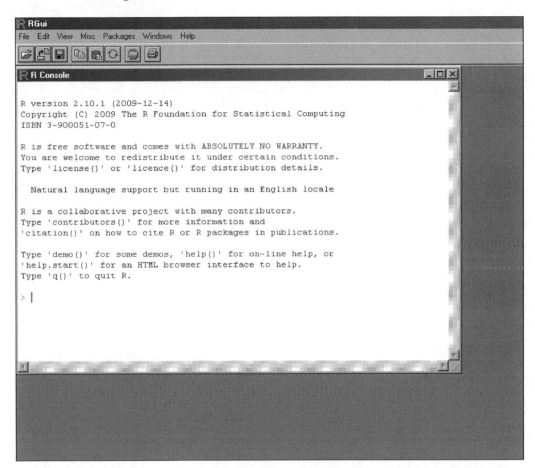

How to do it...

Let's use one of R's built-in datasets called `cars` to look at the relationship between the speed of cars and the distances taken to stop the cars (recorded in the 1920s).

To make your first scatter plot, type the following command in the R prompt:

```
plot(cars$dist~cars$speed)
```

This should bring up a window with the following graph that shows the relationship between the distance travelled by cars plotted with their speeds:

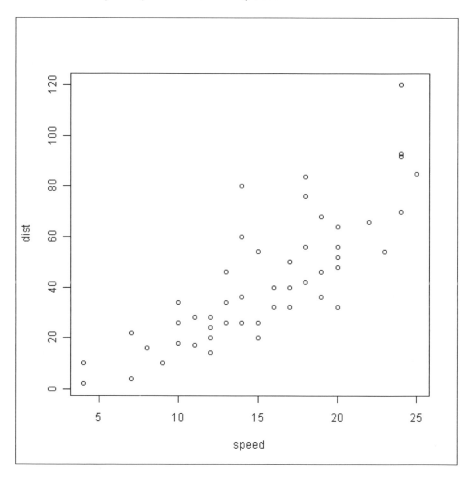

Now, let's tweak the graph to make it look better. Type the following code in the R prompt:

```
plot(cars$dist~cars$speed, # y~x
main="Relationship between car distance & speed", # Plot Title
xlab="Speed (miles per hour)", #X axis title
ylab="Distance travelled (miles)", #Y axis title
xlim=c(0,30), #Set x axis limits from 0 to 30
ylim=c(0,140), #Set y axis limits from 0 to 140
xaxs="i", #Set x axis style as internal
yaxs="i", #Set y axis style as internal
col="red", #Set the color of plotting symbol to red
pch=19) #Set the plotting symbol to filled dots
```

This should produce the following result:

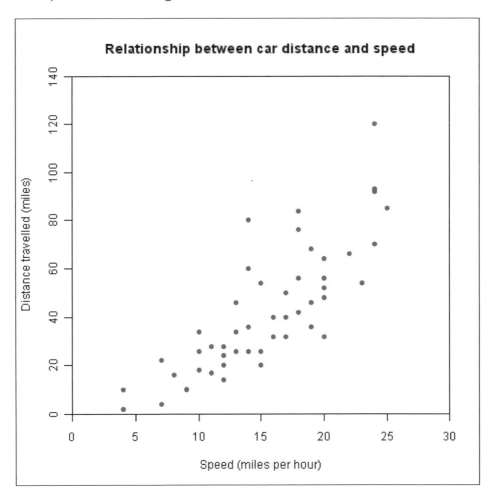

How it works...

R comes preloaded with many datasets. In the example, we used one such dataset called `cars`, which has two columns of data, with the names `speed` and `dist`. To see the data, simply type `cars` in the R prompt and press the *Enter* key:

```
>cars
     speed   dist
1        4      2
2        4     10
3        7      4
4        7     22
 . . .
47      24     92
48      24     93
49      24    120
50      25     85
>
```

As the output from the R command line shows, the cars dataset has 2 columns and 50 rows of data.

The `plot()` command is the simplest way to make scatter plots (and other types of plots, as we'll see in a moment). In the first example, we simply pass the `x` and `y` arguments that we want to plot in the `plot(y~x)` form, that is, we want to plot distance versus speed. This produces a simple scatter plot. In the second example, we pass a few additional arguments that provide R with more information on how we want the graph to look.

The `main` argument sets the plot title; `xlab` and `ylab` set the *x* and *y* axes titles, respectively; `xlim` and `ylim` set the minimum and maximum values of the labels on the *x* and *y* axes, respectively; `xaxs` and `yaxs` set the style of the axes; and `col` and `pch` set the scatter plot symbol color and type, respectively. All of these arguments and more are explained in detail in *Chapter 3, Beyond the Basics – Adjusting Key Parameters*.

There's more...

Instead of the `plot (y~x)` notation used in the preceding examples, you can also use `plot (x,y)`. For more details on all the arguments the `plot ()` command can take, see the help documentation by typing in `?plot` or `help (plot)` at the R prompt, after plotting the first dataset with `plot ()`.

If you want to plot another set of points on the same graph, say from another dataset or the same data points but with another symbol on top, you can use the `points ()` function:

```
points (cars$dist~cars$speed,pch=3)
```

A note on R's built-in datasets

In addition to the cars dataset used in the example, R has many more datasets, which come as part of the base installation in a package called datasets. To see the complete list of available datasets, call the `data ()` function simply by running it at the R prompt:

```
data ()
```

See also

Scatter plots are covered in a lot more detail in *Chapter 4, Creating Scatter Plots*.

Creating line graphs

Line graphs are generally used to look at trends in data over time, so the x variable is usually time expressed as time of day, date, month, year, and so on. In this recipe, we will see how we can quickly plot such data using the same `plot ()` function that was used in the previous recipe to make scatter plots.

Getting ready

First, we need to load the `dailysales.csv` example data file (you can download this file from the code download section of the book's companion website):

```
sales<-read.csv("dailysales.csv", header=TRUE)
```

As the file's name suggests, it contains daily sales data of a product. It has two columns: a date column and a sales column that shows the number of units sold.

How to do it...

Here's the code to make your first line graph:

```
plot(sales$units~as.Date(sales$date,"%d/%m/%y"),
type="l", #Specify type of plot as l for line
main="Unit Sales in the month of January 2010",
xlab="Date",
ylab="Number of units sold",
col="blue")
```

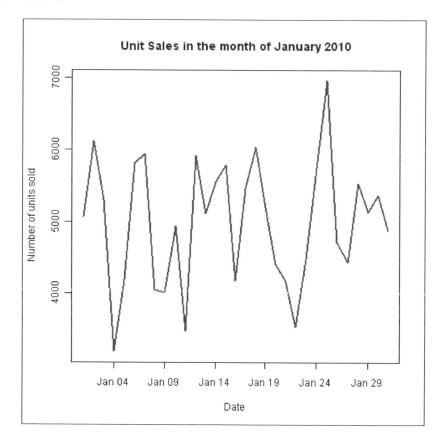

How it works...

We first read the data file using the `read.csv()` function. We passed two arguments to the function: the name of the file we want to read (`dailysales.csv` in double quotes) and `header=TRUE` where we specified that the first row contains column headings. We read the contents of the file and saved it in an object called `sales` with the left arrow notation.

You must have noticed that the plotting code is quite similar to that for producing a scatter plot. The main difference is that this time, we passed the `type` argument. The `type` argument tells the `plot()` function whether you want to plot points, lines, or other symbols. It can take nine different values.

 See the help section on `plot()` for more details. The default value of type is `"p,"` that is, points.

If the type is not specified, R assumes that you want to plot points as it did in the scatter plot example.

The most important part of the example is the way we read the date using the `as.Date()` function. Reading dates in R is a bit tricky. R doesn't automatically recognize date formats. The `as.Date()` function takes two arguments: the first is the variable that contains the date values and the second is the format the date values are stored in. In the example, the dates are in the date/month/year or dd/mm/yyyy format, which we specified as `%d/%m/%y` in the function call. If the date was in the mm/dd/yyyy format, we'd use `%m/%d/%y`.

The plot and axes titles and line color are set using the same arguments as for a scatter plot.

There's more...

If you want to plot another line on the same graph, say daily sales data of a second product, you can use the `lines()` function:

```
lines(sales$units2~as.Date(sales$date,"%d/%m/%y"),
col="red")
```

See also

Line graphs and time series charts are covered in depth in *Chapter 5, Creating Line Graphs and Time Series Charts*.

Creating bar charts

In this recipe, we will learn how to make bar plots that are useful to visualize summary data across various categories, such as sales of products or results of elections.

Getting ready

First, we need to load the `citysales.csv` example data file (you can download this file from the code download section of the book's companion website):

```
sales<-read.csv("citysales.csv",header=TRUE)
```

How to do it...

Just like the `plot()` function we used to make scatter plots and line graphs in the earlier recipes, the `barplot()` and `dotchart()` functions are part of the base graphics library in R. This means that we don't need to install any additional packages or libraries to use these functions.

We can make bar plots using the `barplot()` function as follows:

```
barplot(sales$ProductA,
names.arg= sales$City,
col="black")
```

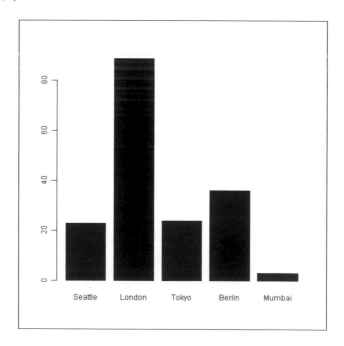

The default setting of orientation for bars is vertical. To change the bars to horizontal, use the `horiz` argument (by default, it is set to `FALSE`):

```
barplot(sales$ProductA,
names.arg= sales$City,
horiz=TRUE,
col="black")
```

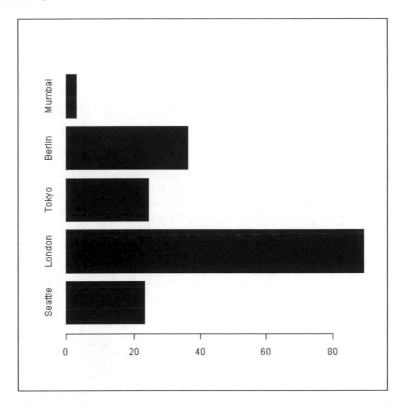

How it works...

The first argument of the `barplot()` function is either a vector or matrix of values that you want to plot as bars, such as the sales data variables in our previous examples. The labels for the bars are specified by the `names.arg` argument, but we use this argument only when plotting single bars. In the example with sales figures for multiple products, we didn't specify `names.arg`. R automatically used the product names as the labels and we had to instead specify the city names as the legend.

As with the other types of plots, the `col` argument is used to specify the color of the bars. This is a common feature throughout R, and `col` is used to set the color of the main feature in any kind of graph.

There's more...

Bar plots are often used to compare the values of groups of values across categories. For example, we can plot the sales in different cities for more than one product using the `beside` argument:

```
barplot(as.matrix(sales[,2:4]), beside=TRUE,
legend=sales$City,
col=heat.colors(5),
border="white")
```

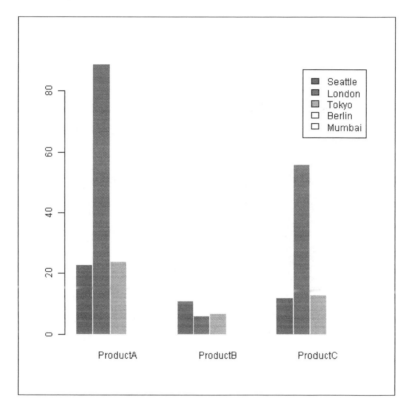

You will notice that when plotting data for multiple products (columns), we used the square bracket notation in the `sales[,2:4]` form. In R, the square bracket notation is used to refer to specific columns and rows of a dataset. For example, `sales[2,3]` refers to the value in the second row and third column.

So, the notation is of the `sales[row,column]` form. If you want to refer to all the rows in a certain column, you can omit the row number. For example, if you want to refer to all the rows in column 2, you would use `sales[,2]`. Similarly, for all the columns of row 3, you would use `sales[3,]`.

So, `sales[,2:4]` refers to all the data in columns 2 to 4, which is the product sales data as shown:

City	ProductA	ProductB	ProductC
San Francisco	23	11	12
London	89	6	56
Tokyo	24	7	13
Berlin	36	34	44
Mumbai	3	78	14

The orientation of bars is set to vertical by default. It is controlled by the optional `horiz` (for horizontal) argument. If we do not use this argument in our `barplot()` function call, it is set to `FALSE`. To make the bars horizontal, we set `horiz` to `TRUE`.

The `beside` argument is used to specify whether we want the bars in a group of data to be stacked or adjacent to each other. By default, `beside` is set to `FALSE`, which produces a stacked bar graph. To make the bars adjacent, we set `beside` to `TRUE`.

To change the color of the border around the bars, we used the `border` argument. The default border color is black. However, if you wish to use another color, say white, you can set it with `border="white"`.

To make the same graph with horizontal bars, we will type:

```
barplot(as.matrix(sales[,2:4]), beside=TRUE,
legend=sales$City,
col=heat.colors(5),
border="white",
horiz=TRUE)
```

See also

Bar charts are explored in a lot more detail with some advanced recipes in *Chapter 6, Creating Bar, Dot, and Pie Charts*.

Creating histograms and density plots

In this recipe, you will learn how to make histograms and density plots, which are useful to look at the distribution of values in a dataset.

How to do it...

The simplest way to demonstrate the use of a histogram is to show a normal distribution:

```
hist(rnorm(1000))
```

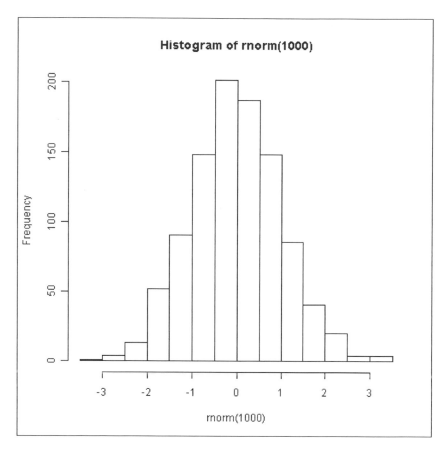

Another example of a histogram is one that shows a skewed distribution:

```
hist(islands)
```

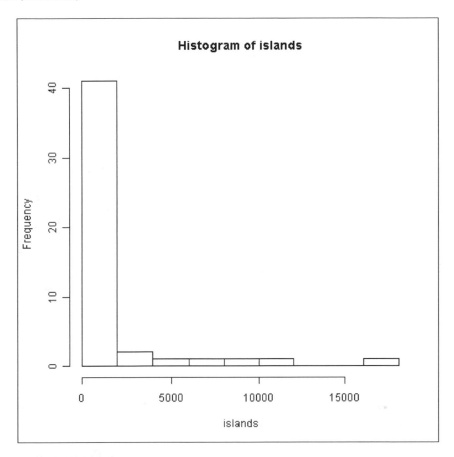

How it works...

The `hist()` function is also a function of R's base graphics library. It takes only one compulsory argument, that is, the variable whose distribution of values we wish to visualize.

In the first example, we passed the `rnorm()` function as the variable. The `rnorm(1000)` function generates a vector of 1000 random numbers with a normal distribution. As you can see in the histogram, it's a bell-shaped curve.

In the second example, we passed the built-in islands dataset (which gives the areas of the world's major landmasses) as the argument to `hist()`. As you can see from these histograms, islands has a distribution skewed heavily towards the lower value range of 0 to 2000 square miles.

There's more...

As you might have noticed in the preceding examples, the default setting for histograms is to display the frequency or number of occurrences of values in a particular range on the *y* axis. We can also display probabilities instead of frequencies by setting the `prob` (for probability) argument to `TRUE` or the `freq` (for frequency) argument to `FALSE`.

Now, let's make a density plot for the same function, `rnorm()`. To do so, we need to use the `density()` function and pass it as our first argument to `plot()` as follows:

```
plot(density(rnorm(1000)))
```

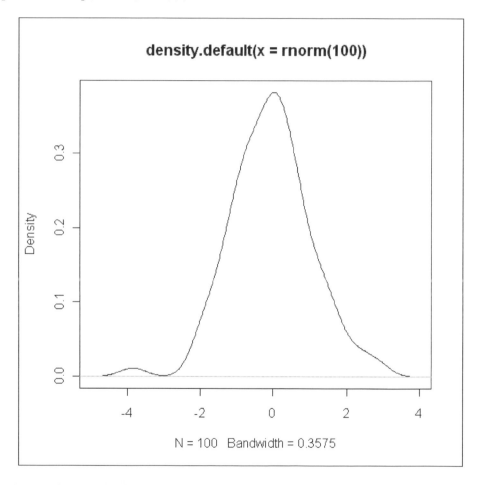

See also

We cover more details such as setting the breaks, density, formatting of bars, and other advanced recipes in *Chapter 7, Creating Histograms*.

Creating box plots

In this recipe, you will learn how to make box plots that are useful in comparing the spread of values in different measurements.

Getting ready

First, we need to load the `metals.csv` example data file that contains measurements of metal concentrations in London's air (you can download this file from the code download section of the book's companion website):

```
metals<-read.csv("metals.csv",header=TRUE)
```

How to do it...

We can make a box plot to summarize the metal concentration data using the `boxplot()` command as follows:

```
boxplot(metals,
xlab="Metals",
ylab="Atmospheric Concentration in ng per cubic metre",
main="Atmospheric Metal Concentrations in London")
```

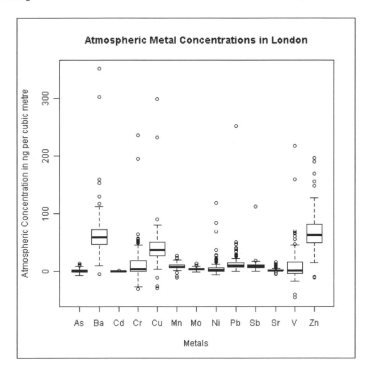

How it works...

The main argument, the `boxplot()` function, takes a set of numeric values (in the form of a vector or data frame). In our first example, we used a dataset containing numerical values of air pollution data from London. The dark line inside the box for each metal represents the median of values for that metal. The bottom and top edges of the box represent the first and third quartiles, respectively. Thus, the length of the box is equal to the interquartile range (IQR, which is the difference between first and third quartiles). The maximum length of a whisker is a multiple of the IQR, (the default multiplier is approximately 1.5). The ends of the whiskers are at data points closest to the maximum length of the whisker.

All the points lying beyond these whiskers are considered outliers.

As with most other plot types, the common arguments such as `xlab`, `ylab`, and `main` can be used to set the titles for the x and y axes and the graph itself, respectively.

There's more...

We can also make another type of box plot where we can group the observations by categories. For example, if we want to study the spread of copper concentrations by the source of the measurements, we can use a formula to include the source. First, we need to read the `copper_site.csv` example data file, as follows:

```
copper<-read.csv("copper_site.csv",header=TRUE)
```

Then, we can add the following code:

```
boxplot(copper$Cu~copper$Source,
xlab="Measurement Site",
ylab="Atmospheric Concentration of Copper in ng per cubic metre",
main="Atmospheric Copper Concentrations in London")
```

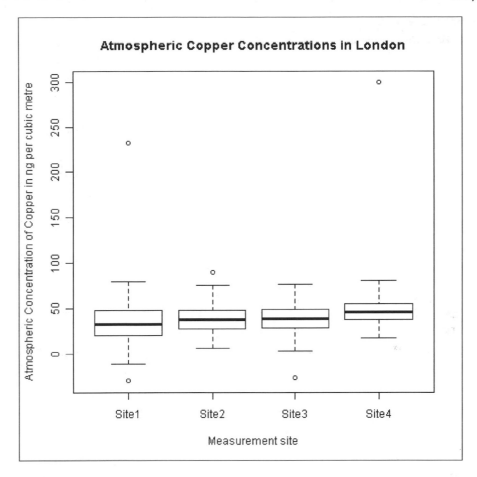

In this example, the `boxplot()` function takes a formula as an argument. This formula, which is in the `value~group` form (`Cu~source`), specifies a column of values and the group of categories it should be summarized over.

See also

More detailed box plot recipes are presented in *Chapter 8, Box and Whisker Plots*.

Adjusting x and y axes' limits

In this recipe, we will learn how to adjust the x and y limits of plots, which is useful in adjusting a graph to suit your presentation needs and adding additional data to the same plot.

How to do it...

We will modify our first scatter plot example to demonstrate how to adjust axes limits:

```
plot(cars$dist~cars$speed,
xlim=c(0,30),
ylim=c(0,150))
```

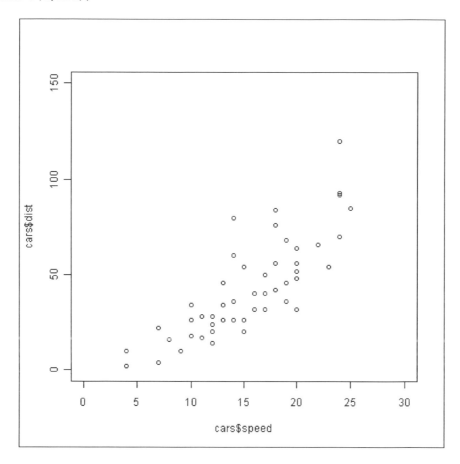

How it works...

In our original scatter plot in the first recipe of this chapter, the x axis limits were set to just below 5 up to 25 and the y axis limits were set from 0 to 120. In this example, we set the x axis limits from 0 to 30 and the y axis limits to 0 to 150 using the xlim and ylim arguments, respectively.

Both `xlim` and `ylim` take a vector of length 2 as valid values in the `c(minimum,maximum)` form, that is, `xlim=c(0,30)` means set the x axis minimum limit to 0 and maximum limit to 30.

There's more...

You might have noticed that even after setting the x and y limit values, there is a gap left at either edge. The two axes' zeroes don't coincide. This is because R automatically adds some additional space at both edges of the axes so that if there any data points at the extremes, they are not cut off by the axes. If you wish to set the axes limits to exact values, in addition to specifying `xlim` and `ylim`, you must also set the `xaxs` and `yaxs` arguments to `"i"`:

```
plot(cars$dist~cars$speed,
xlim=c(0,30),
ylim=c(0,150),
xaxs="i",
yaxs="i")
```

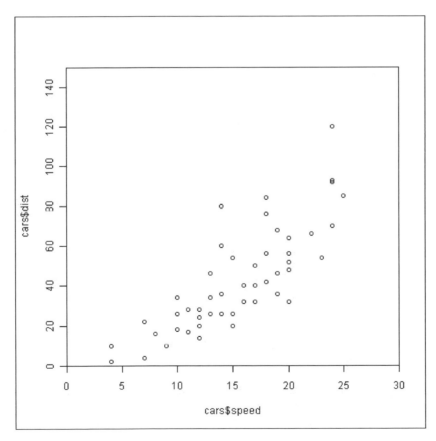

Sometimes, we might wish to reverse a data axis, say, to plot the data in the descending order along one axis. All we have to do is swap the minimum and maximum values in the vector argument supplied as `xlim` or `ylim`. So, if we want the x axis speed values in the preceding graph in the descending order, we need to set `xlim` to `c(30,0)`:

```
plot(cars$dist~cars$speed,
xlim=c(30,0),
ylim=c(0,150),
xaxs="i",
yaxs="i")
```

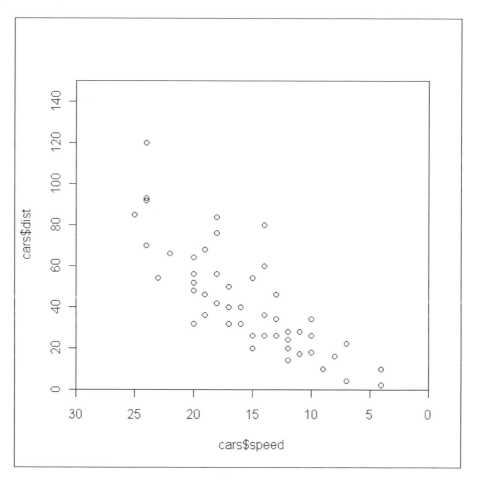

See also

There are a few more recipes on adjusting the axes tick marks and labels in *Chapter 3, Beyond the Basics – Adjusting Key Parameters*.

Creating heat maps

Heat maps are colorful images that are very useful to summarize a large amount of data by highlighting hotspots or key trends in the data.

How to do it...

There are a few different ways to make heat maps in R. The simplest is to use the `heatmap()` function in the base library:

```
heatmap(as.matrix(mtcars),
Rowv=NA,
Colv=NA,
col = heat.colors(256),
scale="column",
margins=c(2,8),
main = "Car characteristics by Model")
```

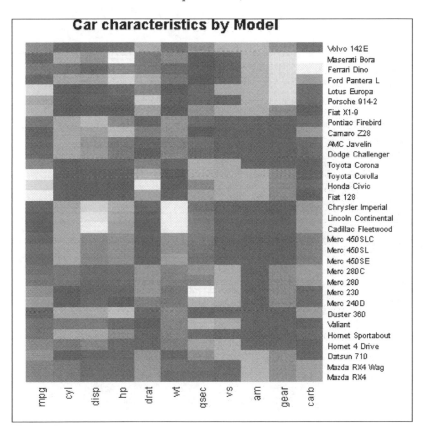

How it works...

The example code has a lot of arguments, so it might look difficult at first sight. However, if we consider each argument in turn, we can understand how it works. The first argument to the `heatmap()` function is the dataset. We are using the built-in dataset `mtcars`, which holds data such as fuel efficiency (`mpg`), number of cylinders (`cyl`), weight (`wt`), and so on for different models of cars. The data needs to be in a matrix format, so we use the `as.matrix()` function. `Rowv` and `Colv` specify whether and how dendrograms should be displayed to the left and top of the heat map.

> See `help(dendrogram)` and `http://en.wikipedia.org/wiki/Dendrogram` for details on dendrograms.

In our example, we suppress them by setting the two arguments to `NA`, which is a logical indicator of a missing value in R. The scale argument tells R in which direction the color gradient should apply. We have set it to column, which means the scale for the gradient will be calculated on a per-column basis.

There's more...

Heat maps are very useful to look at correlations between variables in a large dataset. For example, in bioinformatics, heat maps are often used to study the correlations between groups of genes.

Let's look at an example with the `genes.csv` example data file. Let's first load the file:

```
genes<-read.csv("genes.csv",header=T)
```

Let's use the `image()` function to create a correlation heat map:

```
rownames(genes)<-colnames(genes)

image(x=1:ncol(genes),
y=1:nrow(genes),
z=t(as.matrix(genes)),
axes=FALSE,
xlab="",
ylab="" ,
main="Gene Correlation Matrix")

axis(1,at=1:ncol(genes),labels=colnames(genes),col="white",
las=2,cex.axis=0.8)
axis(2,at=1:nrow(genes),labels=rownames(genes),col="white",
las=1,cex.axis=0.8)
```

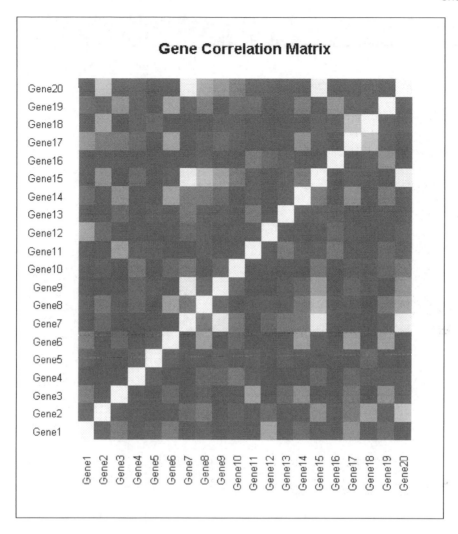

We used a few new commands and arguments in the previous example, especially to format the axes. We discuss these in detail starting in *Chapter 3, Beyond the Basics – Adjusting Key Parameters*, and with more examples in later chapters.

See also

Heat maps are explained in a lot more detail with more examples in *Chapter 9, Creating Heat Maps and Contour Plots*.

Creating pairs plots

A pairs plot is a matrix of scatter plots and is a very handy visualization to quickly scan the correlations between many variables in a dataset.

How to do it...

We will use the built-in `iris` dataset, which gives the measurements in centimeters of the sepal length and sepal width, and petal length and petal width variables, respectively, for 50 flowers from each of three species of iris:

```
pairs(iris[,1:4])
```

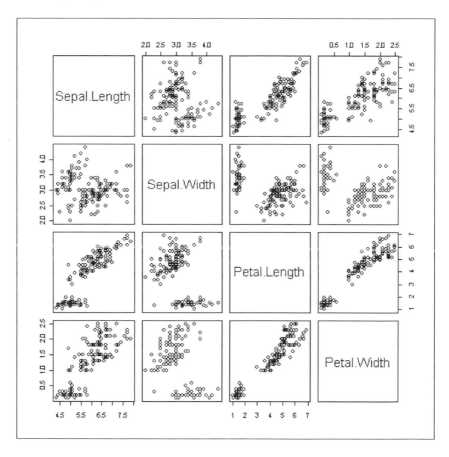

How it works...

As you can see in the preceding figure, the `pairs()` command makes a matrix of scatter plots, where all the variables in the specified dataset are plotted against each other. The variable names, displayed in the diagonal running across from the top-left corner to the bottom-right corner, are the key to reading the graph. For example, the scatter plot in the first row and second column shows the relationship between **Sepal Length** on the *y* axis and **Sepal Width** on the *x* axis.

There's more...

Here's a fun fact: we can produce the preceding graph using the `plot()` function instead of `pairs()` in exactly the same manner:

```
plot(iris[,1:4],
main="Relationships between characteristics of iris flowers",
pch=19,
col="blue",
cex=0.9)
```

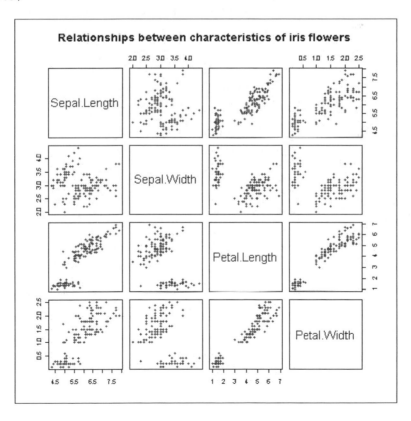

So, if you pass a data frame with more than two variables to the `plot ()` function, it creates a scatter plot matrix by default. We've also added a plot title and modified the plotting symbol style, color, and size using the `pch`, `col`, and `cex` arguments, respectively. We delve into the details of these settings in *Chapter 3, Beyond the Basics – Adjusting Key Parameters*.

See also

We cover some more interesting recipes in *Chapter 4, Creating Scatter Plots*, building upon the things you learned in *Chapter 3, Beyond the Basics – Adjusting Key Parameters*.

Creating multiple plot matrix layouts

In this recipe, you will learn how to present more than one graph in a single image. Pairs plots are one example, which we saw in the last recipe, but here, you will learn how to include different types of graphs in each cell of a graph matrix.

How to do it...

Let's say we want to make a 2 x 3 matrix of graphs, made of two rows and three columns of graphs. We use the `par ()` command as follows:

```
par(mfrow=c(2,3))
plot(rnorm(100),col="blue",main="Plot No.1")
plot(rnorm(100),col="blue",main="Plot No.2")
plot(rnorm(100),col="green",main="Plot No.3")
plot(rnorm(100),col="black",main="Plot No.4")
plot(rnorm(100),col="green",main="Plot No.5")
plot(rnorm(100),col="orange",main="Plot No.6")
```

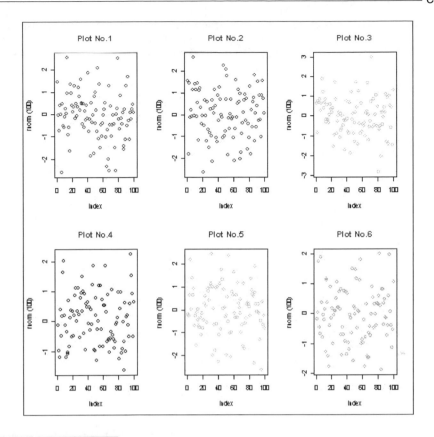

How it works...

The par() command is by far the most important function to customize graphs in R. It is used to set and query many graphical arguments (hence the name), which control the layout and appearance of graphs.

Note that we need to issue the par() command before the actual graph commands. When you first run the par() command, only a blank graphics window appears. The par() command sets the argument for any subsequent graphs made. The mfrow argument is used to specify how many rows and columns of graphs we wish to plot. The mfrow argument takes values in the form of a vector of length 2: c(nrow,ncol). The first number specifies the number of rows and the second specifies the number of columns. In our preceding example, we wanted a matrix of two rows and three columns, so we set mfrow to c(2,3).

Note that there is another argument, `mfcol`, similar to `mfrow`, that can also be used to create multiple plot layouts. The `mfcol` argument also takes a two-value vector that specifies the number of rows and columns in the matrix. The difference is that `mfcol` draws subsequent figures by columns, rather than by rows as `mfrow` does. So, if we used `mfcol` instead of `mfrow` in the earlier example, we will get the following plot:

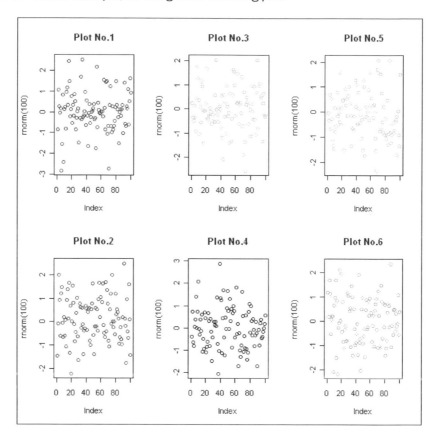

There's more...

Let's look at a practical example where a multiple plot layout would be useful. Let's read the `dailymarket.csv` example file, which contains data on the daily revenue, profits, and number of customer visits for a shop:

```
market<-read.csv("dailymarket.csv",header=TRUE)
```

Now, let's plot all the three variables over time in a plot matrix with the graphs stacked over one another:

```
par(mfrow=c(3,1))
plot(market$revenue~as.Date(market$date,"%d/%m/%y"),
```

```
type="l", #Specify type of plot as l for line
main="Revenue",
xlab="Date",
ylab="US Dollars",
col="blue")

plot(market$profits~as.Date(market$date,"%d/%m/%y"),
type="l", #Specify type of plot as l for line
main="Profits",
xlab="Date",
ylab="US Dollars",
col="red")

plot(market$customers~as.Date(market$date,"%d/%m/%y"),
type="l", #Specify type of plot as l for line
main="Customer visits",
xlab="Date",
ylab="Number of people",
col="black")
```

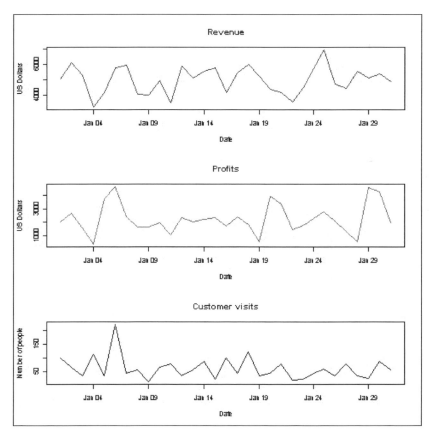

The preceding graph is a good way to visualize variables with different value ranges over the same time period. It helps in identifying where the trends match each other and where they differ.

See also

We will explore more examples and uses of multiple plot layouts in later chapters of the book.

Adding and formatting legends

In this recipe, we will learn how to add and format legends to graphs.

Getting ready

First, we need to load the `cityrain.csv` example data file, which contains monthly rainfall data for four major cities across the world (you can download this file from the code download section of the book's companion website):

```
rain<-read.csv("cityrain.csv",header=TRUE)
```

How to do it...

In the bar plots recipe, we already saw that we can add a legend by passing the legend argument to the `barplot()` function. Now, we see how we can use the `legend()` function to add and customize a legend for any type of graph.

Let's first draw a graph with multiple lines representing the rainfall in cities:

```
plot(rain$Tokyo,type="l",col="red",
ylim=c(0,300),
main="Monthly Rainfall in major cities",
xlab="Month of Year",
ylab="Rainfall (mm)",
lwd=2)
lines(rain$NewYork,type="l",col="blue",lwd=2)
lines(rain$London,type="l",col="green",lwd=2)
lines(rain$Berlin,type="l",col="orange",lwd=2)
```

Now, let's add the legend to mark which line represents which city:

```
legend("topright",
legend=c("Tokyo","NewYork","London","Berlin"),
col=c("red","blue","green","orange"),
lty=1,lwd=2)
```

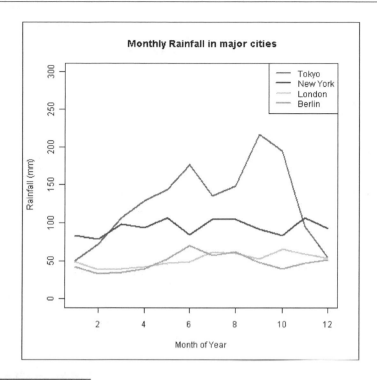

How it works...

In the example code, we first created a graph with multiple lines using the `plot()` and `lines()` commands to represent the monthly rainfall in Tokyo, New York, London, and Berlin in four different colors. However, without a legend, one would have no way of telling which line represents which city. So, we added a legend using the `legend()` function.

The first argument to the `legend()` function is the position of the legend, which we set to `topright`. Other possible values are `"topleft,"` `"top,"` `"left,"` `"center,"` `"right,"` `"bottomleft,"` `"bottom,"` and `"bottomright."` Then, we specify the legend labels by setting the legend argument to a vector of length 4, containing the names of the four cities. The `col` argument specifies the colors of the legend, which should match the colors of the lines in exactly the same order. Finally, the line type and width inside the legend are specified by `lty` and `lwd`, respectively.

There's more...

The placement and look of the legend can be modified in several ways. As a simple example, let's spread the legend across the top of the graph instead of the top-right corner. So first, let's redraw the same base plot:

```
plot(rain$Tokyo,type="l",col="red",
ylim=c(0,250),
```

```
main="Monthly Rainfall in major cities",
xlab="Month of Year",
ylab="Rainfall (mm)",
lwd=2)
lines(rain$NewYork,type="l",col="blue",lwd=2)
lines(rain$London,type="l",col="green",lwd=2)
lines(rain$Berlin,type="l",col="orange",lwd=2)
```

Now, let's add a modified legend:

```
legend("top",
legend=c("Tokyo","NewYork","London","Berlin"),
ncol=4,
cex=0.8,
bty="n",
col=c("red","blue","green","orange"),
lty=1,lwd=2)
```

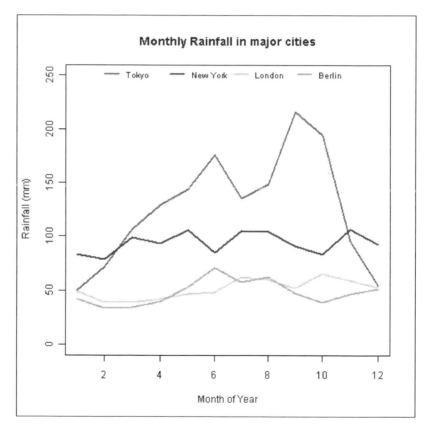

We changed the legend location from toprightto topand added a few other arguments to adjust the look. The ncolargument is used to specify the number of columns over which the legend is displayed. The default value is 1, as we saw in the first example. In our second example, we set ncolto 4 so that all the city names are displayed in one single row. The bty argument specifies the type of box drawn around the legend. We removed it from the graph by setting it to "n." We also modified the size of the legend labels by setting cexto 0.8.

See also

There are plenty of examples of how you can add and customize legends in different scenarios in later chapters of the book.

Creating graphs with maps

In this recipe, you will learn how to plot data on maps.

Getting ready

In order to plot maps in R, we need to install the maps library. Here's how to do it:

```
install.packages("maps")
```

When you run the preceding command, you will most likely be prompted by R to choose from a list of locations where you can download the library. For example, if you are based in the UK, you can choose either the **UK (Bristol)** or **UK (London)** options.

Once the library is installed, we must load it using the library()command:

```
library(maps)
```

 Note that we only need to install any package using install. packages()once but need to load it using library()or require()every time we restart a new session in R.

How to do it...

We can make a simple world map with just one command:

```
map()
```

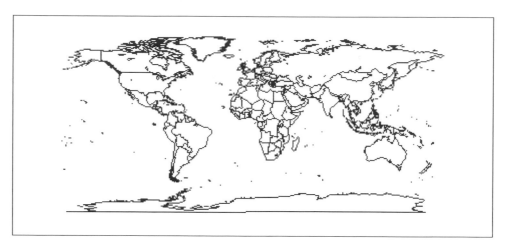

Let's add color:

```
map('world', fill = TRUE,col=heat.colors(10))
```

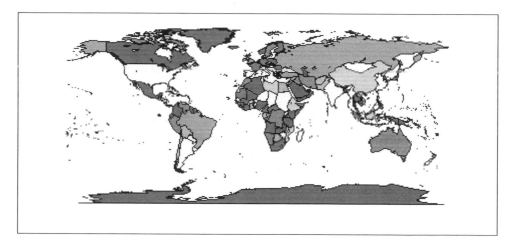

How it works...

The `maps` library provides a way to project world data on to a low-resolution map. It is also possible to make detailed maps of the US. For example, we can make a map that shows the state boundaries as follows:

```
map("state", interior = FALSE)
map("state", boundary = FALSE, col="red", add = TRUE)
```

The `add` argument is set to `TRUE` in the second call to `map()` to add details to the same map created using the first call. This only works if a map has already been drawn on the current graphic device.

There's more...

The examples above are just a basic introduction to the idea of geographical visualisation in R. In order to plot any useful data, we need to use a better maps library. **GADM** (http:// gadm.org) is a free spatial database of the location of the world's administrative areas (or administrative boundaries). The site provides map information as native R objects that can be plotted directly with the use of the `sp` library.

Let's take a look at a quick example. First, we need to install and load the `sp` library, just like we did with the `maps` library:

```
install.packages("sp")
library(sp)
```

GADM provides data for all the countries across the world. Let's load the data for the UK. We can do so by directly reading the data from the GADM website:

```
load(url("http://gadm.org/data/rda/GBR_adm1.RData"))
```

The preceding command loads the boundary data for the group of administrative regions forming the UK. It is stored in memory as a data object named gadm. Now, let's plot a map with the loaded data:

```
spplot(gadm, "Shape_Area")
```

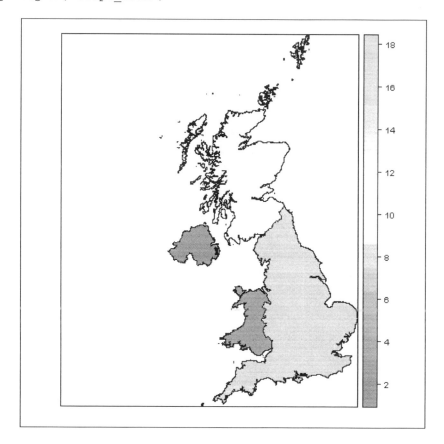

The graph shows the different parts of the UK, color coded by their surface areas. We can just as easily display any other data such as population or crime rates.

See also

We will cover more detailed and practical recipes on maps in *Chapter 10, Creating Maps*.

Saving and exporting graphs

In this recipe, you will learn how to save and export our graphs to various useful formats.

How to do it...

To save a graph as an image file format such as PNG, we can use the png() command:

```
png("scatterplot.png")
plot(rnorm(1000))
dev.off()
```

The preceding command will save the graph as scatterplot.png in the current working directory. Similarly, if we wish to save the graph as JPEG, BMP, or TIFF, we can use the jpeg(), bmp(), or tiff() commands, respectively.

If you are working in Windows, you can also save a graph using the graphical user interface. First, make your graph, make sure that the graph window is the active window by clicking anywhere inside it, and then navigate to **File | Save as | Png** or the format of your choice, as shown in the following screenshot:

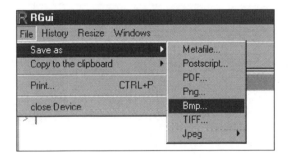

When prompted to choose a name for your saved file, type in a suitable name and click on **Save**. As you can see, you can choose from seven different formats.

How it works...

If you wish to use code to save and export your graphs, it is important to understand how the code works. The first step in saving a graph is to open a graphics device suitable for the format of your choice before you make the graph. For example, when you call the png() function, you are telling R to start the PNG graphics device so that the output of any subsequent graph commands you run will be directed to that device.

By default, the display device on the screen is active. So any graph commands result in showing the graph on your screen. However, you will notice that when you choose a different graphics device such as `png()`, the graphs don't show up on your screen. Finally, you must close the graphics device with the `dev.off()` command to instruct R to save the graph you plotted in the specified format and write it to disk with the specified filename. If you do not run `dev.off()`, the file will not be saved.

There's more...

You can specify a number of arguments to adjust the graph as per your needs. The simplest one that we've already used is the filename. You can also adjust the height and width settings of the graph:

```
png("scatterplot.png",
height=600,
width=600)
```

The default units for height and width are pixels but you can also specify the units in inches, centimeters, or millimeters:

```
png("scatterplot.png",
height=4,
width=4,
units="in")
```

The resolution of the saved image can be specified in **dots per inch** (**dpi**) using the `res` argument:

```
png("scatterplot.png",
res=600)
```

If you want your graphs saved in the vector format, you can also save them as a PDF file using the `pdf()` function:

```
pdf("scatterplot.pdf")
```

Besides maintaining a high resolution of your graphs independent of the size, PDFs are also useful because you can save multiple graphs in the same PDF file.

See also

We will cover the details of saving and exporting graphs, especially for publication and presentation purposes in *Chapter 15, Finalizing Graphs for Publications and Presentations*.

3
Beyond the Basics – Adjusting Key Parameters

In this chapter, we will cover the following recipes:

- ▶ Setting colors of points, lines, and bars
- ▶ Setting plot background colors
- ▶ Setting colors for text elements – axis labels, titles, plot titles, and legends
- ▶ Choosing color combinations and palettes
- ▶ Setting fonts for annotations and titles
- ▶ Choosing plotting point symbol styles and sizes
- ▶ Choosing line styles and width
- ▶ Choosing box styles
- ▶ Adjusting axis labels and tick marks
- ▶ Formatting log axes
- ▶ Setting graph margins and dimensions

Introduction

In this chapter, you will learn about some of the simplest yet most important settings and parameters of graphs in R base graphics. Learning how to adjust colors, sizes, margins, and styles of various graph elements such as points, lines, bars, axes, and titles will give us the ability to improve upon the basic graph commands you learned in *Chapter 1, R Graphics*.

In the previous chapter, we got a glimpse of the different types of graphs that can be created in R using small snippets of code. Now, you will learn how to modify the fundamental building blocks of these graphs to better suit our needs.

The R base library has very powerful graphical capabilities. While you can produce pretty much any type of graph with a couple of lines of code, the default layout and look of the graph is often very basic. Sometimes, you might run into problems such as axis labels and titles getting chopped off at the edges or the legend size or position masking part of your graph. Sometimes, the default color combinations might not be suitable for presentation or publication.

In this chapter, we will go through the relevant names and accepted values of different arguments and arguments to graph functions. We will take a closer look at the `par()` function, which we briefly introduced in the previous chapter.

Reading and trying out all the recipes in this chapter is highly recommended as it will give you a very good hands-on grasp of certain aspects of graph manipulation, which you are likely to use a lot in any visual analysis in R.

Let's get started!

Setting colors of points, lines, and bars

In this recipe, you will learn the simplest way to change the colors of points, lines, and bars in scatter plots, line plots, histograms, and bar plots.

Getting ready

All you need to try out in this recipe is to run R and type the recipe in the command prompt. You can also choose to save the recipe as a script so that you can use it again later on.

How to do it...

The simplest way to change the color of any graph element is using the `col` argument. For example, the `plot()` function takes the `col` argument:

```
plot(rnorm(1000),
col="red")
```

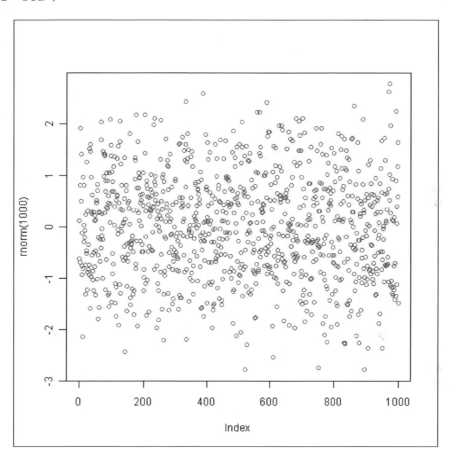

If we choose the plot type as the line, then the color is applied to the plotted line. Let's use the `dailysales.csv` example dataset we used in *Chapter 1, R Graphics*. First, we need to load it:

```
Sales <- read.csv("dailysales.csv",header=TRUE)

plot(sales$units~as.Date(sales$date,"%d/%m/%y"),
type="l", #Specify type of plot as l for line
col="blue")
```

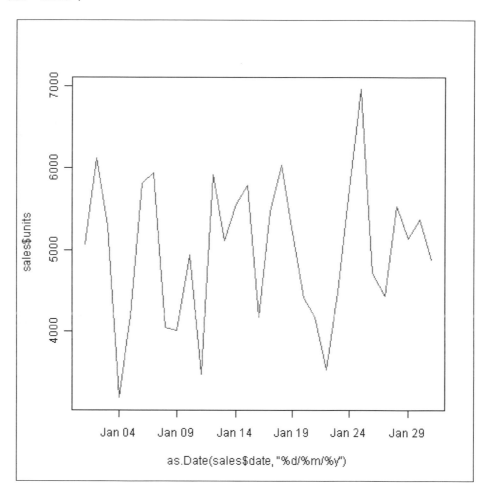

Similarly, the `points()` and `lines()` functions apply the `col` argument's value to the plotted points and lines, respectively.

The `barplot()` and `hist()` functions also take the `col` argument and apply the respective value to the plotted bars. So, the following code will produce a bar plot with blue bars:

```
barplot(sales$ProductA~sales$City,
col="blue")
```

The `col` argument for the `boxplot()` function is applied to the color of the plotted boxes.

How it works...

The `col` argument automatically applies the specified color to the elements being plotted, based on the plot type. So, if we do not specify a plot type or choose points, then the color is applied to points. Similarly, if we choose the plot type as the line, then the color is applied to the plotted line, and if we use the `col` argument in the `barplot()` or `histogram()` commands, then the color is applied to the bars.

The `col` argument accepts names of colors such as `red`, `blue`, and `black`. The `colors()` (or `colours()`) function lists all the built-in colors (more than 650) that are available in R. We can also specify colors as hexadecimal codes such as #FF0000 (for red), #0000FF (for blue), and #000000 (for black). If you have ever created any web pages, you would know that these hex codes are used in HTML to represent colors.

The `col` argument can also take numeric values. When it is set to a numeric value, the color corresponding to that index in the current color palette is used. For example, in the default color palette, the first color is black and the second color is red. So `col=1` and `col=2` refers to black and red, respectively. Index 0 corresponds to the background color.

There's more...

In many settings, `col` can also take a vector of multiple colors instead of a single color. This is useful if you wish to use more than one color in a graph. For example, in *Chapter 1, R Graphics*, we created a bar plot of sales data for three products across five cities. In that example, we used a vector of five colors to represent each of the five cities with the help of the `heat.colors()` function. The `heat.colors()` function takes a number as an argument and returns a vector of those many colors. So, `heat.colors(5)` produces a vector of five colors.

Type the following at the R prompt:

```
heat.colors(5)
```

You should get the following output:

```
[1] "#FF0000FF" "#FF5500FF" "#FFAA00FF" "#FFFF00FF" "#FFFF80FF"
```

These are the five colors in the hexadecimal format.

Another way of specifying a vector of colors is to construct it:

```
barplot(as.matrix(sales[,2:4]), beside=T,
legend=sales$City,
col=c("red","blue","green","orange","pink"),
border="white")
```

In the preceding example, we set the value of col to c("red","blue","green","orange","pink"), which is a vector of five colors.

We have to take care to create a vector that matches the length of the number of elements, in this case, the bars that we are plotting. If the two numbers don't match, R will *recycle* values by repeating colors from the beginning of the vector. For example, if we had fewer colors in the vector than the number of elements, say, if we had four colors in the previous plot, then R would apply the four colors to the first four bars and then apply the first color to the fifth bar. This is called recycling in R:

```
barplot(as.matrix(sales[,2:4]), beside=T,
legend=sales$City,
col=c("red","blue","green","orange"),
border="white")
```

In the example, both the bars for the first and last data rows (Seattle and Mumbai) would be of the same color (red), making it difficult to distinguish one from the other.

One good way to ensure that you always have the correct number of colors is to find out the length of the number of elements first and pass that as an argument to one of the color palette functions. For example, if we did not know the number of cities in the preceding example, we could execute the following to make sure that the number of colors matches the number of plotted bars:

```
barplot(as.matrix(sales[,2:4]), beside=T,
legend=sales$City,
col=heat.colors(length(sales$City)),
border="white")
```

We used the length() function to find out the length or the number of elements in the sales$City vector and passed that as the argument to heat.colors(). So, regardless of the number of cities, we will always have the right number of colors.

See also

In the next four recipes, we will see how to change the colors of other elements. The fourth recipe is especially useful; we look at color combinations and palettes there.

Setting plot background colors

The default background color of all plots in R is white, which is usually the best choice as it is least distracting for data analysis. However, sometimes, we might wish to use another color. We will see how to set background colors in this recipe.

Getting ready

All you need to try out in this recipe is to run R and type the recipe in the command prompt. You can also choose to save the recipe as a script so that you can use it again later on.

How to do it...

To set the plot background color to gray, we use the bg argument in the par() command:

```
par(bg="gray")
plot(rnorm(100))
```

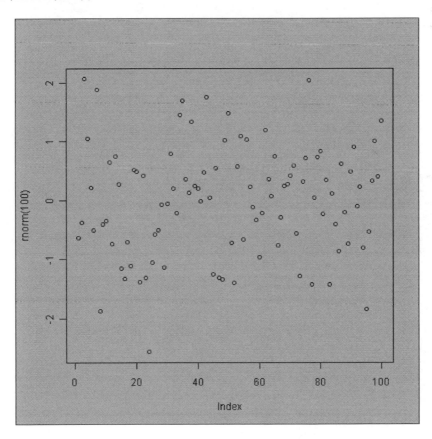

How it works...

The `bg` argument of the `par()` command sets the background color for the entire plotting area, including the margins for any subsequent plots on the same device. Until the plotting device is closed or a new device is initiated, the background color stays the same.

There's more...

It is more likely that we want to set the background color only for the plot region (within the axes) but there is no straightforward way to do this in R. We must draw a rectangle of the desired color in the background and then create our graph on top of it:

```
plot(rnorm(1000),type="n")
x<-par("usr")
rect(x[1],x[3],x[2],x[4],col="lightgray ")
points(rnorm(1000))
```

First, we draw the plot with the `type` parameter set to `n` so that the plotted elements are invisible. This does not show the graph points or lines but sets the axes up, which we need for the next step.

The `par("usr")` part gets us the coordinates of the plot region in a vector of form `c(xleft, xright, ybottom, ytop)`. We then use the `rect()` function to draw a rectangle with a fill color that we wish to use for the plot background. Note that `rect()` takes a set of arguments that represent the `xleft`, `ybottom`, `xright`, and `ytop` coordinates. So, we must pass the values we obtained from `par("usr")` in the correct order. Then, finally, we redraw the graph with the correct type (points or lines). The redrawn graph looks like the following figure:

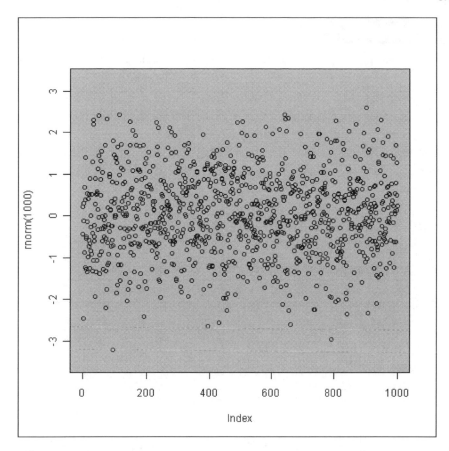

Setting colors for text elements – axis annotations, labels, plot titles, and legends

Axis annotations are the numerical or text values placed beside tick marks on an axis. Axis labels are the names or titles of axes, which tell the reader what the values on a particular axis represent. In this recipe, you will learn how to set the colors for these elements and legends.

Getting ready

All you need to try out this recipe is to run R and type the recipe in the command prompt. You can also choose to save the recipe as a script so that you can use it again later on.

How to do it...

Let's say that we want to make the axis value annotations black, the labels of the axes gray, and the plot title dark blue. For this, you should use the following code:

```
plot(rnorm(100),
main="Plot Title",
col.axis="blue",
col.lab="red",
col.main="darkblue")
```

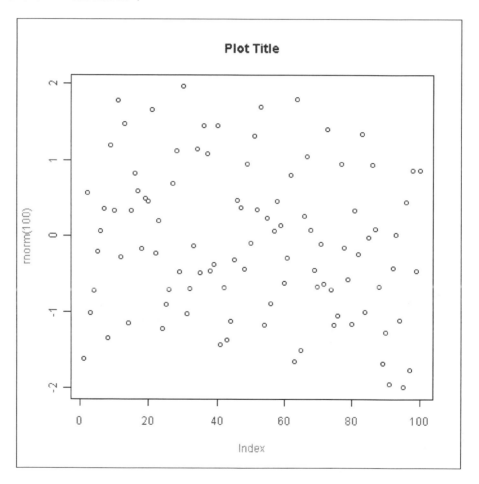

How it works...

Colors for axis annotations, labels, and plot titles can be set either using the `par()` command before creating the graph or in the graph command, such as `plot()` itself. The arguments for setting the colors for axis annotations, labels, and plot titles are `col.axis`, `col.lab`, and `col.main`, respectively.

These are similar to the `col` argument and take names of colors or hex codes as values, but they do not take a vector of more than one color.

There's more...

If we use the `par()` command, the difference is that `par()` will apply these settings to every subsequent graph until it is reset either by specifying the settings again or starting a new graphics device:

```
par(col.axis="black",
col.lab="#444444",
col.main="darkblue")

plot(rnorm(100),main="plot")
```

The `col.axis` argument can also be passed to the `axis()` function, which is useful for creating a custom axis if you do not want to use the default axis. The `col.lab` argument does not work with `axis()` and must be specified in `par()` or the main graph function such as `plot()` or `barplot()`.

The `col.main` argument can also be passed to the `title()` function, which is useful for adding a custom plot title if you do not want to use the default title:

```
title("Sales Figures for 2010", col.main="blue")
```

Axis labels can also be specified with `title()`:

```
title(xlab="Month",ylab="Sales",col.lab="red")
```

This is handy because you can specify two different colors for the x and y axes:

```
title(xlab="X axis",col.lab="red")
title(ylab="Y axis",col.lab="blue")
```

When setting the axis titles with the `title()` command, we must set `xlab` and `ylab` to the `" "` empty strings in the original plot command in order to avoid overlapping titles.

Choosing color combinations and palettes

We often need more than one color to represent various elements in graphs. Palettes are combinations of colors, which is a convenient way to use multiple colors without choosing individual colors separately. R provides inbuilt color palettes as well as the ability to create our own custom palettes. Using palettes is a good way to avoid repeatedly choosing or setting colors in multiple locations, which can be a source of error and confusion. This helps in separating the presentation settings of a graph from the construction.

Getting ready

All you need to try out in this recipe is to run R and type the recipe in the command prompt. You can also choose to save the recipe as a script so that you can use it again later on. One new library needs to be installed, which is also explained.

How to do it...

We can change the current palette by passing a character vector of colors to the `palette()` function as shown in the following code:

```
palette(c("red","blue","green","orange"))
```

To use the colors in the current palette, we can refer to them by the index number. For example, `palette()[1]` will be `red`.

How it works...

R has a default palette of colors that can be accessed by calling the `palette()` function. If we run the `palette()` command just after starting R, we get the default palette:

```
palette()
[1] "black"    "red"      "green3"   "blue"     "cyan"      "magenta"
"yellow"
[8] "gray"
```

To revert to the default palette type, use the following code:

```
palette("default")
```

When a vector of color names is passed to the `palette()` function, it sets the current palette to those colors. We must enter valid color names; otherwise, we will get an invalid color name error.

There's more...

Besides the default palette provided by the `palette()` function, R has many more built-in palettes and additional palette libraries. One of the most commonly used palettes is the `heat.colors()` palette, which provides a range of colors from red through yellow to white, based on number of colors specified by the n argument. For example, `heat.colors(10)` produces a palette of ten warm colors from red to white.

Other palettes are `rainbow()`, `terrain.colors()`, `cm.colors()`, and `topo.colors`, which take the number of colors as an argument.

`RColorBrewer` is a very good color palette package that creates nice-looking color palettes, especially for thematic maps. This is an R implementation of the `RColorBrewer` palettes, which provides three types of palettes: sequential, diverging, and qualitative. More information on this is available at `http://www.colorbrewer.org`.

To use `RColorBrewer`, we need to install and load it:

```
install.packages("RColorBrewer")
library(RColorBrewer)
```

To see all the `RColorBrewer` palettes, run the following command on the R prompt:

```
display.brewer.all()
```

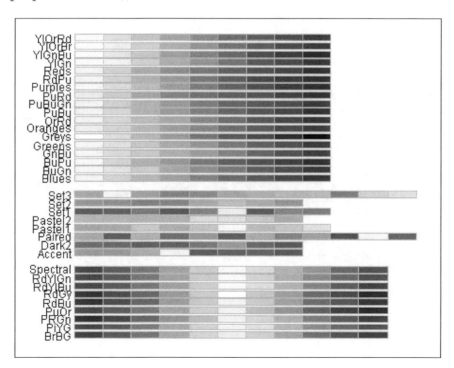

The names of the palettes are displayed in the left-hand margin, and the colors in each palette are displayed in each row running to the right.

To use one of the palettes, let's say `YlOrRd` (which, as the names suggests, is a combination of yellows and reds), we can use the `brewer.pal()` function:

```
brewer.pal(7,"YlOrRd")
[1] "#FFFFB2" "#FED976" "#FEB24C" "#FD8D3C" "#FC4E2A" "#E31A1C"
"#B10026"
```

The `brewer.pal` function takes two arguments: the number of colors we wish to choose and the name of the palette. The minimum number of colors is three but the maximum varies from palette to palette.

We can view the colors of an individual palette using the `display.brewer.pal()` command:

```
display.brewer.pal(7,"YlOrRd")
```

To use a specific color of the palette, we can refer to the color by its index number. So, the first color in the palette is `brewer.pal(7,"YlOrRd")[1]`, the second is `brewer.pal(7,"YlOrRd")[2]`, and so on.

We can set the current palette to the preceding one using the `palette()` function:

```
palette(brewer.pal(7,"YlOrRd"))
```

Now, we can refer to the individual colors as `palette()[1]`, `palette()[2]`, and so on. We can also store the palette as a vector:

```
pal1<- brewer.pal(7,"YlOrRd")
```

See also

We will see the use of a lot of color palettes throughout the recipes in this book, starting from *Chapter 4, Creating Scatter Plots*.

Setting fonts for annotations and titles

For most data analysis, we can just use the default fonts for titles. However, sometimes, we might want to choose different fonts for presentation and publication purposes. Selecting fonts can be tricky, as this depends on the operating system and the graphics device. We will see some simple ways to choose fonts in this recipe.

Getting ready

All you need to try out in this recipe is to run R and type the recipe in the command prompt. You can also choose to save the recipe as a script so that you can use it again later on.

How to do it...

The font family and face can be set with the `par()` command:

```
par(family="serif",font=2)
```

How it works...

A font is specified in two parts: a font `family` (such as Helvetica or Arial) and a font `face` within `family` (such as **bold** or *italic*).

The available font families vary by operating system and graphics devices. So, R provides some proxy values that are mapped on to the relevant available fonts irrespective of the system. Standard values for `family` are `serif`, `sans`, and `mono`.

The `font` argument takes numerical values: 1 corresponds to plain text (the default), 2 to bold face, 3 to italic, and 4 to bold italic.

For example, `par(family="serif",font=2)` sets the font to a bold Times New Roman font on Windows. You can check the other font mappings by running the `windowsFonts()` command at the R prompt.

The fonts for axis annotations, labels, and plot main title can be set separately using the `font.axis`, `font.lab`, and `font.main` arguments, respectively.

There's more...

The choice of fonts is very limited if we just use the proxy family names. However, we can use a wide range of fonts if we are exporting our graphs in the PostScript or PDF formats. The `postscriptFonts()` and `pdfFonts()` functions show us all the available fonts for these devices. To see the PDF fonts, run the following command:

```
names(pdfFonts())
 [1] "serif"            "sans"                "mono"
 [4] "AvantGarde"       "Bookman"             "Courier"
 [7] "Helvetica"        "Helvetica-Narrow"    "NewCenturySchoolbook"
[10] "Palatino"         "Times"               "URWGothic"
[13] "URWBookman"       "NimbusMon"           "NimbusSan"
[16] "URWHelvetica"     "NimbusSanCond"       "CenturySch"
```

```
[19]  "URWPalladio"        "NimbusRom"          "URWTimes"
[22]  "Japan1"             "Japan1HeiMin"       "Japan1GothicBBB"
[25]  "Japan1Ryumin"       "Korea1"             "Korea1deb"
[28]  "CNS1"               "GB1"
```

To use one of these font families in a PDF, we can pass the family argument to the `pdf()` function:

```
pdf(family="AvantGarde")  pdf(paste(family="AvantGarde")
```

See also

In *Chapter 15, Finalizing Graphs for Publications and Presentations*, we will see some more practical recipes on setting fonts for publications and presentations.

Choosing plotting point symbol styles and sizes

In this recipe, we will see how we can adjust the styling of plotting symbols, which is useful and necessary when we plot more than one set of points that represent different groups of data on the same graph.

Getting ready

All you need to try out in this recipe is to run R and type the recipe in the command prompt. You can also choose to save the recipe as a script so that you can use it again later on. We will also use the `cityrain.csv` example data file that we used in the first chapter. Please read the file into R as follows:

```
rain<-read.csv("cityrain.csv")
```

How to do it...

The plotting symbol and size can be set using the `pch` and `cex` arguments:

```
plot(rnorm(100),pch=19,cex=2)
```

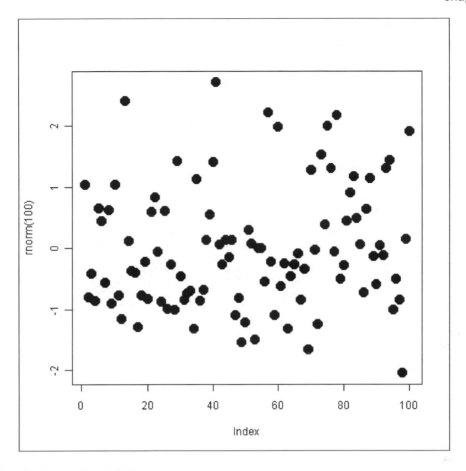

How it works...

The pch argument stands for the plotting character (the symbol). It can take numerical values (usually between 0 and 25) as well as single character values. Each numerical value represents a different symbol. For example, 1 represents circles, 2 represents triangles, 3 represents plus signs, and so on. If we set the value of pch to a character such as * or £ in inverted commas, then the data points are drawn as that character instead of the default circles.

The size of the plotting symbol is controlled by the cex argument, which takes numerical values starting at 0, giving us the amount by which plotting symbols should be magnified, relative to the default. Note that cex takes relative values (the default is 1). So, the absolute size might vary depending on the defaults of the graphic device in use. For example, the size of plotting symbols with the same cex value might be different for a graph saved as a PNG file versus a graph saved as a PDF.

There's more...

The most common use of `pch` and `cex` is when we don't want to use colors to distinguish between different groups of data points. This is often the case in scientific journals that do not accept color images. For example, let's plot the city rainfall data we looked at in *Chapter 1, R Graphics*, as a set of points instead of lines:

```
plot(rain$Tokyo,
ylim=c(0,250),
main="Monthly Rainfall in major cities",
xlab="Month of Year",
ylab="Rainfall (mm)",
pch=1)

points(rain$NewYork,pch=2)
points(rain$London,pch=3)
points(rain$Berlin,pch=4)

legend("top",
legend=c("Tokyo","New York","London","Berlin"),
ncol=4,
cex=0.8,
bty="n",
pch=1:4)
```

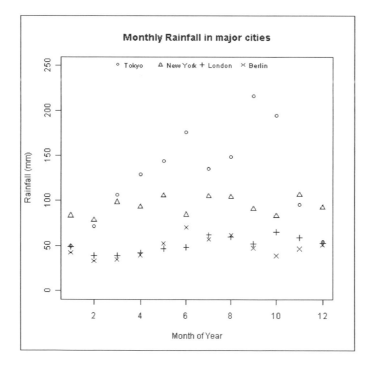

See also

We will see more examples of symbol settings later in the book, especially in the next chapter on scatter plots.

Choosing line styles and width

Similar to plotting point symbols, R provides simple ways to adjust the style of lines in graphs.

Getting ready

All you need to try out in this recipe is to run R and type the recipe in the command prompt. You can also choose to save the recipe as a script so that you can use it again later on. We will use the `cityrain.csv` data file that we read in the last recipe again.

How to do it...

Line styles can be set using the `lty` and `lwd` arguments (for the line type and width, respectively) in the `plot()`, `lines()`, and `par()` commands. Let's take our rainfall example and apply different line styles, keeping the color the same:

```
plot(rain$Tokyo,
ylim=c(0,250),
main="Monthly Rainfall in major cities",
xlab="Month of Year",
ylab="Rainfall (mm)",
type="l",
lty=1,
lwd=2)

lines(rain$NewYork,lty=2,lwd=2)
lines(rain$London,lty=3,lwd=2)
lines(rain$Berlin,lty=4,lwd=2)

legend("top",
legend=c("Tokyo","New York","London","Berlin"),
ncol=4,
```

```
cex=0.8,
bty="n",
lty=1:4,
lwd=2)
```

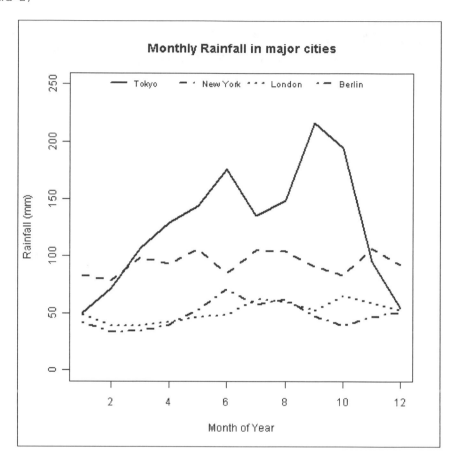

How it works...

Both the line type and width can be set with numerical values, as shown in the preceding example. The line type number values correspond to types of lines:

▸   0: blank

▸   1: solid (the default)

▸   2: dashed

▸   3: dotted

- ▶ 4: dotdash
- ▶ 5: longdash
- ▶ 6: twodash

We can also use the character strings instead of numbers, for example, lty="dashed" instead of lty=2.

The line width argument, lwd, takes positive numerical values. The default value is 1. In the example, we used a value of 2, thus making the lines thicker than the default.

See also

We will explore more examples of line styles in subsequent chapters, especially in *Chapter 5, Creating Line Graphs and Time Series Charts*, in which we will see some advanced line graph recipes.

Choosing box styles

The styles of various boxes drawn in a graph such as the one around the plotting region and the legend can be adjusted in a similar way to the line styles we saw in the last recipe.

Getting ready

All you need to try out in this recipe is to run R and type the recipe in the command prompt. You can also choose to save the recipe as a script so that you can use it again later on.

How to do it...

Let's say we want to create an L-shaped box around a graph such that the default top and right borders are not drawn. We can do so using the `bty` argument in the `par()` command:

```
par(bty="l")
plot(rnorm(100))
```

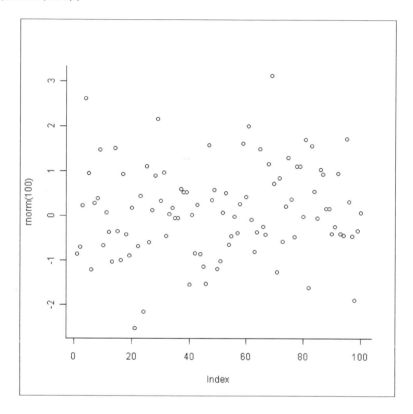

How it works...

The `bty` argument stands for the box type and takes single characters in inverted commas as values. The resulting box resembles the corresponding uppercase letter. For example, the default value is o, thus creating a box with all four edges. Other possible values are l, 7, c, u, and]. If we do not wish to draw a box at all, we can set `bty` to n.

Note that setting `bty` to n doesn't suppress the drawing of axes. If we wish to suppress these too, then we would also have to set `xaxt` and `yaxt` to n. Alternatively, we can simply set the `axes` argument to FALSE in the `plot()` function call.

There's more...

Box styles can be controlled in a finer way using the box () command. In addition to the lty and lwd arguments, we can also specify where the box should be drawn using the which parameter, which can take values of plot, figure, inner, and outer.

Let's say we want to draw a graph with an L-shaped box for the plot area and a full box around the figure including the axis annotations and titles. Then, we can use the following code:

```
par(oma=c(1,1,1,1))
plot(rnorm(100),bty="l")
box(which="figure")
```

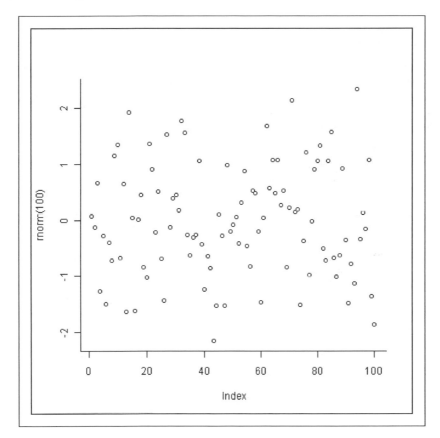

Note that we had to first set the outer margins by setting the oma argument with the par() function. You will learn more about this argument later in this chapter. If we did not set the outer margins, the box around the figure would be right at the edge of the plot and get cut off because the default margins are set to zero.

Adjusting axis annotations and tick marks

The default axis settings are often not adequate to deal with all kinds of data. For example, we might wish to change the number of tick marks along an axis or change the orientation of the annotations if they are too long in order to fit them horizontally. In this recipe, we will cover some settings that can be used to customize axes as per our requirements.

Getting ready

All you need to try out in this recipe is to run R and type the recipe in the command prompt. You can also choose to save the recipe as a script so that you can use it again later on.

How to do it...

We can set the `xaxp` and `yaxp` arguments with the `par()` command in order to specify coordinates of the extreme tick marks and the number of intervals between tick marks in the `c(min,max,n)` form:

```
plot(rnorm(100),xaxp=c(0,100,10))
```

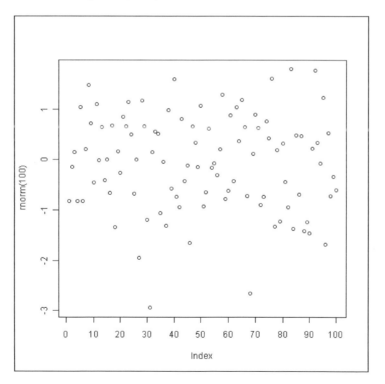

How it works...

When `xaxp` or `yaxp` is not specified, R automatically calculates the number of tick marks and their values. By default, R extends the axis limits by adding 4 percent at each end and then draws an axis that fits within the extended range. This means that even if we set the axis limits using `xlim` or `ylim`, the graph corners don't exactly correspond with these values. To make sure they do, we need to change the axis style using the `xaxs` argument, which takes one of the two possible values: `r` (the regular or default) and `i` (internal). We need to set `xaxs` to `i`.

A vector of the `c(x1, x2, n)` form gives the coordinates of the extreme tick marks and the number of intervals between tick marks.

There's more...

To change the orientation of axis value annotations, we need to set the `las` argument of the `par()` command. This takes one of the four possible numeric values:

- ▸ 0: This is always parallel to the axis (the default)
- ▸ 1: This is always horizontal
- ▸ 2: This is always perpendicular to the axis
- ▸ 3: This is always vertical

We can also use the `axis()` command to create a custom axis by specifying a number of arguments. The basic arguments are as follows:

- ▸ `side`: This takes numeric values (1=below, 2=left, 3=above, and 4=right)
- ▸ `at`: This takes a vector of coordinates where tick marks are to be drawn
- ▸ `labels`: This takes a vector of tick mark annotations

We can set the line width for the axis lines and the tick marks separately by passing the `lwd` and `lwd.ticks` arguments, respectively. Similarly, colors can be set using the `col` and `col.ticks` arguments.

See also

We will come across various examples of custom axes in the following chapters as we explore more advanced recipes.

Formatting log axes

In scientific analysis, we often need to represent data on a logarithmic scale. In this recipe, we will see how we can do this easily in R.

Getting ready

All you need to try out in this recipe is to run R and type the recipe in the command prompt. You can also choose to save the recipe as a script so that you can use it again later on.

How to do it...

The simplest way to create an axis logarithmic is to use the `log` argument in the `plot()` command:

```
plot(10^c(1:5),log="y",type="b")
```

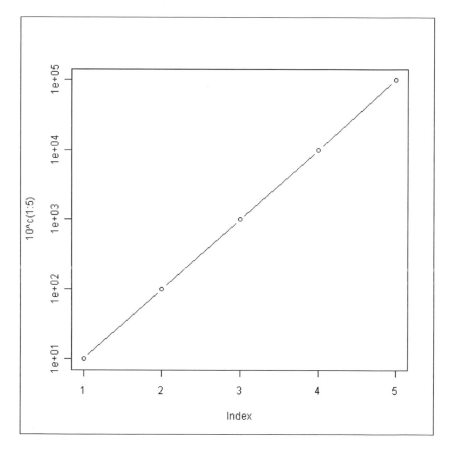

How it works...

The log argument takes character values, specifying which axes should be logarithmic: x for the x-axis only, y for the y-axis only, and xy or yx for both axes.

There's more...

We can also set scales to be logarithmic by setting the xlog and ylog arguments to TRUE with the par() command. This can be handy if we wish to have the same setting for multiple plots as par() applies the settings to all subsequent plots on the same device.

Note that R will not create the plot if our data contains zero or negative values.

Setting graph margins and dimensions

In this recipe, we will learn how to adjust graph margins and dimensions.

Getting ready

All you need to try out in this recipe is to run R and type the recipe in the command prompt. You can also choose to save the recipe as a script so that you can use it again later on.

How to do it...

We can use the fin and pin arguments of the par() command to set the figure region and plot dimensions:

```
par(fin=c(6,6),
pin=c(4,4))
```

We can use the mai and omi arguments to adjust the inner and outer margins, respectively:

```
par(mai=c(1,1,1,1),
omi=c(0.1,0.1,0.1,0.1))
```

How it works...

All the mentioned arguments accept values in inches as a pair of width and height values. The default values for fin and pin are approximately 7 x 7 and 5.75 x 5.15. We have to be careful not to specify higher values for pin than fin, or we would get an error.

Adjusting fin and pin is one way of setting the figure margins that contain the axis annotations and labels. Another way is to use the mai or mar arguments. In the example mentioned, we used mai, which takes a vector values in inches, whereas mar takes a vector of numerical values in terms of the number of lines of margins. It is better to use mar or mai because they adjust the figure margins irrespective of the figure or plot size.

We can also set an outer margin that is set to zero by default. This margin is useful if we wish to contain the entire graph including axis labels within a box, as we saw in an earlier recipe. Like figure margins, outer margins can be set in inches with `omi` or in number of lines of text using `oma`.

R Graphics by Paul Murrell (CRC Press) is an excellent reference with visual explanations of how margins work in R. See the book's homepage for more details at `http://www.stat.auckland.ac.nz/~paul/RGraphics/rgraphics.html`.

This talk by Paul Murrell also contains figures from the book, explaining the same concepts: `http://www.stat.auckland.ac.nz/~paul/Talks/Rgraphics.pdf`.

See also

We will come across examples of figure margin settings in some of the recipes in the following chapters.

4

Creating Scatter Plots

In this chapter, we will cover the following recipes:

- ► Grouping data points within a scatter plot
- ► Highlighting grouped data points by size and symbol type
- ► Labeling data points
- ► Correlation matrix using pairs plot
- ► Adding error bars
- ► Using jitter to distinguish closely packed data points
- ► Adding linear model lines
- ► Adding nonlinear model curves
- ► Adding nonparametric model curves with lowess
- ► Creating three-dimensional scatter plots
- ► Creating Quantile-Quantile plots
- ► Displaying the data density on axes
- ► Creating scatter plots with a smoothed density representation

Introduction

In this chapter, we will learn about scatter plots in depth by looking at some advanced recipes. Scatter plots are one of the most commonly used type of graphs in data analysis. In the first chapter, we learned how to create a basic scatter plot. Now, we will learn how we can create more enhanced plots by adjusting various arguments and using some new functions.

So far, we have mostly only used the base graphics functions such as `plot()`, but in this chapter, we have recipes that use other graph libraries such as `lattice` and `ggplot2`, which offer more advanced control over graphs. It is possible to create these advanced graphs using the base library too, but the additional libraries give us ways to achieve the same results with less code and often produce better-looking graphs with the least amount of effort.

A lot of new functions will be introduced in this chapter. It is a good practice to look up the help file whenever you encounter a new function. For example, to look up the help file for the `plot()` function, you can type `?plot` or `help(plot)` in the R command prompt.

As the recipes in this chapter are slightly more advanced than the earlier chapters, you may require some practice with multiple datasets before you are comfortable with using all the functions. Example datasets are used in each recipe, but it is highly recommended that you also work with your own datasets and modify the recipes to suit your own analysis.

Grouping data points within a scatter plot

A basic scatter plot has a set of points plotted at the intersection of their values along *x* and *y* axes. Sometimes, we might wish to further distinguish between these points based on another value associated with the points. In this recipe, we will learn how we can group data points using colors.

Getting ready

To try out this recipe, start R and type the recipe in the command prompt. You can also choose to save the recipe as a script so that you can use it again later on.

We will also need the `lattice` and `ggplot2` packages. The `lattice` package is included automatically in the base R installation, but we will need to install the `ggplot2` package. To do this, run the following command in the R prompt:

```
install.packages("ggplot2")
```

How to do it...

As a first example, let's use the `xyplot()` command of the lattice library:

```
library(lattice)

xyplot(mpg~disp,
data=mtcars,
groups=cyl,
auto.key=list(corner=c(1,1)))
```

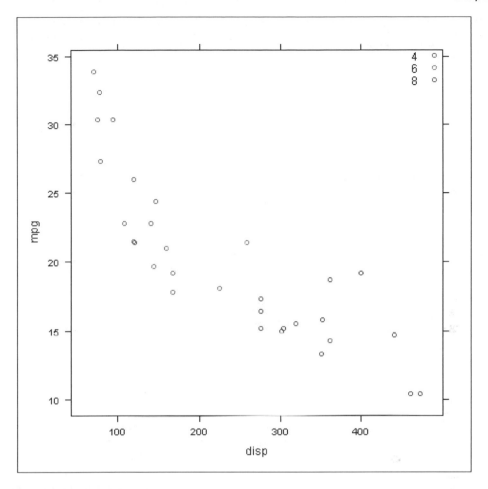

How it works...

In this example, we used the `xyplot()` command to plot **mpg** versus **disp** from the preloaded `mtcars` dataset. We will understand this better if we look at the actual dataset. Type `mtcars` in the R prompt and hit the *Enter* key. Let's look at a sample of the data in order to see the row names and first three columns of data:

```
mtcars[1:6,1:3]
                   mpg   cyl   disp
Mazda RX4          21.0    6    160
Mazda RX4 Wag      21.0    6    160
Datsun 710         22.8    4    108
Hornet 4 Drive     21.4    6    258
Hornet Sportabout  18.7    8    360
Valiant            18.1    6    225
```

So, we plotted `mpg` against `disp`, but we also used the `groups` argument to group the data points by `cyl`. This tells `xyplot()` that we would like to highlight the data points by different colors based on the number of cylinders (`cyl`) each car has. Finally, the `auto.key` argument is set to add a legend so that we know what values of `cyl` each color represents. The `auto.key` argument can take a list of values. The only one we have provided here is the location given by the corner argument, which we set to `c(1,1)`, representing the top-right corner. We can also simply set `auto.key` to `TRUE`, which will draw the legend in the top margin outside the plotting area.

There's more...

The `xyplot()` function has slightly obscure arguments. If you look at the help file on `xyplot()` (by running `?xyplot`), you will see that there are a lot of arguments that can be used to control many different aspects of the graph. A simpler alternative to `xyplot()` is using the functions from the `ggplot2` package. Let's draw the same plot using `ggplot2`:

```
library(ggplot2)
qplot(disp,mpg,data=mtcars,col= as.factor(cyl))
```

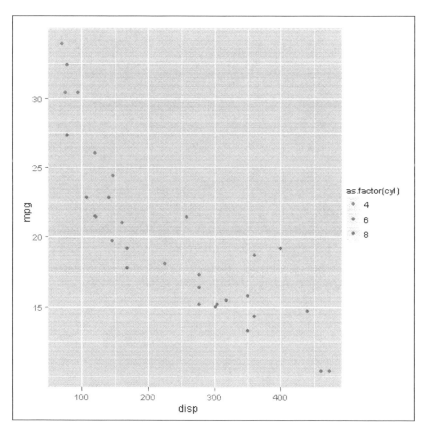

First, we load the ggplot2 library and then we use the qplot () function to create the preceding graph. We passed disp and mpg as the x and y variables, respectively (note that we can't use the y~x notation in qplot). To group by cyl, all we had to do was set the col argument to cyl. This tells qplot that we want to group the points based on the values of cyl and represent them by different colors. The legend is automatically drawn to the right.

Note that we set col to as.factor(cyl) and not just cyl. This is to make sure that cyl is read as a factor (or a categorical value). If we just use cyl, then the plot is still the same, but the color scale and legend uses all the values between 4 and 8 as it takes cyl as a numerical variable.

Thus, it is easier and more intuitive to produce a better-looking graph with ggplot2.

See also

We will use ggplot2 to group data points by size and symbol instead of color in the next recipe.

Highlighting grouped data points by size and symbol type

Sometimes, we might not want to use different colors to represent different groups of data points. For example, some journals accept graphs only in grayscale. In this recipe, we will learn how we can highlight grouped data points by symbol size and type.

Getting ready

We will use the ggplot2 library, so let's load it by running the following command:

```
library(ggplot2)
```

How to do it...

First, let's group points by the symbol type. Once again, we use the `qplot()` function:

```
qplot(disp,mpg,data=mtcars,shape=as.factor(cyl))
```

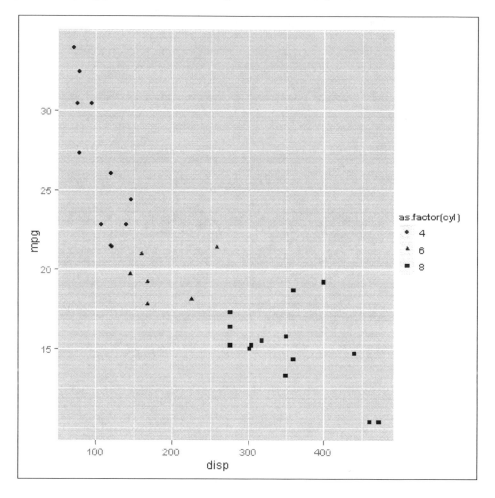

Next, let's group the points simply by the size of the plotting symbol:

```
qplot(disp,mpg,data=mtcars,size=as.factor(cyl))
```

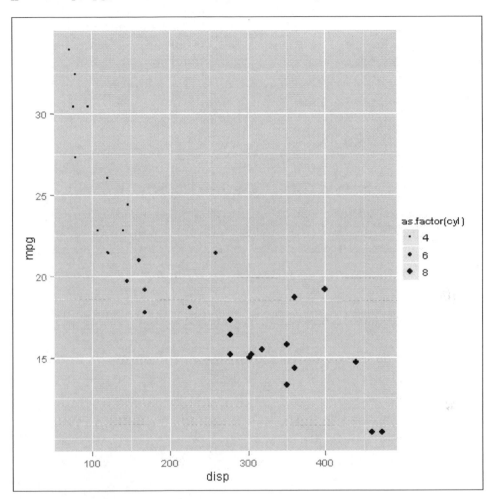

How it works...

Highlighting groups of points by symbol type and size works exactly like colors using the `qplot()` functions. Instead of the `col` argument, we used the `shape` and `size` arguments and set them to the factor we want to group the points by (in this case, `cyl`). We can also use combinations of any of these arguments. For example, we can use colors to represent `cyl` and size to represent the gear.

Labeling data points

In this recipe, we will learn how to label individual or multiple data points with text.

Getting ready

For this recipe, we don't need to load any additional libraries. We just need to type the recipe in the R prompt or run it as a script.

How to do it...

Let's say we want to highlight one data point in the cars' scatter plot that we used in the previous few recipes. We can label it using the `text()` command:

```
plot(mpg~disp, data=mtcars)
text(258,22,"Hornet")
```

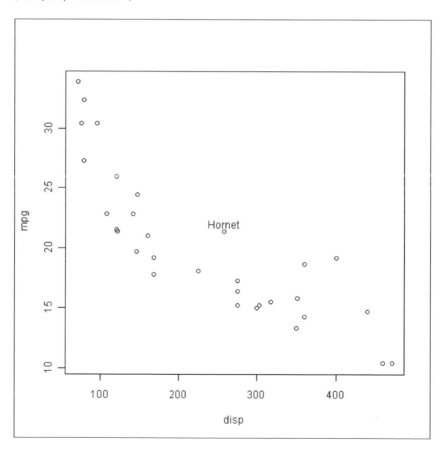

How it works...

In the preceding example, we first plotted the graph and then used the `text()` function to overlay a label at a specific location. The `text()` function takes the x and y coordinates and the text of the label as arguments. We specified the location as `(258,22)` and the label text as `Hornet`. This function is especially useful when we want to label outliers.

There's more...

We can also use the `text()` function to label all the data points in a graph instead of just one or two. Let's look at another example where we wish to plot the life expectancy in countries versus their health expenditure. Instead of representing the data as points, let's use the name of countries to represent the values. We will use the `HealthExpenditure.csv` example dataset:

```
health<-read.csv("HealthExpenditure.csv",header=TRUE)
plot(health$Expenditure,health$Life_Expectancy,type="n")
text(health$Expenditure,health$Life_Expectancy,health$Country)
```

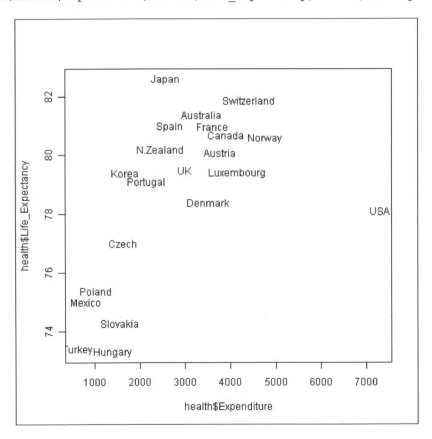

We first use the `plot()` command to create a graph of life expectancy versus expenditure. Note that we set `type` equal to `"n"`, which means that only the graph layout and axes are drawn but no data points are drawn. Then, we use the `text()` function to place country names as labels at the x-y locations of all the data points. Thus, `text()` accepts vectors as values for (x, y) and labels in order to dynamically label all the data points with the corresponding country names. If the text labels overlap, we can use the `jitter()` function or remove some labels to reduce the overlap.

Correlation matrix using pairs plots

In this recipe, we will learn how to create a correlation matrix, which is a handy way of quickly finding out which variables in a dataset are correlated with each other.

Getting ready

To try out this recipe, simply type it in the command prompt. You can also choose to save the recipe as a script so that you can use it again later on.

How to do it...

We will use the `iris` flowers dataset that we first used in the pairs plot recipe in *Chapter 1, R Graphics*:

```
panel.cor <- function(x, y, ...)
{
    par(usr = c(0, 1, 0, 1))
    txt <- as.character(format(cor(x, y), digits=2))
    text(0.5, 0.5, txt,  cex = 6* abs(cor(x, y)))
}

pairs(iris[1:4], upper.panel=panel.cor)
```

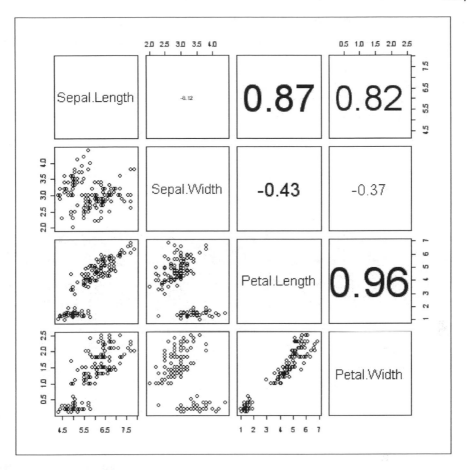

How it works...

We have basically used the `pairs()` function to create the graph, but in addition to the dataset, we also set the `upper.panel` argument to `panel.cor`, which is a function that we define beforehand. The `upper.panel` argument refers to the squares in the top-right half of the preceding graph, the diagonal moving from the top-left corner to the bottom-right corner. Correspondingly, there is also a `lower.panel` argument for the bottom-left half of the graph.

The `panel.cor` value is defined as a function using the following notation:

```
newfunction<-function(arg1, arg2, ...)
{
#function code here
}
```

The `panel.cor` function does a few different things. First, it sets the individual panel block axes limits to `c(0,1,0,1)` using the `par()` command. Then, it calculates the correlation coefficient value between a pair of variables up to two decimal values and formats it as a text string so that it can then be passed to the `text()` function, which places it in the center of each block. Also note that the size of the labels is set using the `cex` argument to a multiple of the absolute value of the correlation coefficient. Thus, the size of the value label also indicates how important the correlation is.

Panel functions are, in fact, one of the most powerful features of the lattice package. To learn more about them and the package, please refer to the excellent book *Lattice: Multivariate Data Visualization with R* by Deepayan Sarkar (Springer), who is also the author of the package. The book's website is located at `http://lmdvr.r-forge.r-project.org/figures/figures.html`.

Adding error bars

In most scientific data visualizations, error bars are required to show the level of confidence in the data. However, there is no predefined function in the base R library to draw error bars. In this recipe, we will learn how to draw error bars in scatter plots.

Getting ready

All you need for the next recipe is to type it at the R prompt as we will use some base library functions to define a new error bar function. You can also save the recipe's code as a script so that you can use it again later on.

How to do it...

Let's draw vertical error bars with 5 percent errors on our cars' scatter plot using the `arrows()` function:

```
plot(mpg~disp,data=mtcars)

arrows(x0=mtcars$disp,
y0=mtcars$mpg*0.95,
x1=mtcars$disp,
y1=mtcars$mpg*1.05,
angle=90,
code=3,
length=0.04,
lwd=0.4)
```

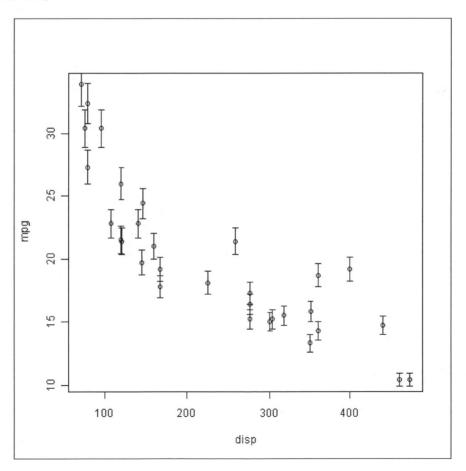

To add horizontal error bars (also 5 percent in both directions) to the same graph, run the following code after creating the preceding graph:

```
arrows(x0=mtcars$disp*0.95,
y0=mtcars$mpg,
x1=mtcars$disp*1.05,
y1=mtcars$mpg,
angle=90,
code=3,
length=0.04,
lwd=0.4)
```

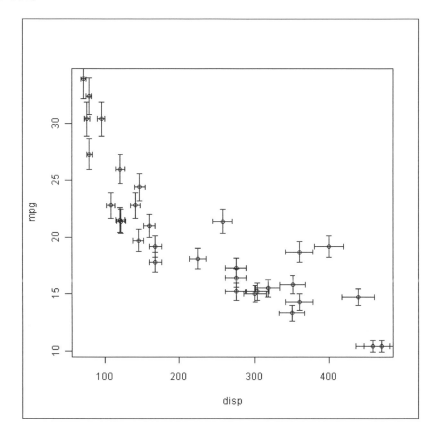

How it works...

In the previous two examples, we used the `arrows()` function to draw horizontal and vertical error bars. The `arrows()` function is a base graphics function that draws different kinds of arrows. It provides various arguments to adjust the size, location, and shape of the arrows such that they can be used as error bars.

The first four arguments define the location of the start and end points of the arrows. The first two arguments, which are x0 and y0, are coordinates of the starting points and the next two arguments, which are x1 and y1, are coordinates of the endpoints of the arrows.

To draw vertical error bars, say, with a 5 percent error both ways, we set both x0 and x1 to the x location of the data points (in this case, mtcars$disp), and we set y0 and y1 to the y values of the data points' plus and minus the error margin (1.05*mtcars$mpg and 0.95*mtcars$mpg, respectively).

Similarly, to draw horizontal error bars, we have the same y coordinate for the start and end, but add and subtract the error margin from the x coordinates of the data points.

The angle argument is to set the angle between the shaft of the arrow and the edge of the arrowhead. The default value is 30 (which looks more like an arrow), but to use as an error bar, we set it to 90 (to flatten out the arrowhead in a way).

The code argument sets the type of arrow to be drawn. Setting it to 3 means drawing an arrowhead at both ends.

The length and lwd arguments set the length of the arrowheads and the line width of the arrow, respectively.

There's more...

The Hmisc package has the errbar function, which can be used to draw vertical error bars. The plotrix package has the plotCI function, which can be used to draw error bars or confidence intervals. If we do not wish to write our own error bars function using arrows(), it's easier to use one of these packages.

Using jitter to distinguish closely packed data points

Sometimes, when working with large datasets, we might find that a lot of data points on a scatter plot overlap each other. In this recipe, we will learn how to distinguish between closely packed data points by adding a small amount of noise with the jitter() function.

Getting ready

All you need for the next recipe is to type it in the R prompt as we will use some base library functions to define a new error bar function. You can also save the recipe code as a script so that you can use it again later on.

How to do it...

First, let's create a graph that has a lot of overlapping points:

```
x <- rbinom(1000, 10, 0.25)
y <- rbinom(1000, 10, 0.25)
plot(x,y)
```

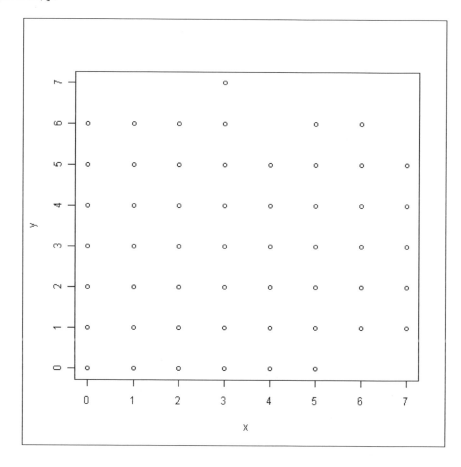

Now, let's add some noise to the data points to see whether there are overlapping points:

```
plot(jitter(x), jitter(y))
```

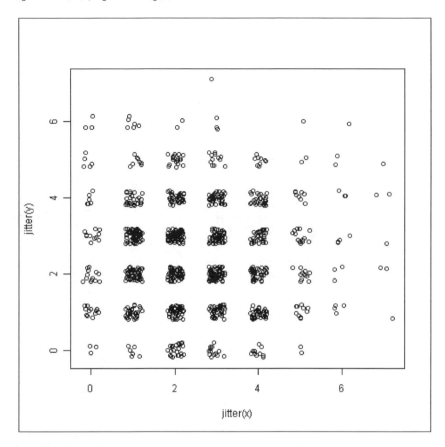

How it works...

In the first graph, we plotted 1,000 random data points generated with the `rbinom()` function. However, as you can see in the first graph, only a few data points are visible because there are multiple data points in the exact same location. Then, when we plotted the points by applying the `jitter()` function to the x and y values, we saw a lot more of the thousand points. We can also see that most of the data is in the range of x and y values of 2 to 4, respectively.

Adding linear model lines

In this recipe, we will learn how to fit a linear model and plot the linear regression line on a scatter plot.

Getting ready

All you need for the next recipe is to type it at the R prompt as we will only use some base functions. You can also save the recipe code as a script so that you can use it again later on.

How to do it...

Once again, let's use the `mtcars` dataset and draw a linear fit line for `mpg` versus `disp`:

```
plot(mtcars$mpg~mtcars$disp)
lmfit<-lm(mtcars$mpg~mtcars$disp)
abline(lmfit)
```

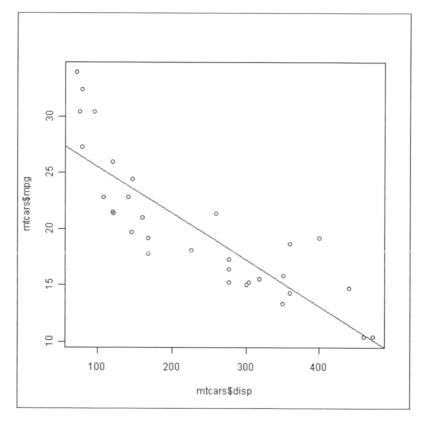

How it works...

We first draw the basic scatter plot of `mpg` versus `disp`. Then, we fit a linear model to the data using the `lm()` function, which takes a formula in the form `y~x` as its argument. Finally, we pass the linear fit to the `abline()` function, which reads the intercept and slope saved in the `lmfit` object to draw a line.

Adding nonlinear model curves

In this recipe, we will learn how to fit and draw a nonlinear model curve to a dataset.

Getting ready

All you need for the next recipe is to type it at the R prompt as we will only use some base functions. You can also save the recipe code as a script so that you can use it again later on.

How to do it...

Plot an exponential plot:

```
x <- -(1:100)/10
y <- 100 + 10 * exp(x / 2) + rnorm(x)/10
nlmod <- nls(y ~  Const + A * exp(B * x), trace=TRUE)

plot(x,y)
lines(x, predict(nlmod), col="red")
```

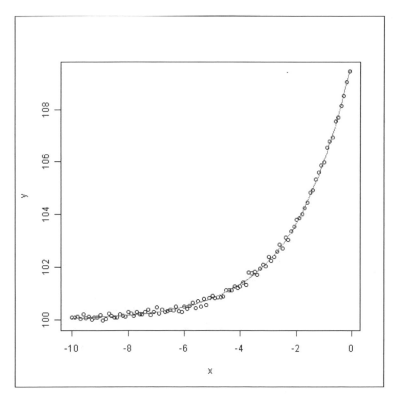

How it works...

We first plot y against x, where x is a variable defined using the : sequence operator and y is an exponential function of x. Then, we fit a nonlinear model to the data using the `nls()` function. We save the model fit as `nlmod` and finally draw the model predicted values by passing x and `predict(nlmod)` to the `lines()` function.

Adding nonparametric model curves with lowess

In this recipe, we will learn how to use lowess, which is a nonparametric model, and add the resulting prediction curve to a scatter plot.

Getting ready

For this recipe, we don't need to load any additional libraries. We just need to type the recipe in the R prompt or run it as a script.

How to do it...

First, let's create a simple scatter plot with the preloaded `cars` dataset and add a couple of lowess lines to it:

```
plot(cars, main = "lowess(cars)")
lines(lowess(cars), col = "blue")
lines(lowess(cars, f=0.3), col = "orange")
```

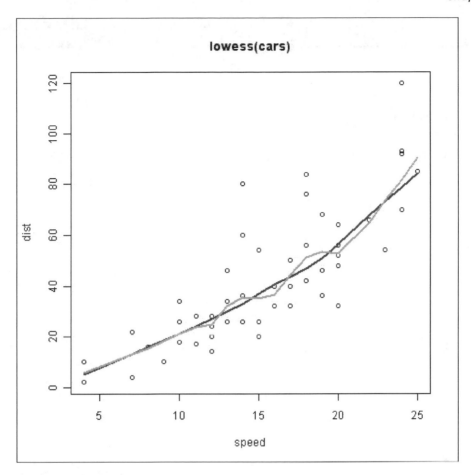

How it works...

Standard R sessions include the `lowess()` function. It is a smoother that uses locally weighted polynomial regression. The first argument, in this instance, is a data frame called `cars` that gives the x and y variables (**speed** and **dist**). So we apply the `lowess` function to the `cars` dataset and in turn pass that result to the `lines()` function. The result of `lowess` is a list with components named x and y. The `lines()` function automatically detects this and uses the appropriate values to draw a smooth line through the scatter plot. The second smooth line has an additional argument, `f`, which is known as the smoother span. This gives us the proportion of points in the plot that influence the smoothening at each value. Larger values give us more smoothness. The default value is approximately `0.67`, so when we change it to `0.3` we get a less smooth fit.

Creating three-dimensional scatter plots

In this recipe, we will learn how to create three-dimensional scatter plots that can be very useful when we want to explore the relationships between more than two variables at a time.

Getting ready

We need to install and load the scatterplot3d package in order to run this recipe:

```
install.packages("scatterplot3d")
library(scatterplot3d)
```

How to do it...

Let's create the simplest default three-dimensional-scatter plot with our mtcars dataset:

```
scatterplot3d(x=mtcars$wt,
              y=mtcars$disp,
              z=mtcars$mpg)
```

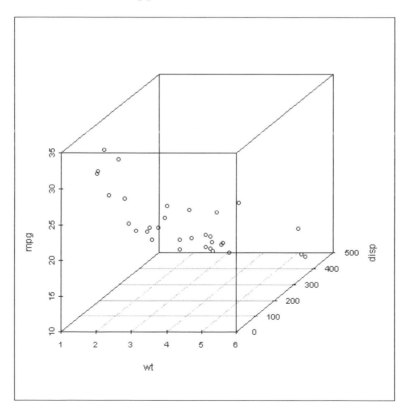

How it works...

That was easy! The `scatterplot3d()` functions much like the basic `plot()` function. In the preceding example, all we had to provide was `wt`, `disp`, and `mpg` from the `mtcars` dataset as the `x`, `y`, and `z` arguments, respectively.

There's more...

Just like `plot()` and other graph functions, `scatterplot3d()` accepts a number of additional arguments using which we can configure the graph in many ways. Let's try some of these additional settings.

Let's add a title to the graph, change the plotting symbol and the angle of viewing, add highlighting, and add vertical drop lines to the x-y plane:

```
scatterplot3d(mtcars$wt,mtcars$disp,mtcars$mpg,
pch=16, highlight.3d=TRUE, angle=20,
xlab="Weight",ylab="Displacement",zlab="Fuel Economy (mpg)",
type="h",
main="Relationships between car specifications")
```

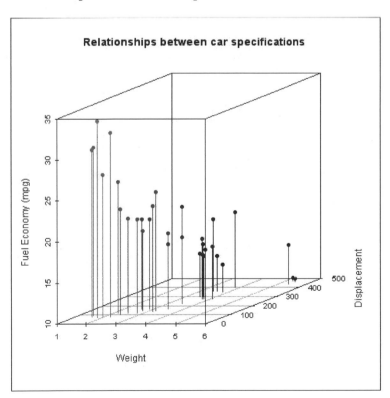

As you can see, we changed some of the graph settings using arguments we used in the `plot()` function previously. These include the axis titles, graph title, and symbol type. In addition, we added some color highlighting by setting the `highlight.3d` argument to TRUE, which draws the points in different colors related to the y coordinates (`disp`). The `angle` argument is used to set the angle between the x and y axes, which controls the point from which we view the data. Finally, setting `type` to h adds the vertical lines to the x-y plane, which makes reading the graph easier.

For more advanced three-dimensional data visualization in R, please have a look at the `rggobi` package, which allows interactive analysis with 3D plots. The package can be installed like any other R package:

```
install.packages("rggobi")
```

Please refer to the package's website for more details: `http://www.ggobi.org/rggobi/`.

Creating Quantile-Quantile plots

In this recipe, we will create **Quantile-Quantile (Q-Q)** plots, which are useful for comparing two probability distributions.

Getting ready

For this recipe, we don't need to load any additional libraries. We just need to type the recipe in the R prompt or run it as a script.

How to do it...

Let's see how the distribution of `mpg` in the `mtcars` dataset compares with a normal distribution using the `qnorm()` function:

```
qqnorm(mtcars$mpg)
qqline(mtcars$mpg)
```

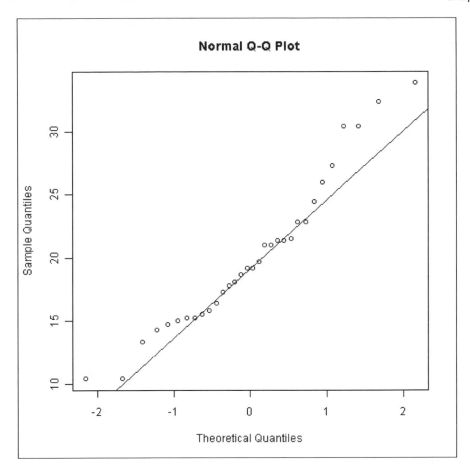

How it works...

In this, we used the qqnorm() function to create a normal Q-Q plot of mpg values. We added a straight line with the qqline() function. The closer the dots are to this line, the closer the distribution to a normal Q-Q plot.

There's more...

Another way of creating a Q-Q plot is by calling the `plot()` function on a model fit. For example, let's plot the following linear model fit:

```
lmfit<-lm(mtcars$mpg~mtcars$disp)
par(mfrow=c(2,2))
plot(lmfit)
```

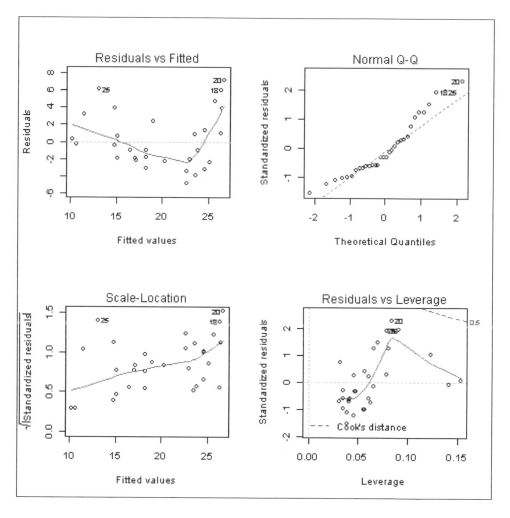

The second plot is a Q-Q plot that compares the model fit to a normal distribution.

Displaying the data density on axes

In this recipe, we will learn how to show the density of data points on a scatter plot in the margin of the X or Y axes.

Getting ready

For this recipe, we don't need to load any additional libraries.

How to do it...

We will use the `rug()` function in the base graphics library. As a simple example to illustrate the use of this function, let's see the data density of a normal distribution:

```
x<-rnorm(1000)
plot(density(x))
rug(x)
```

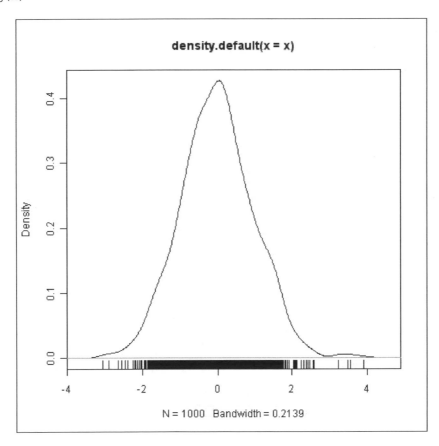

How it works...

As can be seen from this example, the `rug()` function adds a set of lines just above the x-axis. A line or tick mark is placed wherever there is a point at that particular X location. So, the more closely packed together the lines are, the higher the data density around those X values is. The example is obvious, as we know that in a normal distribution, most values are around the mean value (in this case, zero).

The `rug()` function, in its simplest form, only takes one numeric vector as its argument. Note that it draws on top of an existing plot.

There's more...

Let's take another example and explore some of the additional arguments that can be passed to `rug()`. We will use the example `metals.csv` dataset:

```
metals<-read.csv("metals.csv")
plot(Ba~Cu,data=metals,xlim=c(0,100))
rug(metals$Cu)
rug(metals$Ba,side=2,col="red",ticksize=0.02)
```

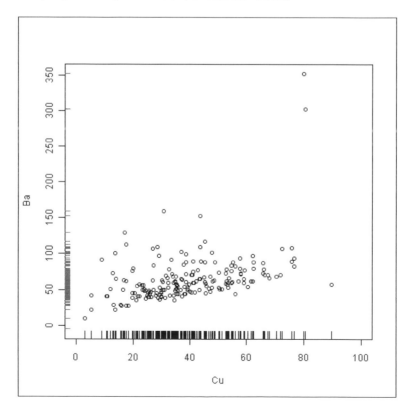

We first read the `metals.csv` file and plot barium (Ba) concentrations against copper (Cu) concentrations. Next, we added a `rug` of Cu values on the X axis using the default settings. Then, we added another `rug` for Ba values on the Y axis by setting the `side` argument to 2. The `side` argument takes four values:

- ▶ 1: Bottom axis (the default)
- ▶ 2: Left
- ▶ 3: Top
- ▶ 4: Right

We also set the color of the tick marks to red using the `col` argument. Finally, we adjusted the size of the tick marks using the `ticksize` argument that reads numeric values as a fraction of the width of the plotting area. Positive values draw inward ticks and negative values draw ticks on the outside.

Creating scatter plots with a smoothed density representation

Smoothed density scatter plots are a good way of visualizing large datasets. In this recipe, we will learn how to create them using the `smoothScatter()` function.

Getting ready

For this recipe, we don't need to load any additional libraries. We just need to type the recipe in the R prompt or run it as a script.

How to do it...

We will use the `smoothScatter()` function that is part of the base graphics library. We will use an example from the help file that can be accessed from the R prompt with the help command:

```
n <- 10000
x  <- matrix(rnorm(n), ncol=2)
y  <- matrix(rnorm(n, mean=3, sd=1.5), ncol=2)
smoothScatter(x,y)
```

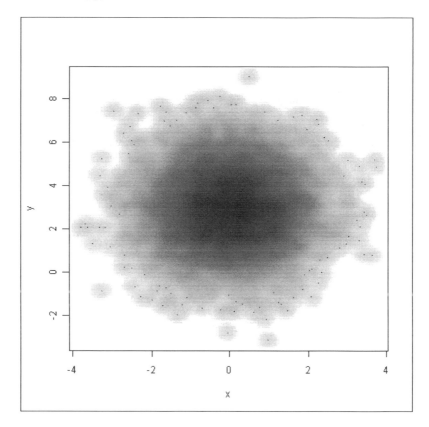

How it works...

The `smoothScatter()` function produces a smoothed color density representation of the scatter plot, which is obtained through a kernel density estimate. We passed the x and y variables that represented the data to be plotted. The gradient of the blue color shows us the density of the data points, with most points in the center of the graph. The dots in the outer light blue circles are outliers.

There's more...

We can pass a number of arguments to `smoothScatter()` in order to adjust the smoothing, for example, `nbin` for specifying the number of equally spaced grid points for the density estimation and `nrpoints` to specify how many points are to be shown as dots. In addition, we can also pass standard arguments such as `xlab`, `ylab`, `pch`, and `cex` in order to modify axis and plot symbol characteristics.

5

Creating Line Graphs and Time Series Charts

In this chapter, we will cover the following recipes:

- ▶ Adding customized legends for multiple-line graphs
- ▶ Using margin labels instead of legends for multiple-line graphs
- ▶ Adding horizontal and vertical grid lines
- ▶ Adding marker lines at specific X and Y values using abline
- ▶ Creating sparklines
- ▶ Plotting functions of a variable in a dataset
- ▶ Formatting time series data for plotting
- ▶ Plotting the date or time variable on the X axis
- ▶ Annotating axis labels in different human-readable time formats
- ▶ Adding vertical markers to indicate specific time events
- ▶ Plotting data with varying time averaging periods
- ▶ Creating stock charts

Introduction

In *Chapter 1, R Graphics*, and *Chapter 3, Beyond the Basics – Adjusting Key Parameters*, we learned some basics of how to make line graphs and customize them by setting certain arguments as per our needs. In this chapter, we will learn some intermediate to advanced recipes to customize line graphs even further. We will look at ways to improve and speed up line graphs with multiple lines that represent more than one variable.

One of the most used forms of line graphs is time trends or time series, where the x variable is some measure of time such as year, month, week, day, hour, and so on. Reading, formatting, and plotting dates can be quite tricky in R. In this chapter, we will see how to deal with dates and process them to make time series charts with custom annotations, grid lines, uncertainty bounds, and markers.

We will also learn to make some interesting and popular types of time series charts such as sparklines and stock charts.

As the recipes in this chapter are slightly more advanced than the earlier chapters, it might take some practice with multiple datasets before you are comfortable with using all the functions. Example datasets are used in each recipe, but it is highly recommended you also work with your own datasets and modify the recipes to suit your own analysis.

Adding customized legends for multiple-line graphs

Line graphs with more than one line, representing more than one variable, are quite common in any kind of data analysis. In this recipe, we will learn how to create and customize legends for such graphs.

Getting ready

We will use the base graphics library for this recipe, so all you need to do is run the recipe at the R prompt. It is good practice to save your code as a script for use again later.

How to do it...

Once again we will use the `cityrain.csv` example dataset that we used in *Chapter 1, R Graphics*, and *Chapter 3, Beyond the Basics – Adjusting Key Parameters*:

```
rain<-read.csv("cityrain.csv")
plot(rain$Tokyo,type="b",lwd=2,
xaxt="n",ylim=c(0,300),col="black",
xlab="Month",ylab="Rainfall (mm)",
main="Monthly Rainfall in major cities")
axis(1,at=1:length(rain$Month),labels=rain$Month)
lines(rain$Berlin,col="red",type="b",lwd=2)
lines(rain$NewYork,col="orange",type="b",lwd=2)
lines(rain$London,col="purple",type="b",lwd=2)

legend("topright",legend=c("Tokyo","Berlin","New York","London"),
```

```
lty=1,lwd=2,pch=21,col=c("black","red","orange","purple"),
ncol=2,bty="n",cex=0.8,
text.col=c("black","red","orange","purple"),
inset=0.01)
```

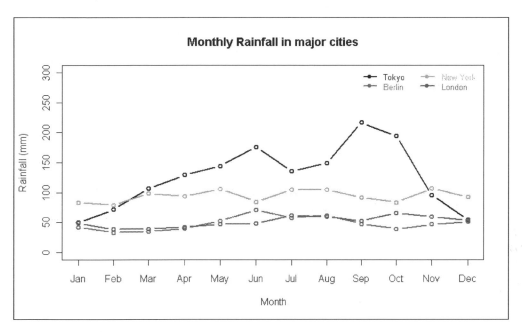

How it works...

We used the `legend()` function that we have already come across in earlier chapters. It is quite a flexible function and allows us to adjust the placement and styling of the legend in many ways.

The first argument we passed to `legend()` specifies the position of the legend within the plot region. We used `"topright"`. Other possible values are `"bottomright"`, `"bottom"`, `"bottomleft"`, `"left"`, `"topleft"`, `"top"`, `"right"`, and `"center"`. We can also specify the location of legend with the x and y coordinates, as we will soon see.

The other important arguments specific to lines are `lwd` and `lty` that specify the line width and type drawn in the legend box, respectively. It is important to keep these the same as the corresponding values in the `plot()` and `lines()` commands. We also set `pch` to 21 to replicate the `type="b"` argument in the `plot()` command. The `cex` and `text.col` parameters set the size and colors of the legend text, respectively. Note that we set the text colors to the same colors as the lines they represent. Setting `bty` (box type) to `"n"` ensures no box is drawn around the legend. This is good practice as it keeps the look of the graph clean. The `ncol` parameter sets the number of columns over which the legend labels are spread and inset sets the inset distance from the margins as a fraction of the plot region.

There's more...

Let's experiment by changing some of the arguments discussed:

```
legend(1,300,legend=c("Tokyo","Berlin","New York","London"),
lty=1,lwd=2,pch=21,col=c("black","red","orange","purple"),
horiz=TRUE,bty="n",bg="yellow",cex=1,
text.col=c("black","red","orange","purple"))
```

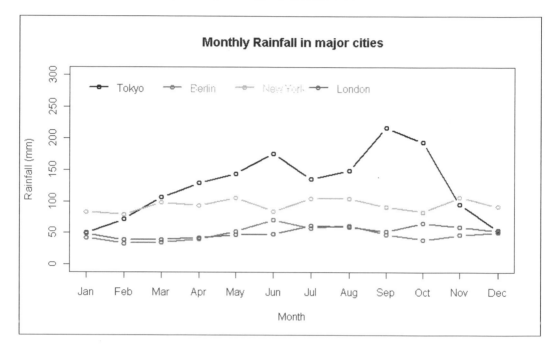

This time we used the x and y coordinates instead of a keyword to position the legend. We also set the `horiz` argument to `TRUE`. As the name suggests, `horiz` makes the legend labels horizontal instead of the default vertical. Specifying `horiz` overrides the `ncol` argument. Finally, we made the legend text bigger by setting `cex` to `1` and did not use the inset argument.

An alternative way of creating the previous plot without have to call `plot()` and `lines()` multiple times is to use the `matplot()` function. To see details on how to use this function, see the help file by running `?matplot` or `help(matplot)` on the R prompt.

See also

Have a look at the next recipe that shows a way to label lines directly instead of using a legend.

Using margin labels instead of legends for multiple-line graphs

While legends are the most commonly used method of providing a key to read multiple-variable graphs, they are often not the easiest to read. Labeling lines directly is one way of getting around this problem.

Getting ready

We will use the base graphics library for this recipe, so all you need to do is run the recipe at the R prompt. It is good practice to save your code as a script for use again later.

How to do it...

Let's use the `gdp.txt` example dataset to look at the trends in annual GDP of five countries:

```
gdp<-read.table("gdp_long.txt",header=T)

library(RColorBrewer)
pal<-brewer.pal(5,"Set1")

par(mar=par()$mar+c(0,0,0,2),bty="l")

plot(Canada~Year,data=gdp,type="l",lwd=2,lty=1,ylim=c(30,60),
col=pal[1],main="Percentage change in GDP",ylab="")

mtext(side=4,at=gdp$Canada[length(gdp$Canada)],text="Canada",
col=pal[1],line=0.3,las=2)

lines(gdp$France~gdp$Year,col=pal[2],lwd=2)

mtext(side=4,at=gdp$France[length(gdp$France)],text="France",
col=pal[2],line=0.3,las=2)

lines(gdp$Germany~gdp$Year,col=pal[3],lwd=2)

mtext(side=4,at=gdp$Germany[length(gdp$Germany)],text="Germany",
col=pal[3],line=0.3,las=2)

lines(gdp$Britain~gdp$Year,col=pal[4],lwd=2)
```

```
mtext(side=4,at=gdp$Britain[length(gdp$Britain)],text="Britain",
col=pal[4],line=0.3,las=2)

lines(gdp$USA~gdp$Year,col=pal[5],lwd=2)

mtext(side=4,at=gdp$USA[length(gdp$USA)]-2,
text="USA",col=pal[5],line=0.3,las=2)
```

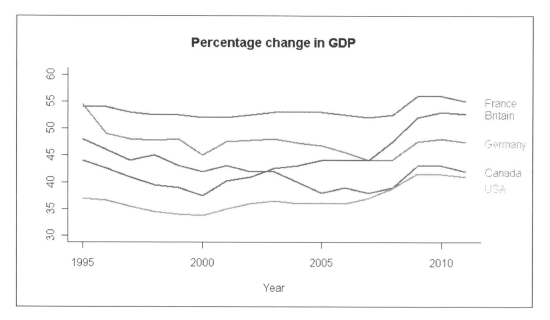

How it works...

We first read the `gdp.txt` data file using the `read.table()` function. Next, we loaded the `RColorBrewer` color palette library and set our color palette, `pal`, to "Set1" (with five colors).

Before drawing the graph, we used the `par()` command to add extra space to the right margin, so that we have enough space for the labels. Depending on the size of the text labels, you might have to experiment with this margin until you get it right. Finally, we set the box type (`bty`) to an L shape ("l") so that there is no line on the right margin. We can also set it to "c" if we want to keep the top line.

We used the `mtext()` function to label each of the lines individually in the right margin. The first argument we passed to the function is the side where we want the label to be placed. Sides (margins) are numbered starting from 1 for the bottom side and going round in a clockwise direction so that 2 is left, 3 is top, and 4 is right.

The `at` argument was used to specify the Y coordinate of the label. This is a bit tricky because we have to make sure we place the label as close to the corresponding line as possible. So, here we have used the last value of each line. For example, `gdp$France[length(gdp$France)` picks the last value in the `France` vector by using its length as the index. Note that we had to adjust the value for USA by subtracting 2 from its last value so that it doesn't overlap the label for Canada.

We used the `text` argument to set the text of the labels as country names. We set the `col` argument to the appropriate element of the `pal` vector by using a number index. The `line` argument sets an offset in terms of margin lines, starting at 0 counting forward. Finally, setting `las` to 2 rotates the labels so they're perpendicular to the axis, instead of the default value of 1, which makes them parallel to the axis.

There's more...

Sometimes, simply using the last value of a set of values might not work because the value might be missing. In that case, we can use the second-last value or visually choose a value that places the label closest to the line. Also, the size of the plot window and the proximity of the final values can cause overlapping of labels. So, we might need to iterate a few times before we get the placement right. We can write functions to automate this process but it is still good to visually inspect the outcome.

Adding horizontal and vertical grid lines

In this recipe, we will learn how to add and customize grid lines to graphs.

Getting ready

We will use the base graphics for this recipe, so all you need to do is run the recipe at the R prompt. It is good practice to save your code as a script for use again later.

How to do it...

Let's use the city rainfall example again to see how we can add grid lines to that graph:

```
rain<-read.csv("cityrain.csv")
plot(rain$Tokyo,type="b",lwd=2,
xaxt="n",ylim=c(0,300),col="black",
xlab="Month",ylab="Rainfall (mm)",
main="Monthly Rainfall in Tokyo")
```

```
axis(1,at=1:length(rain$Month),labels=rain$Month)

grid()
```

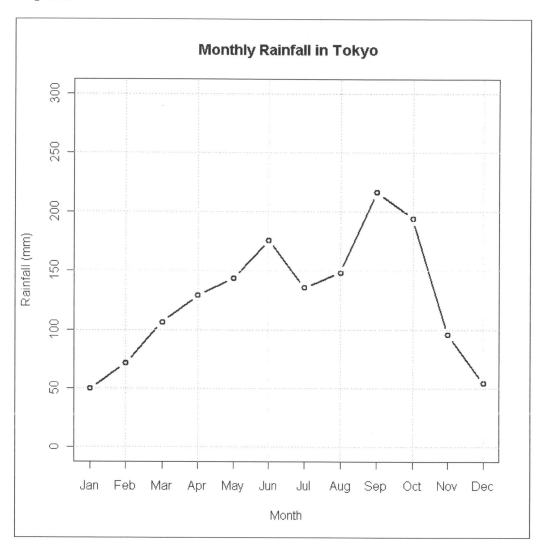

How it works...

It's as simple as that! Adding a simple default grid just necessitates calling the `grid()` function without passing any arguments. The `grid()` function automatically computes the number of cells in the grid and aligns with the tick marks on the default axes. It uses the `abline()` function (that we will see again in the next recipe) to draw the grid lines.

There's more...

We can specify the location of the grid lines using the nx and ny arguments, corresponding to vertical and horizontal grid lines, respectively. By default, these two arguments are set to NULL, which results in the default grid lines in both X and Y directions. If we do not wish to draw grid lines in a particular direction, we can set nx or ny to NA. If nx is set to NA, no vertical grid lines are drawn; if ny is set to NA, no horizontal grid lines are drawn.

The default grid lines are very thin and light-colored; they can barely be seen. We can customize the styling of the grid lines using the lwd, lty, and col arguments:

```
grid(nx=NA, ny=8,
lwd=1,lty=2,col="blue")
```

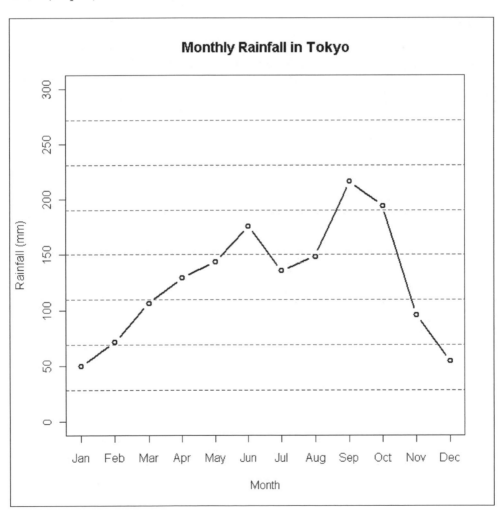

See also

In the next recipe, we will learn to use the `abline()` function, which we can use to draw lines at any specific X and Y locations.

Adding marker lines at specific x and y values using abline

Sometimes, we might only want to draw one or a few lines to indicate specific cutoff or threshold values. In this recipe, we will learn how to do this using the `abline()` function.

Getting ready

We will use the base graphics library for this recipe, so all you need to do is run the recipe at the R prompt. It is good practice to save your code as a script for use again later.

How to do it...

Let's draw a vertical line against the month of September in the rainfall graph for Tokyo:

```
rain <- read.csv("cityrain.csv")
plot(rain$Tokyo,type="b",lwd=2,
xaxt="n",ylim=c(0,300),col="black",
xlab="Month",ylab="Rainfall (mm)",
main="Monthly Rainfall in Tokyo")
axis(1,at=1:length(rain$Month),labels=rain$Month)

abline(v=9)
```

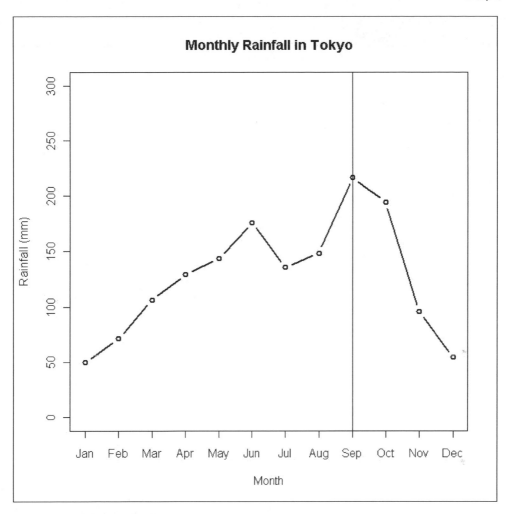

How it works...

To draw marker lines with `abline()` at specific X or Y locations, we have to set the `v` (as in vertical) or `h` (as in horizontal) arguments, respectively. In the example, we set `v=9` (the index of the month September in the `Month` vector).

There's more...

Now, let's add a red dotted horizontal line to the graph to denote a high rainfall cutoff of 150 mm:

```
abline(h=150,col="red",lty=2)
```

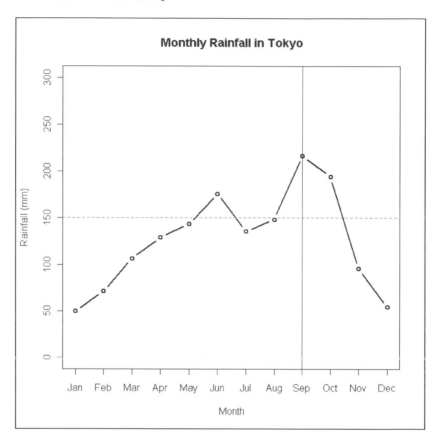

Creating sparklines

Sparklines are small and simple line graphs, useful to summarize trend data in a small space. The word *sparklines* was coined by Prof. Edward Tufte. In this recipe, we will learn how to make sparklines using a basic `plot()` function.

Getting ready

We will use the base graphics library for this recipe, so all you need to do is run the recipe at the R prompt. It is good practice to save your code as a script for use again later.

How to do it...

Let's represent our city rainfall data in the form of sparklines:

```
rain <- read.csv("cityrain.csv")

par(mfrow=c(4,1),mar=c(5,7,4,2),omi=c(0.2,2,0.2,2))

for(i in 2:5)
{
    plot(rain[,i],ann=FALSE,axes=FALSE,type="l",
    col="gray",lwd=2)

    mtext(side=2,at=mean(rain[,i]),names(rain[i]),
    las=2,col="black")

    mtext(side=4,at=mean(rain[,i]),mean(rain[i]),
    las=2,col="black")

    points(which.min(rain[,i]),min(rain[,i]),pch=19,col="blue")
    points(which.max(rain[,i]),max(rain[,i]),pch=19,col="red")
}
```

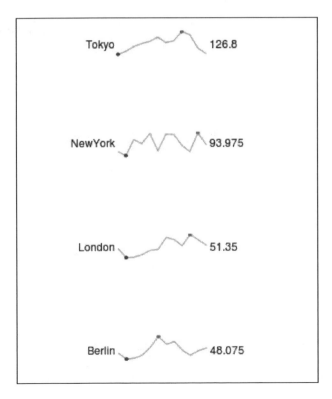

How it works...

The key feature of sparklines is to show the trend in the data with just one line without any axis annotations. In the example, we have shown the trend with a gray line. The minimum and maximum values for each line is represented by blue and red dots, respectively, while the mean value is displayed on the right margin.

As sparklines have to be very small graphics, we first set the margins such that the plot area is small and the outer margins are large. We did this by setting the outer margins in inches using the `omi` argument of the `par()` function. Depending on the dimensions of the plot, sometimes R produces an error that says that the figure margins are too large, and does not draw the graph. In this case, we need to try lower values for the margins. Note that we also set up a 4 x 1 layout with the `mfrow` argument.

Next, we set up a for loop to draw a sparkline for each of the four cities. We drew the line with the `plot()` command, setting both annotations, `ann` and `axes`, to `false`. Then, we used the `mtext()` function to place the name of the city and the mean value of rainfall to the left and right of the line, respectively. Finally, we plotted the minimum and maximum values using the `points()` command. Note that we used the `which.min()` and `which.max()` functions to get the indices of the minimum and maximum values, respectively, and used them as the x value for the `points()` function calls.

Plotting functions of a variable in a dataset

Sometimes, we might wish to visualize the effect of applying a mathematical function to a set of values, instead of the original variable itself. In this recipe, we will learn a simple method to plot functions of variables.

Getting ready

We will use the base graphics library for this recipe, so all you need to do is run the recipe at the R prompt. It is good practice to save your code as a script for use again later.

How to do it...

Let's say we want to plot the difference in rainfall between Tokyo and London. We can do this just by passing the correct expression to the `plot()` function:

```
rain <- read.csv("cityrain.csv")

plot(rain$Berlin-rain$London,type="l",lwd=2,
xaxt="n",col="blue",
xlab="Month",ylab="Difference in Rainfall (mm)",
```

```
main="Difference in Rainfall between Berlin and London (Berlin-
London)")

axis(1,at=1:length(rain$Month),labels=rain$Month)

abline(h=0,col="red")
```

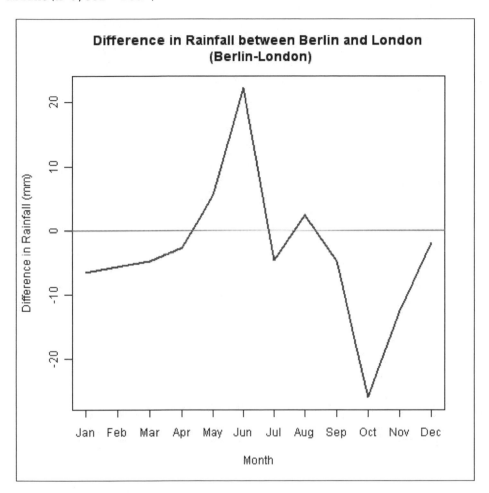

How it works...

So, plotting a function of a variable is as simple as passing an expression to the plot()
function. In the example, the function consisted of two variables in the dataset. We can
also plot transformations applied to any one variable.

There's more...

As another simple example, let's see how we can plot a polynomial function of a set of numbers:

```
x<-1:100
y<-x^3-6*x^2+5*x+10
plot(y~x,type="l",main=expression(f(x)==x^3-6*x^2+5*x+10))
```

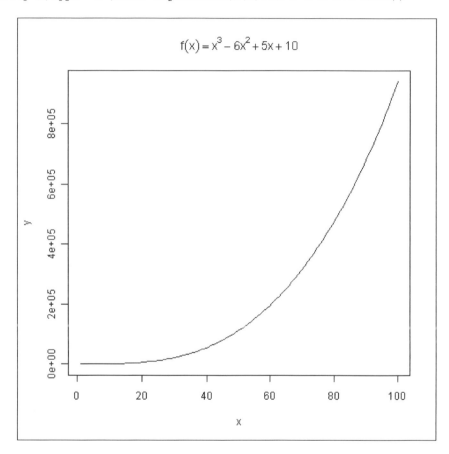

In the preceding example, we defined y as a polynomial function of a vector of the numbers 1 to 100 and then plotted it using the plot() function. Note that we used the expression() function to format the title of the graph. By using expression(), we can get the power values as superscripts.

Formatting time series data for plotting

Time series or trend charts are the most common form of line graphs. There are a lot of ways in R to plot such data. However, it is important to first format the data in a suitable format that R can understand. In this recipe, we will look at some ways of formatting time series data using the base and some additional packages.

Getting ready

In addition to the basic R functions, we will also be using the zoo package in this recipe. So, first we need to install it:

```
install.packages("zoo")
```

How to do it...

Let's use the `dailysales.csv` example dataset and format its `date` column:

```
sales<-read.csv("dailysales.csv")

d1<-as.Date(sales$date,"%d/%m/%y")

d2<-strptime(sales$date,"%d/%m/%y")

data.class(d1)
[1] "Date"

data.class(d2)
[1] "POSIXt"
```

How it works...

We have seen two different functions to convert a character vector into dates. If we did not convert the `date` column, R will not automatically recognize the values in the column as dates. Instead, the column will be treated as a character vector or a factor.

The `as.Date()` function takes at least two arguments: the character vector to be converted to dates and the format to which we want it converted. It returns an object of the `Date` class, represented as the number of days since 1970-01-01, with negative values for earlier dates. The values in the `date` column are in the DD/MM/YYYY format (you can verify this by typing in `sales$date` at the R prompt). So, we specify the format argument as `"%d/%m/%y"`. Note that this order is important. If we instead use `"%m/%d/%y"`, then our days will be read as months and vice versa. The quotes around the value are also necessary.

The strptime() function is another way to convert character vectors into dates. However, strptime() returns a different kind of object of the POSIXlt class, which is a named list of vectors that represent the different components of a date and time, such as year, month, day, hour, seconds, and minutes.

POSIXlt is one of the two basic classes of date/time in R. The other POSIXct class represents the (signed) number of seconds since the beginning of 1970 (in the UTC time zone) as a numeric vector. POSIXct is more convenient for including in data frames, and POSIXlt is closer to human-readable forms. Being a virtual class, POSIXt inherits from both of the classes. That's why, when we ran the data.class() function on d2 earlier, we got POSIXt as the result.

The strptime() function also takes a character vector to be converted and the format as arguments.

There's more...

The zoo package is handy for dealing with time series data. The zoo() function takes an x argument that can be a numeric vector, matrix, or factor. It also takes an order.by argument that has to be an index vector with unique entries by which the observations in x are ordered:

```
library(zoo)

d3<-zoo(sales$units,as.Date(sales$date,"%d/%m/%y"))

data.class(d3)
[1] "zoo"
```

See the help on DateTimeClasses to find out more details about the ways dates can be represented in R.

Plotting the date or time variable on the x axis

In this recipe, we will learn how to plot formatted date or time values on the x axis.

Getting ready

For the first example, we only need to use the plot() base graphics function.

How to do it...

We will use the `dailysales.csv` example dataset to plot the number of units of a product sold daily in a month:

```
sales<-read.csv("dailysales.csv")
plot(sales$units~as.Date(sales$date,"%d/%m/%y"),type="l",
xlab="Date",ylab="Units Sold")
```

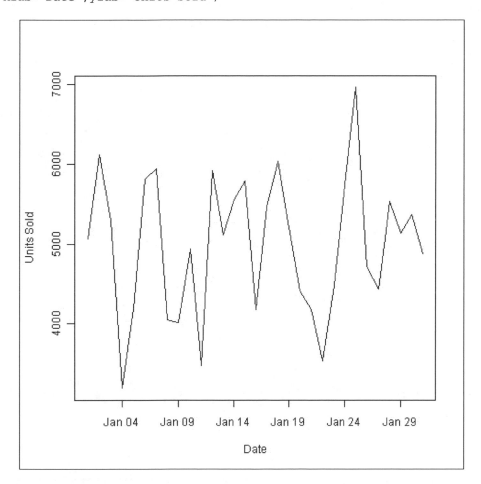

How it works...

Once we have formatted the series of dates using `as.Date()`, we can simply pass it to the `plot()` function as the x variable in either the `plot(x,y)` or `plot(y~x)` format.

We can also use `strptime()` instead of using `as.Date()`. However, we cannot pass the object returned by `strptime()` to `plot()` in the `plot(y~x)` format. We must use the `plot(x,y)` format as follows:

```
plot(strptime(sales$date,"%d/%m/%Y"),sales$units,type="l",
xlab="Date",ylab="Units Sold")
```

There's more...

We can plot the example using the `zoo()` function as follows (assuming zoo is already installed):

```
library(zoo)
plot(zoo(sales$units,as.Date(sales$date,"%d/%m/%y")))
```

Note that we don't need to specify x and y separately when plotting using `zoo`; we can just pass the object returned by `zoo()` to `plot()`. We also need not specify the type as `"l"`.

Let's look at another example that has full date and time values on the *x* axis, instead of just dates. We will use the `openair.csv` example dataset for this example:

```
air<-read.csv("openair.csv")

plot(air$nox~as.Date(air$date,"%d/%m/%Y %H:%M"),type="l",
xlab="Time", ylab="Concentration (ppb)",
main="Time trend of Oxides of Nitrogen")
```

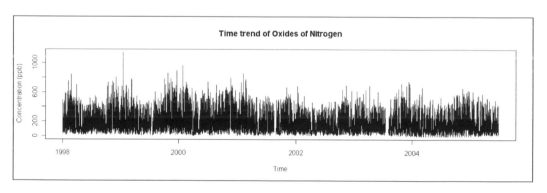

The same graph can be made using `zoo` as follows:

```
plot(zoo(air$nox,as.Date(air$date,"%d/%m/%Y %H:%M")),
xlab="Time", ylab="Concentration (ppb)",
main="Time trend of Oxides of Nitrogen")
```

Annotating axis labels in different human-readable time formats

In this recipe, we will learn how to choose the formatting of time axis labels, instead of just using the defaults.

Getting ready

We will only use the basic R functions for this recipe. Make sure that you are at the R prompt and load the `openair.csv` dataset:

```
air<-read.csv("openair.csv")
```

How to do it...

Let's redraw our original example involving plotting air pollution data from the last recipe, but with labels for each month and year pairing:

```
plot(air$nox~as.Date(air$date,"%d/%m/%Y %H:%M"),type="l",
xaxt="n",
xlab="Time", ylab="Concentration (ppb)",
main="Time trend of Oxides of Nitrogen")

xlabels<-strptime(air$date, format = "%d/%m/%Y %H:%M")
axis.Date(1, at=xlabels[xlabels$mday==1], format="%b-%Y")
```

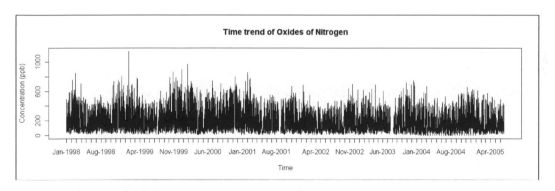

How it works...

In our original example involving plotting air pollution data in the last recipe, we only formatted the date/time vector to pass as a x argument to `plot()`, but the axis labels were chosen automatically by R as the years 1998, 2000, 2002, and 2004. In this example, we drew a custom axis with labels for each month and year pairing.

We first created an `xlabels` object of the `POSIXlt` class by using the `strptime()` function. Then, we used the `axis.Date()` function to add the *x* axis. The `axis.Date()` function is similar to the `axis()` function and takes the `side` and `at` arguments. In addition, it also takes the format argument that we can use to specify the format of the labels. We specified the `at` argument as a subset of `xlabels` for only the first day of each month by setting `mday=1`. The `"%b-%Y"` format value means an abbreviated month name with full year.

There's more...

See the help on `strptime()` to see all the possible formatting options.

Adding vertical markers to indicate specific time events

We might wish to indicate specific points of importance or measurements in a time series, where there is a significant event or change in the data. In this recipe, we will learn how to add vertical markers using the `abline()` function.

Getting ready

We will only use the basic R functions for this recipe. Make sure that you are at the R prompt and load the `openair.csv` dataset:

```
air<-read.csv("openair.csv")
```

How to do it...

Let's take our air pollution time series example again and draw a red vertical line on Christmas day, `25/12/2003`:

```
plot(air$nox~as.Date(air$date,"%d/%m/%Y %H:%M"),type="l",
xlab="Time", ylab="Concentration (ppb)",
main="Time trend of Oxides of Nitrogen")

abline(v=as.Date("25/12/2003","%d/%m/%Y"))
```

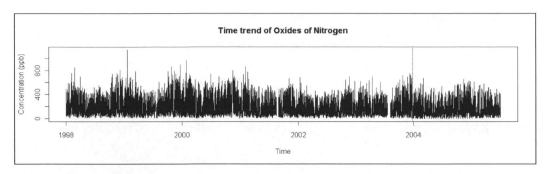

How it works...

As we have seen before in the recipe introducing `abline()`, we drew a vertical line in the example by setting the `v` argument to the date we want to mark. We specified `25/12/2003` as the X coordinate by using the `as.Date()` function. Note that the original time series plotted also contains the timestamp in addition to the dates. As we didn't specify a time, the line was plotted at the start of the specified date, `25/12/2003 00:00`.

There's more...

Let's look at another example, where we want to draw a vertical marker line on Christmas every year:

```
markers<-seq(from=as.Date("25/12/1998","%d/%m/%Y"),
to=as.Date("25/12/2004","%d/%m/%Y"),
by="year")

abline(v=markers,col="red")
```

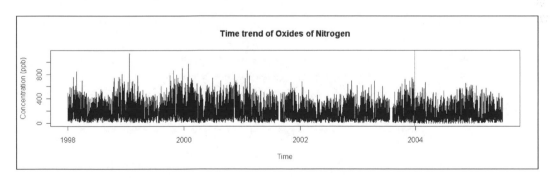

We created a sequence of the Christmas dates for each year using the `seq()` function, which takes the `from`, `to`, and `by` arguments. Then, we passed this vector to the `abline()` function as `v`.

One important thing to note is that, by default, R does not deal with gaps in a time series. There can be missing values denoted by NA and, as you can see in the previous examples, the graphs show gaps in those places. However, if any dates or time intervals are missing from the actual dataset, then R draws a line connecting the data points before and after the gap instead of leaving it blank. In order to remove this connecting line, we must fill in the missing time intervals in the gap and set the y values to NA.

Plotting data with varying time-averaging periods

In this recipe, we will learn how we can plot the same time series data by averaging it over different time periods using the aggregate() function.

Getting ready

We will only use the basic R functions for this recipe. Make sure that you load the openair. csv dataset.

```
air<-read.csv("openair.csv")
```

How to do it...

Let's plot the air pollution time series with weekly and daily averages instead of hourly values:

```
air$date = as.POSIXct(strptime(air$date, format = "%d/%m/%Y %H:%M",
"GMT"))
means <- aggregate(air["nox"], format(air["date"],"%Y-%U"),mean, na.rm
= TRUE)
means$date <- seq(air$date[1], air$date[nrow(air)],length =
nrow(means))
plot(means$date, means$nox, type = "l")
```

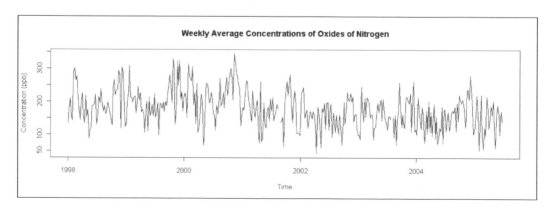

```
means <- aggregate(air["nox"], format(air["date"],"%Y-%j"),mean, na.rm
= TRUE)
means$date <- seq(air$date[1], air$date[nrow(air)],length =
nrow(means))
plot(means$date, means$nox, type = "l",
xlab="Time", ylab="Concentration (ppb)",
main="Daily  Average Concentrations of Oxides of Nitrogen")
```

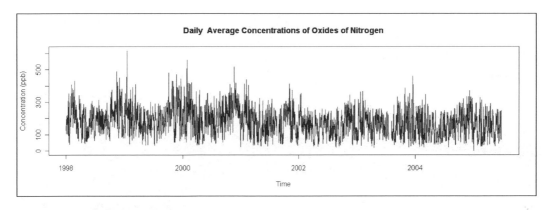

How it works...

The key function in these examples is the `aggregate()` function. Its first argument is the R object, `x`, which has to be aggregated and in this case is `air["nox"]`. The next argument is the list of grouping elements over which `x` has to be aggregated. This is the part where we specify the time period over which to average the values. In the first example, we set it to `format(air["date"],"%Y-%U")`, which extracts all the weeks out of the `date` column using the `format()` function. The third argument is FUN or the name of the function to apply to the selected values, in our case, `mean`. Finally, we set `na.rm` to TRUE, thus telling R to ignore missing values denoted by NA.

Once we have the mean values saved in a data frame, we add a date field to this new vector using the `seq()` function and then plot the means against the date using `plot()`.

In the second example, we use `format(air["date"],"%Y-%j")` to calculate daily means.

Creating stock charts

Given R's powerful analysis and graphical capabilities, it is no surprise that R is very popular in the world of finance. In this recipe, we will learn how to plot data from the stock market using some special libraries.

Getting ready

We need the `tseries` and `quantmod` packages to run the following recipes. Let's install and load these two packages:

```
install.packages("quantmod")
install.packages("tseries")
library(quantmod)
library(tseries)
```

How to do it...

Let's first see an example using the `tseries` library function, `get.hist.quotes()`. We will compare the stock prices of three technology companies:

```
aapl<-get.hist.quote(instrument = "aapl", quote = c("Cl", "Vol"))

goog <- get.hist.quote(instrument = "goog", quote = c("Cl", "Vol"))

msft <- get.hist.quote(instrument = "msft", quote = c("Cl", "Vol"))

plot(msft$Close,main = "Stock Price Comparison",
ylim=c(0,800)    ,col="red"  ,type="l"   ,lwd=0.5,
pch=19  ,cex=0.6  ,xlab="Date" ,ylab="Stock Price (USD)")

lines(goog$Close,col="blue",lwd=0.5)
lines(aapl$Close,col="gray",lwd=0.5)

legend("top",horiz=T,legend=c("Microsoft","Google","Apple"),
col=c("red","blue","gray"),lty=1,bty="n")
```

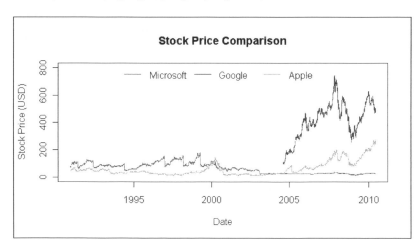

How it works...

The `get.hist.quote()` function retrieves historical financial data from one of the two providers, `yahoo` (for Yahoo!) or `oanda` (for OANDA), `yahoo` being the default. We passed the `instrument` and `quote` arguments to this function, which specifies the name of the stock and the measure of stock data we want. In our example, we used the function three times to pull the closing price and volume for Microsoft (`msft`), Google (`goog`), and Apple (`aapl`). We then plotted the three stock prices on a line graph using the `plot()` and `lines()` functions.

There's more...

Now, let's make some charts using the `quantmod` package. This package provides in-built graphics functions to visualize the stock data:

```
getSymbols("AAPL",src="yahoo")
barChart(AAPL)
```

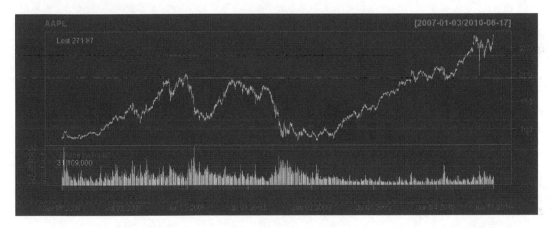

First, we obtained stock data for Apple using the `getSymbols()` function by specifying the stock name and source. Again, the default source is Yahoo!. The stock data is stored in an R object with the same name as the stock symbol (`AAPL` for Apple, `GOOG` for Google, and so on). Then, we passed this object to the `barChart()` function to produce the preceding graph. Of course, it is more than just a bar chart.

A similar chart in a different color scheme can be drawn using the following line of code:

```
candleChart(AAPL,theme="white")
```

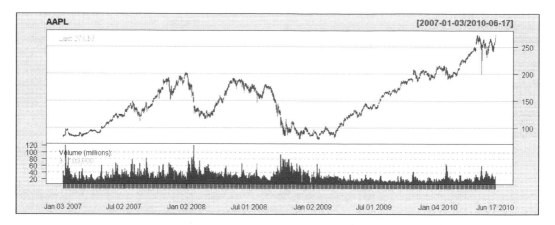

For more detailed information about the `quantmod` package, visit its website at `http://www.quantmod.com`.

6

Creating Bar, Dot, and Pie Charts

In this chapter, we will cover the following recipes:

- ▶ Creating bar charts with more than one factor variable
- ▶ Creating stacked bar charts
- ▶ Adjusting the orientation of bars – horizontal and vertical
- ▶ Adjusting bar widths, spacing, colors, and borders
- ▶ Displaying values on top of or next to the bars
- ▶ Placing labels inside bars
- ▶ Creating bar charts with vertical error bars
- ▶ Modifying dot charts by grouping variables
- ▶ Making better readable pie charts with clockwise-ordered slices
- ▶ Labeling a pie chart with percentage values for each slice
- ▶ Adding a legend to a pie chart

Introduction

In this chapter, we will look at bar, dot, and pie charts in detail. Bar charts are used commonly in reporting business data and scientific analysis. We will see how we can enhance the basic bar charts in R by adjusting some parameters in the base graphics library. There are a few different packages that can be used to make bar charts (most notably `lattice` and `ggplot2`). However, in this chapter, we will see how we can create many useful variations of bar graphs by using only the base library functions.

We will also look at a few recipes on pie charts—easily the most criticized type of chart in the scientific community, but also one of the most popular in the business world. While it is true that pie charts often obscure the data and are hard to read, the recipes in this chapter offer some ways to make pie charts more readable.

Some of the parameters are obscure and, sometimes, it might not be absolutely clear as to what values an argument can take. It is best to experiment as you go along and try out the recipes. You might not understand a function or its arguments fully until you have tried to graph a few of your own datasets. If you get stuck at any point, first look at the help file of the relevant function. If you are still stuck after having read the help files, then you can search the R mailing list (http://www.r-project.org/mail.html) and forums (http://r.789695.n4.nabble.com/ and http://stackoverflow.com/questions/tagged/r). Often, the problems one comes across are common and might have already been addressed by the R community in response to someone else's question.

Creating bar charts with more than one factor variable

In this first recipe, we will learn how to make bar charts for data with more than one category. Such bar charts are commonly used to compare values of the same measure across different categories.

Getting ready

We will use the base library `barplot()` function, but we will also use the `RColorBrewer` package to choose a good color palette. So, let's first install and load that package:

```
install.packages("RColorBrewer") #if not already installed
library(RColorBrewer)
```

How to do it...

Let's reuse the `citysales.csv` example dataset that we used in the first chapter:

```
citysales<-read.csv("citysales.csv")
barplot(as.matrix(citysales[,2:4]), beside=TRUE,
legend.text=citysales$City,
args.legend=list(bty="n",horiz=TRUE),
col=brewer.pal(5,"Set1"),
border="white",ylim=c(0,100),
ylab="Sales Revenue (1,000's of USD)",
main="Sales Figures")
box(bty="l")
```

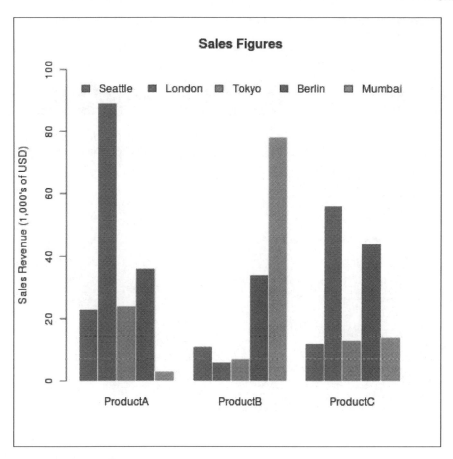

How it works...

The key argument for drawing bar charts with more than one category is the `beside` argument, which must be set to `TRUE`. The first argument is the input data, which must be in the form of a matrix. The columns of the matrix are the categories (in this case, `ProductA`, `ProductB`, and `ProductC`), while the rows are the set of values for each category. If we do not set the `beside` argument to `TRUE`, we will get a stacked bar chart (as we will see later in this chapter).

Most of the other arguments of the `barplot()` function work the same way as they do for `plot()`. The `args.legend` argument takes a list of arguments and passes them on to the `legend()` function. We can instead also call the `legend()` function separately after the `barplot()` call.

See also

In the next recipe, we will learn how to make stacked bar charts.

Creating stacked bar charts

Stacked bar charts are another form of bar chart used to compare values across categories. As the name implies, the bars for each category are stacked on top of each other instead of being placed next to each other.

Getting ready

We will use the same dataset and color scheme as the last recipe, so ensure that you have the RColorBrewer package installed and loaded:

```
install.packages("RColorBrewer")
library(RColorBrewer)
```

How to do it...

Let's draw a stacked bar chart of sales figures across the five cities:

```
citysales<-read.csv("citysales.csv")

barplot(as.matrix(citysales[,2:4]),
legend.text=citysales$City,
args.legend=list(bty="n",horiz=TRUE),
col=brewer.pal(5,"Set1"),border="white",
ylim=c(0,200),ylab="Sales Revenue (1,000's of USD)",
main="Sales Figures")
```

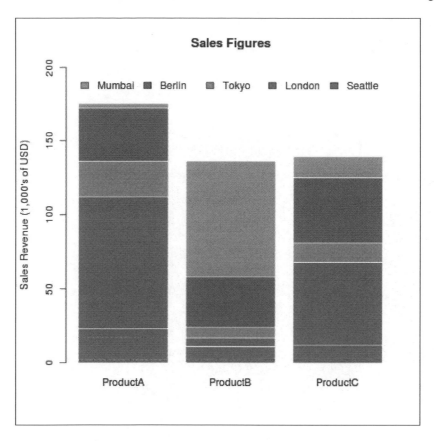

How it works...

If you compare the code for this example and the last recipe, you will see that the main difference is that we did not use the beside argument. By default, it is set to FALSE, which results in a stacked bar chart. We extended the top y axis limit from 100 to 200.

There's more...

Another common use of stacked charts is to compare the relative proportion of values across categories. Let's use the example dataset, citysalesperc.csv, which contains the percentage values of sales data by city for each of the three products A, B, and C:

```
citysalesperc<-read.csv("citysalesperc.csv")

par(mar=c(5,4,4,8),xpd=T)

barplot(as.matrix(citysalesperc[,2:4]),
```

```
col=brewer.pal(5,"Set1"),border="white",
ylab="Sales Revenue (1,000's of USD)",
main="Percentage Sales Figures")

legend("right",legend=citysalesperc$City,bty="n",
inset=c(-0.3,0),fill=brewer.pal(5,"Set1"))
```

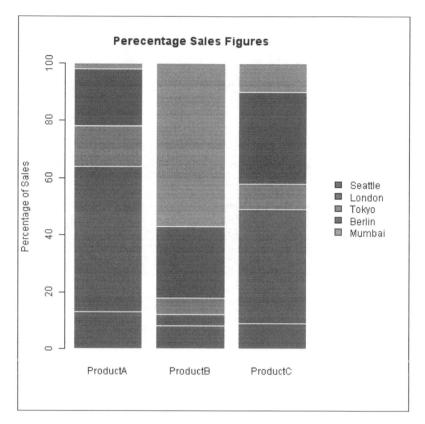

In the graph, the *y* axis shows the percentage of sales of a product in a city. It is a good way to quickly visually compare the relative proportion of product sales in cities. The code we used for the main graph is the same as the previous example. One difference is that we drew the legend separately using the `legend()` command. Note that we drew the legend outside the plot region by setting the `x` part of the inset to a negative value. We also had to create a larger margin to the right using the `mar` argument in the `par()` function and also setting `xpd` to TRUE to allow the legend to be drawn outside the plot region.

Adjusting the orientation of bars – horizontal and vertical

In this recipe, we will learn how to adjust the orientation of bars to horizontal or vertical.

Getting ready

We will use the same dataset we used in the last few recipes (`citysales.csv`) and the `RColorBrewer` color palette package.

How to do it...

Let's make a bar chart with horizontal bars:

```
barplot(as.matrix(citysales[,2:4]), beside=TRUE,horiz=TRUE,
legend.text=citysales$City, args.legend=list(bty="n"),
col=brewer.pal(5,"Set1"),border="white",
xlim=c(0,100), xlab="Sales Revenue (1,000's of USD)",
main="Sales Figures")
```

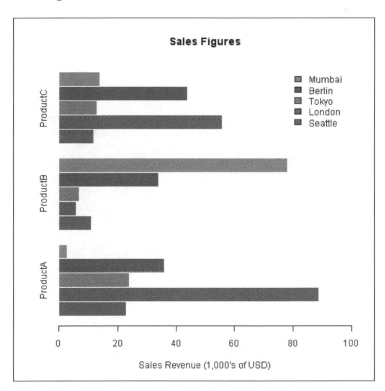

How it works...

In the example, we set the `horiz` argument to TRUE, which makes the bars horizontal. By default, `horiz` is set to FALSE, making the bars vertical. While it's really easy to make the bars horizontal, we must remember that the axes are reversed when we do that. So, in the example, we had to set the limits for the *x* axis (`xlim` instead of `ylim`) and set `xlab` (instead of `ylab`) to `"Sales Revenue"`. We also removed the `horiz=TRUE` argument from the legend arguments list because that would have plotted some of the legend labels on top of the **ProductC** bars. Removing the `horiz` argument puts the legend back into its default top-right position.

There's more...

Let's draw the stacked bar chart from the last recipe with horizontal bars:

```
par(mar=c(5,4,4,8),xpd=T)

barplot(as.matrix(citysalesperc[,2:4]), horiz=TRUE,
col=brewer.pal(5,"Set1"),border="white",
xlab="Percentage of Sales",
main="Perecentage Sales Figures")

legend("right",legend=citysalesperc$City,bty="n",
inset=c(-0.3,0),fill=brewer.pal(5,"Set1"))
```

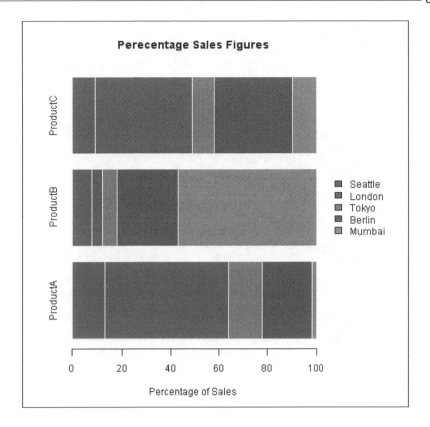

Again, we had to simply set the `horiz` argument to `TRUE` and adjust the margins to accommodate the legend to the right, outside the plot region.

Adjusting bar widths, spacing, colors, and borders

In this recipe, we will learn how to adjust the styling of bars by setting their width, the space between them, colors, and borders.

Getting ready

We will continue using the `citysales.csv` example dataset in this recipe. Make sure that you have loaded it into R and type in the recipe at the R prompt. You might also want to save the recipe as a script so that you can easily run it again later.

How to do it...

Let's adjust all the arguments at once to make the same graph as in the *Creating bar charts with more than one factor variable* recipe but with different visual settings:

```
barplot(as.matrix(citysales[,2:4]), beside=TRUE,
legend.text=citysales$City, args.legend=list(bty="n",horiz=T),
col=c("#E5562A","#491A5B","#8C6CA8","#BD1B8A","#7CB6E4"),
border=FALSE,space=c(0,5),
ylim=c(0,100),ylab="Sales Revenue (1,000's of USD)",
main="Sales Figures")
```

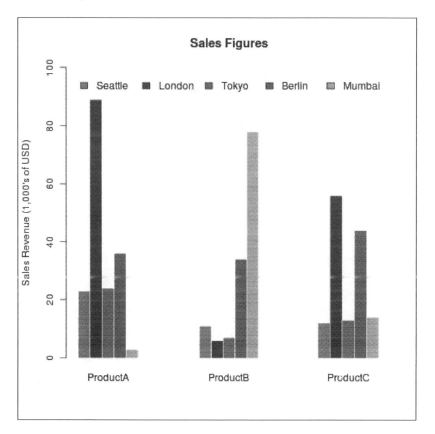

How it works...

Firstly, we changed the colors of the bars by setting the `col` argument to a vector of five colors we formed by hand, instead of using a `RColorBrewer` palette. If we do not set the `col` argument, R automatically uses shades from the grayscale.

Next, we set the `border` argument to `FALSE`. This tells R not to draw borders around each individual bar. By default, black borders are drawn around bars, but they usually don't look very good. So, we set the border to `"white"` in the earlier recipes of this chapter.

Finally, we set the `space` argument to `c(0,5)`, a vector of two numbers, to set the space between bars within each category and between the groups of bars, representing each category respectively. We left no space between bars within a category and increased the space between categories.

Adjusting the space between bars automatically adjusts the width of the bars too. There is also a `width` argument that we can use to set the width when plotting data for a single category, but the `width` argument is ignored when plotting for multiple categories. So, it's best to use `space` instead.

There's more...

The following is an example that shows the previous graph with the default settings for color, spacing, and borders:

```
barplot(as.matrix(citysales[,2:4]), beside=T,
legend.text=citysales$City,args.legend=list(bty="n",horiz=T),
ylim=c(0,100),ylab="Sales Revenue (1,000's of USD)",
main="Sales Figures")
```

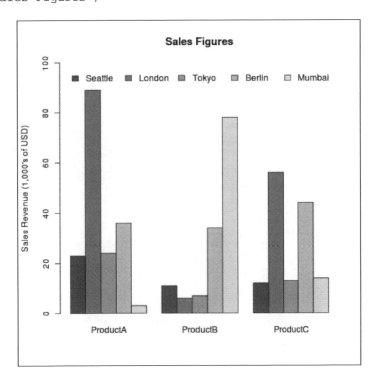

Displaying values on top of or next to the bars

Sometimes, it is useful to have the exact values displayed on a bar chart to enable quick and accurate reading. There is no built-in function in R to do this. In this recipe, we will learn how to do this by writing some custom code.

Getting ready

Once again, we will use the `citysales.csv` dataset and build upon the graph from the first recipe in this chapter.

How to do it...

Let's make the graph with vertical bars and display the sales values just on top of the bars:

```
x<-barplot(as.matrix(citysales[,2:4]), beside=TRUE,
legend.text=citysales$City, args.legend=list(bty="n",horiz=TRUE),
col=brewer.pal(5,"Set1"),border="white",
ylim=c(0,100),ylab="Sales Revenue (1,000's of USD)",
main="Sales Figures")

y<-as.matrix(citysales[,2:4])

text(x,y+2,labels=as.character(y))
```

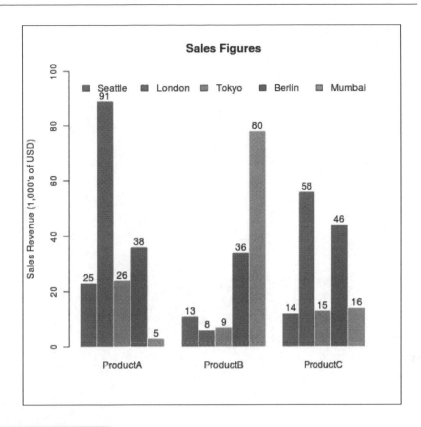

How it works...

In the example, we have used the text() function to label the bars with the corresponding values. To do so, we constructed two vectors, x and y, with the X and Y coordinates of the labels. We first created the barplot and saved it as an R object called x. When the result of the barplot() function call is assigned to an object, a vector that contains the X coordinates of the center of each of the bars is returned and saved in that object. You can verify this by typing in x at the R prompt and hitting the *Enter* key.

For the y vector, we created a matrix of the sales value columns. Finally, we passed the x and y values to text() as coordinates and set the label's argument to y values transformed into characters using the as.character() function. Note that we added 2 to each y value so that the labels are placed slightly above the bar. We might have to add a different value, depending on the scale of the graph.

There's more...

We can place the value labels next to the bars in a horizontal bar chart simply by swapping the x and y vectors in the text() function call:

```
y<-barplot(as.matrix(citysales[,2:4]), beside=TRUE,horiz=TRUE,
legend.text=citysales$City,args.legend=list(bty="n"),
col=brewer.pal(5,"Set1"),border="white",
xlim=c(0,100),xlab="Sales Revenue (1,000's of USD)",
main="Sales Figures")

x<-as.matrix(citysales[,2:4])

text(x+2,y,labels=as.character(x))
```

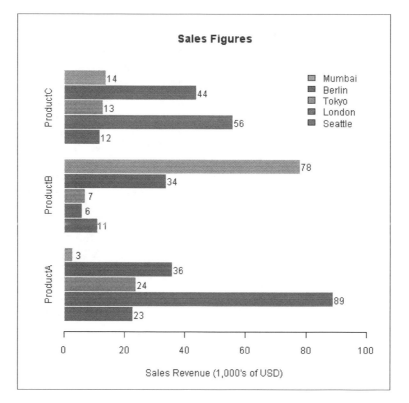

See also

In the next recipe, we will learn how to place text labels inside bars.

Placing labels inside bars

Sometimes, we might wish to label bars by placing text inside the bars instead of using a legend. In this recipe, we will learn how to do this based on code, similar to the previous recipe.

Getting ready

We will use the `cityrain.csv` example dataset. We don't need to load any additional packages for this recipe.

How to do it...

We will plot the rainfall in the month of January in four cities as a horizontal bar chart:

```
rain<-read.csv("cityrain.csv")

y<-barplot(as.matrix(rain[1,-1]),horiz=T,col="white",
yaxt="n",main=" Rainfall in January",xlab="Rainfall (mm)")

x<-0.5*rain[1,-1]
text(x,y,colnames(rain[-1]))
```

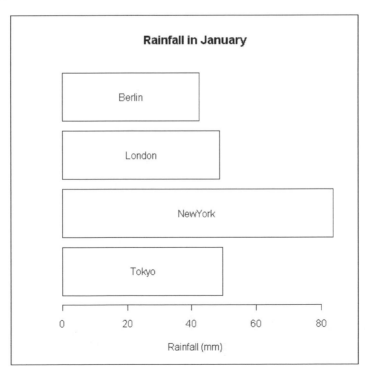

How it works...

The example is very similar to the one in the previous recipe. The only difference is that now we are plotting one set of bars, not groups of bars. As we want to place the labels inside the bars, we turned off the y axis labels by setting `yaxt="n"`. Otherwise, the city names would appear along the y axis to the left of the bars. We retrieve the y axis coordinates of the bars by setting y to the `barplot` function call. We created the vector x so as to place the labels in the middle of each of the bars by multiplying the rainfall values by `0.5`. Note that these X coordinates represent the center of each label, not its start. Finally, we pass the x and y coordinates and city names to `text()` to label the bars.

There's more...

As we have seen in the example and the previous recipe, once we retrieve the x or y coordinates of the center of bars, we can place labels in any position relative to those coordinates.

Creating bar charts with vertical error bars

Bar charts with error bars are commonly used in analyzing and reporting results of scientific experiments. In this recipe, we will learn how to add error bars to a bar chart in a similar way to the recipe for scatter plots in *Chapter 4, Creating Scatter Plots*.

Getting ready

We will continue using the `citysales.csv` example dataset in this recipe. Make sure that you have loaded it into R and type in the recipe at the R prompt. You might also want to save the recipe as a script so that you can easily run it again later.

How to do it...

One change we will make in this recipe is that we will use the transpose of the `citysales` dataset (turns rows into columns and columns into rows). So, first let's create the transpose as a new dataset:

```
sales<-t(as.matrix(citysales[,-1]))
colnames(sales)<-citysales[,1]
```

Now, let's make a bar plot with 5-percent-error bars that show the sales of the three products across the five cities as categories:

```
x<-barplot(sales,beside=T,legend.text=rownames(sales),
args.legend=list(bty="n",horiz=T),
col=brewer.pal(3,"Set2"),border="white",ylim=c(0,100),
```

```
ylab="Sales Revenue (1,000's of USD)",
main="Sales Figures")
arrows(x0=x,y0=sales*0.95,
x1=x,y1=sales*1.05,
angle=90,
code=3,
length=0.04,
lwd=0.4)
```

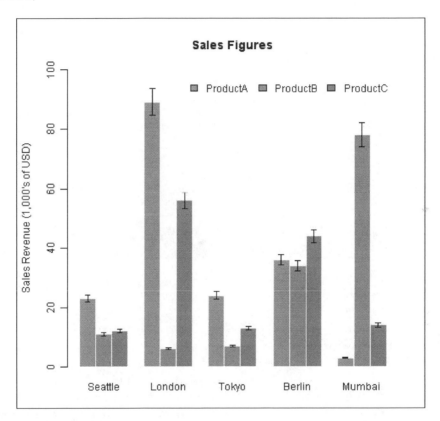

How it works...

We first created the bar chart with the transposed data so that the sales data is represented as groups of three products for each of the cities. We saved the X coordinates of these bars as a vector x. Then, we used the arrows() function, just as we used it in *Chapter 4, Creating Scatter Plots*, to make error bars on scatter plots. The first four arguments are the X and Y coordinate pairs of the start and end points of the error bars. The X coordinates, x0 and x1, are both set equal to x and the Y coordinates are sales values 5 percent above and below the original values. The angle and code set the type of arrow and flatten the arrow head relative to the length of the arrow, and length and lwd set the length and line width of the arrows.

There's more...

The code to draw the error bars can be saved as a function and used with any `barplot`. This can be especially useful when comparing experimental values with control values, trying to look for a significant effect:

```
errorbars<-function(x,y,upper,lower=upper,length=0.04,lwd=0.4,...) {
arrows(x0=x,y0=y+upper,
x1=x,y1=y-lower,
angle=90,
code=3,
length=length,
lwd=lwd)
}
```

Now, error bars can be added to the preceding graph and can be drawn simply by using the following code:

```
errorbars(x,sales,0.05*sales)
```

In practice, scaled estimated standard deviation values or other formal estimates of error would be used to draw error bars instead of a blanket percentage error as shown here.

Modifying dot charts by grouping variables

In this recipe, we will learn how to make dot charts with grouped variables. Dot charts are often preferred to bar charts because they are less cluttered and convey the same information more clearly with less ink.

Getting ready

We will continue using the `citysales.csv` example dataset in this recipe. Make sure that you have loaded it into R and type in the recipe at the R prompt. You might also want to save the recipe as a script so that you can easily run it again later. We will need the `reshape` package to change the structure of the dataset. So, let's make sure we have it installed and loaded:

```
install.packages("reshape")
library(reshape)
```

How to do it...

We will first apply the `melt()` function to the `citysales` dataset to convert it to long form and then use the `dotchart()` function:

```
sales<-melt(citysales)

sales$color[sales[,2]=="ProductA"] <- "red"
sales$color[sales[,2]=="ProductB"] <- "blue"
sales$color[sales[,2]=="ProductC"] <- "violet"

dotchart(sales[,3],labels=sales$City,groups=sales[,2],
col=sales$color,pch=19,
main="Sales Figures",
xlab="Sales Revenue (1,000's of USD)")
```

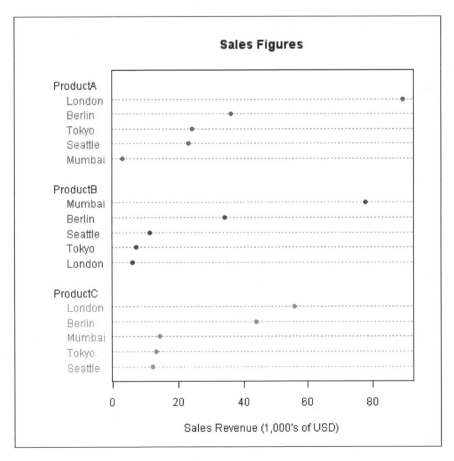

How it works...

We first converted the data into long form by applying the `melt()` function from the `reshape` library. This is what the new dataset looks like:

City	Variable	Value
Mumbai	ProductA	3
London	ProductB	6
Tokyo	ProductB	7
Seattle	ProductB	11
Seattle	ProductC	12
Tokyo	ProductC	13
Mumbai	ProductC	14
Seattle	ProductA	23
Tokyo	ProductA	24
Berlin	ProductB	34
Berlin	ProductA	36
Berlin	ProductC	44
London	ProductC	56
Mumbai	ProductB	78
London	ProductA	89

Then we add a column called `color` that holds a different value of color for each product (`red`, `blue`, and `violet`).

Finally, we call the `dotchart()` function with the values column as the first argument. We set the `labels` argument to the city names and group the points by the second column (product). The color is set to the color column using the `col` argument. This results in a dot chart with the data points grouped and colored by products on the *y* axis.

Making better, readable pie charts with clockwise-ordered slices

Pie charts are very popular in business data reporting. However, they are not preferred by scientists and are often criticized for being hard to read and obscuring data. In this recipe, we will learn how to make better pie charts by ordering the slices by size.

Getting ready

In this recipe, we will use the `browsers.txt` example dataset that contains data about the usage percentage share of different Internet browsers.

How to do it...

First, we will load the `browsers.txt` dataset and then use the `pie()` function to draw a pie chart:

```
browsers<-read.table("browsers.txt",header=TRUE)
browsers<-browsers[order(browsers[,2]),]

pie(browsers[,2],
labels=browsers[,1],
clockwise=TRUE,
radius=1,
col=brewer.pal(7,"Set1"),
border="white",
main="Percentage Share of Internet Browser usage")
```

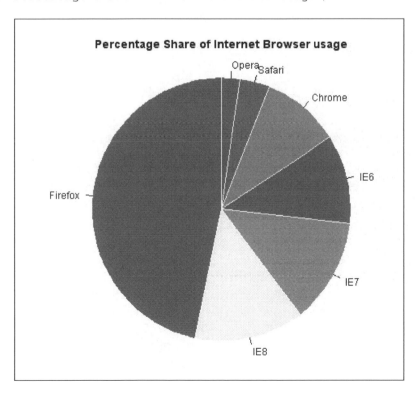

How it works...

The important thing about the graph is that the slices are ordered in the ascending order of their sizes. We have done this because one of the main criticisms of pie charts is that, when there are many slices and they are in a random order, it is not easy (often impossible) to tell whether one slice is bigger than another. By ordering the slices by size in a clockwise direction, we can directly compare the slices.

We ordered the dataset by using the `order()` function, which returns the index of its argument in the ascending order. So, if we just type in `order(browsers[,2])` at the R prompt, we get the following output:

```
[1]  7 6 5 3 2 1 4
```

This is a vector of the index of the share values in the ascending order in the original dataset. For example, Firefox, which has the largest share, is in the fourth row, so the last number in the vector is 4. We then use the index to reassign the browser dataset in the ascending order of share by using the square bracket notation.

Then, we pass the share values in the second column as the first argument to the `pie()` function of the base R graphics library. We set labels to the first column, the names of browsers (note that IE stands for Internet Explorer). We also set the `clockwise` argument to `TRUE`. By default, slices are drawn counterclockwise.

See also

In the next two recipes, we will see how we can further enhance pie charts with percentage value labels.

Labeling a pie chart with percentage values for each slice

In this recipe, we will learn how to add the percentage values in addition to the names of slices, thus making them more readable.

Getting ready

Once again in this recipe, we will use the `browsers.txt` example dataset, which contains data about the usage percentage share of different Internet browsers.

How to do it...

First, we will load the `browsers.txt` dataset and then use the `pie()` function to draw a pie chart:

```
browsers<-read.table("browsers.txt",header=TRUE)
browsers<-browsers[order(browsers[,2]),]

pielabels <- sprintf("%s = %3.1f%s", browsers[,1],
100*browsers[,2]/sum(browsers[,2]), "%")

pie(browsers[,2],
labels=pielabels,
clockwise=TRUE,
radius=1,
col=brewer.pal(7,"Set1"),
border="white",
cex=0.8,
main="Percentage Share of Internet Browser usage")
```

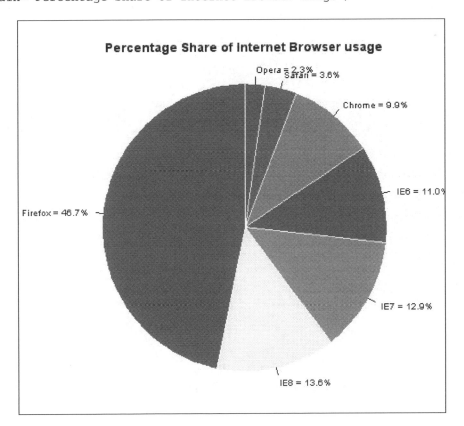

How it works...

In the example, instead of using just the browser names as labels, we first created a vector of labels that concatenated the browser names and percentage share values. We used the `sprintf()` function that returns a character vector that contains a formatted combination of text and variable values. The first argument to `sprintf()` is the full character string in double quotes, where the % notation is used to fill in values dynamically and thus create a vector of strings for each slice. %s refers to a character string (`browsers[,1]` which is the second argument). %3.1 refers to a three-digit value with one significant decimal place (the percentage share value calculated as the third argument). The second %s refers to the character "%" itself, which is the last argument.

We make the pie chart using the same `pie()` function call as in the last recipe, except that we set `labels` to the newly constructed vector, `pielabels`.

There's more...

We can adjust the size of the chart and the text labels by using the `radius` and `cex` arguments, respectively.

See also

In the next recipe, we will see how to add a legend to a pie chart.

Adding a legend to a pie chart

Sometimes, we might wish to use a legend to annotate a pie chart instead of using labels. In this recipe, we will learn how to do this using the `legend()` function.

Getting ready

Once again in this recipe, we will use the `browsers.txt` example dataset, which contains data about the usage percentage share of different Internet browsers.

How to do it...

First, we will load the `browsers.txt` dataset and then use the `pie()` function to draw a pie chart:

```
browsers<-read.table("browsers.txt",header=TRUE)
browsers<-browsers[order(browsers[,2]),]

pielabels <- sprintf("%s = %3.1f%s", browsers[,1],
```

```
100*browsers[,2]/sum(browsers[,2]), "%")

pie(browsers[,2],
labels=NA,
clockwise=TRUE,
col=brewer.pal(7,"Set1"),
border="white",
radius=0.7,
cex=0.8,
main="Percentage Share of Internet Browser usage")

legend("bottomright",legend=pielabels,bty="n",
fill=brewer.pal(7,"Set1"))
```

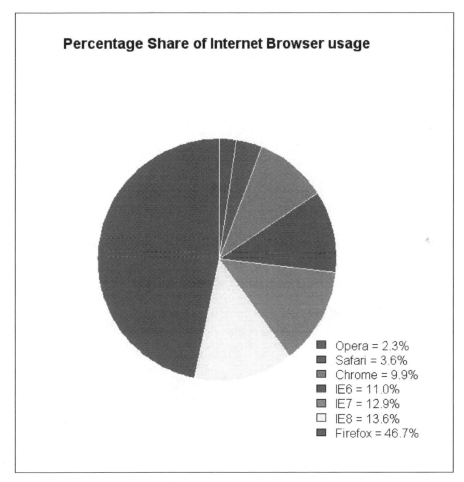

How it works...

Once again we ordered the `browser` dataset, created a vector of labels, and made the pie chart with the `pie()` function call, just as in the previous recipe. However, we set `labels` to `NA` this time as we want to create a legend instead of labeling the slices directly.

We added a legend to the bottom-right corner by calling the `legend()` function. We passed the `pielabels` vector as the `legend` argument and set the `fill` argument to the same `RColorBrewer` color palette we used for the pie slices.

There's more...

Depending on the number of slices and the desired size of the chart, we can experiment with placing the legend in different places. In this case, we have a lot of slice labels: otherwise, we can place the legend in one single row on top of the chart by setting `x` to `"top"` and `horiz` to `TRUE`.

7
Creating Histograms

In this chapter, we will cover the following recipes:

- ▶ Visualizing distributions as count frequencies or probability densities
- ▶ Setting bin size and the number of breaks
- ▶ Adjusting histogram styles – bar colors, borders, and axes
- ▶ Overlaying a density line over a histogram
- ▶ Multiple histograms along the diagonal of a pairs plot
- ▶ Histograms in the margins of line and scatter plots

Introduction

In this chapter, we will look at histograms in detail. They are a very useful form of visualization for rapidly viewing the distribution of values of a variable. They are usually one of the first graphs looked at to see whether a variable follows a normal distribution or has a skewed distribution.

We will see how we can enhance the basic histogram in R by adjusting some parameters in the base graphics library. We will learn how to change certain settings to control the format in which the histogram is plotted (the frequency or probability of values) and also how the values are grouped into bins. We will also look at the usual parameters to change the styling of histogram bars, such as color, width, and border. In addition, we will also look at some advanced recipes combining histograms with other types of graphs.

As with the previous chapters, it is best to try out each recipe first with the example shown here and then with your own datasets, so that you can fully understand each line of code.

Visualizing distributions as count frequencies or probability densities

Histograms can represent the distribution of values either as frequency (the absolute number of times values fall within specific ranges) or as probability density (the proportion of the values that falls within specific ranges). In this recipe, we will learn how to choose one or the other.

Getting ready

We are only using base graphics functions for this recipe. So, just open up the R prompt and type in the following code. We will use the `airpollution.csv` example dataset for this recipe. So, let's first load it:

```
air<-read.csv("airpollution.csv")
```

How to do it...

We will use the `hist()` base graphics function to make our histogram, first showing the frequency and then probability density of nitrogen oxide concentrations:

```
hist(air$Nitrogen.Oxides,
xlab="Nitrogen Oxide Concentrations",
main="Distribution of Nitrogen Oxide Concentrations")
```

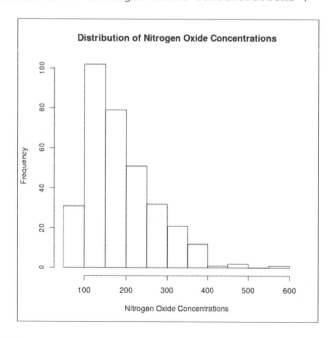

Now, let's make the same histogram but with probability instead of frequency:

```
hist(air$Nitrogen.Oxides, freq=FALSE,
xlab="Nitrogen Oxide Concentrations",
main="Distribution of Nitrogen Oxide Concentrations")
```

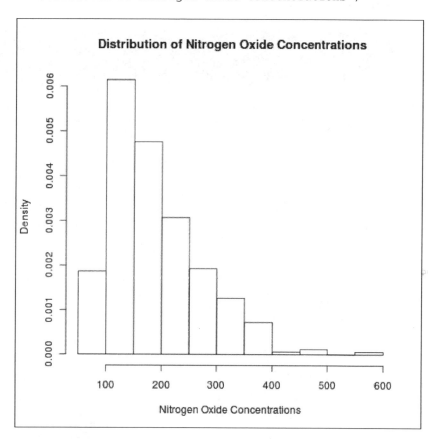

How it works...

The first example, which shows the frequency counts of different value ranges of nitrogen oxides, simply uses a call to the hist() function in the base graphics library. The variable is passed as the first argument; by default, the histogram plotted shows frequency. In the second example, we pass an extra freq argument and set it to FALSE, which results in a histogram that shows probability densities. This suggests that, by default, freq is set to TRUE. The help section on hist() (?hist) states that freq defaults to TRUE if, and only if, the breaks are equidistant and the probability is not specified.

There's more

An alternative to using the `freq` argument is the `prob` argument that, as the name suggests, takes the opposite value to `freq`. So, by default, it is set to `FALSE`; if we want to show probability densities, then we need to set `prob` to `TRUE`.

Setting the bin size and the number of breaks

As we saw in the previous recipe, the `hist()` function automatically computes the number of breaks and the size of bins in which the values of the variable will be grouped. In this recipe, we will learn how we can control this and specify exactly how many bins we want or where to have breaks between bars.

Getting ready

Once again, we will use the `airpollution.csv` example dataset, so make sure that you have loaded it:

```
air<-read.csv("airpollution.csv")
```

How to do it...

First, let's see how to specify the number of breaks. Let's make 20 breaks in the nitrogen oxides histogram instead of the default 11:

```
hist(air$Nitrogen.Oxides,
breaks=20,xlab="Nitrogen Oxide Concentrations",
main="Distribution of Nitrogen Oxide Concentrations")
```

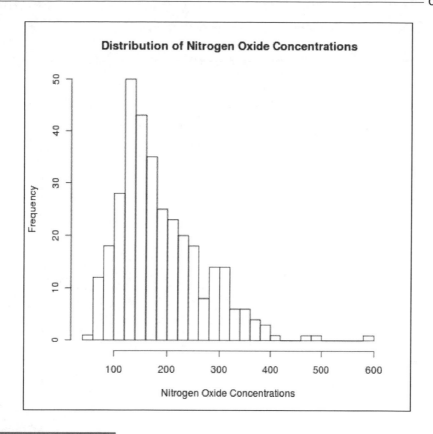

Distribution of Nitrogen Oxide Concentrations

How it works...

We used the `breaks` argument to specify the number of bars for the histogram. We set `breaks` to `20`. However, the graph shows more than 20 bars because R uses the value specified only as a suggestion and computes the best way to bin the data with breaks as close to the value specified as possible.

There's more

We can also specify the exact values at which we want the breaks to occur. In this case, R does use the value we specify. Once again, we use the `breaks` argument but, this time, we have to set it to a numerical vector that contains the values at which we want the breaks. The `breaks` vector must cover the full range of values of the x variable.

Let's say we want breaks at every `100` units of concentration:

```
hist(air$Nitrogen.Oxides,
breaks=c(0,100,200,300,400,500,600),
xlab="Nitrogen Oxide Concentrations",
main="Distribution of Nitrogen Oxide Concentrations")
```

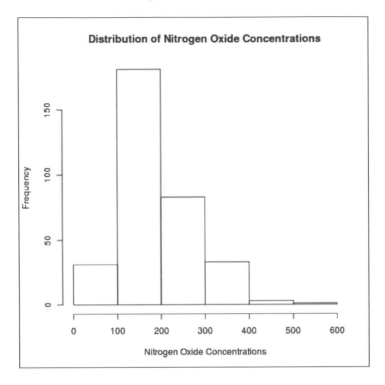

So, as you might have noticed, the `breaks` argument can take different types of values: a single value that suggests the number of breaks or a vector that specifies exact bin breaks. In addition, `breaks` can also take a function that computes the number of bins.

Finally, `breaks` can also take a character string as a value that names an algorithm to calculate the number of bins. By default, it is set to `"Sturges"`. Other names for which algorithms are supplied are `"Scott"` and `"FD"` (or `"Freedman-Diaconis"`).

Adjusting histogram styles – bar colors, borders, and axes

The default styling of histograms does not look great and might not be suitable for publications. In this recipe, we will learn how to improve the look by setting bar colors and borders, and adjusting the axes.

Getting ready

Once again we will use the `airpollution.csv` example. So, let's make sure it is loaded by running the following command at the R prompt:

```
air<-read.csv("airpollution.csv")
```

How to do it...

Let's visualize the probability distribution of respirable particle concentrations with black bars and white borders:

```
hist(air$Respirable.Particles,
prob=TRUE,col="black",border="white",
xlab="Respirable Particle Concentrations",
main="Distribution of Respirable Particle Concentrations")
```

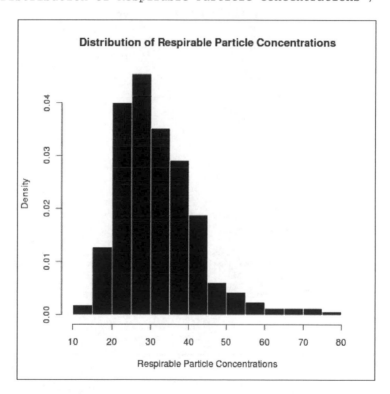

How it works...

By now, you might have guessed how to do this yourself. We used the `col` and `border` arguments to set the bar and border colors to black and white, respectively.

There's more

You might have noticed that, in all of the previous examples, the x axis is detached from the base of the bars. This gives the graphs a bit of an unclean look. Also notice that the y axis labels are rotated vertically, which makes them harder to read. Let's improve the graph by fixing these two visual settings:

```
par(yaxs="i",las=1)
hist(air$Respirable.Particles,
prob=TRUE,col="black",border="white",
xlab="Respirable Particle Concentrations",
main="Distribution of Respirable Particle Concentrations")
box(bty="l")
grid(nx=NA,ny=NULL,lty=1,lwd=1,col="gray")
```

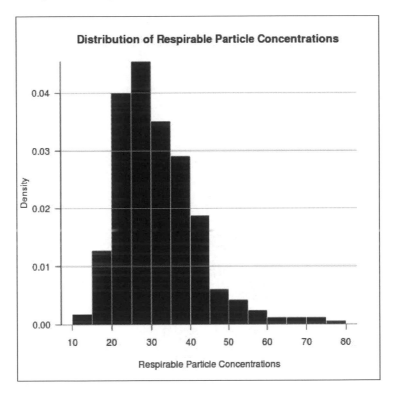

So, we used a couple of extra function calls to change the look of the graph. First, we called the par() function and set yaxs to "i" so that the y axis joins the x axis instead of having a detached x axis. We also set las equal to 1 to make all the axis labels horizontal, thus making it easier to read the y axis labels. Then, we ran the hist() function call as before and called box() with the type equal to "l" to make an L-shaped box running along the axes. Finally, we added horizontal grid lines using the grid() function.

Overlaying a density line over a histogram

In this recipe, we will learn how to superimpose a kernel density line on top of a histogram.

Getting ready

We will continue using the `airpollution.csv` example dataset. You can simply type in the recipe code at the R prompt. If you wish to use the code later, you should save it as a script file. First, let's load the data file.

```
air<-read.csv("airpollution.csv")
```

How to do it...

Let's overlay a line that shows the kernel density of respirable particle concentrations on top of a probability distribution histogram:

```
par(yaxs="i",las=1)
hist(air$Respirable.Particles,
prob=TRUE,col="black",border="white",
xlab-"Respirable Particle Concentrations",
main="Distribution of Respirable Particle Concentrations")
box(bty="l")

lines(density(air$Respirable.Particles,na.rm=T),col="red",lwd=4)
grid(nx=NA,ny=NULL,lty=1,lwd=1,col="gray")
```

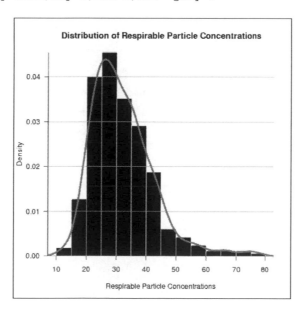

How it works...

The code for the histogram itself is exactly the same as in the previous recipe. After making the `hist()` function call, we used the `lines()` function to plot the density line on top. We passed the result of the `density()` function call to the `lines()` function. The default kernel used is Gaussian, although other values can be specified. Take a look at the help file for `density()` for more details (run `?density` at the R prompt).

To make the line prominent, we set its type to solid (`lty=1`), color to red (`col="red"`), and width to `4` (`lwd=4`).

Multiple histograms along the diagonal of a pairs plot

In this recipe, we will look at some slightly advanced code to embed histograms inside another kind of graph. We learned how to make pairs plots (a matrix of scatter plots) in *Chapter 1, R Graphics*, and *Chapter 4, Creating Scatter Plots*. In those pairs plots, the diagonal cells running from the top-left to the bottom-right showed the names of the variables, while the other cells showed the relationship between any two pairs of variables. It will be useful if we can also see the probability distribution of each variable in the same plot. Here, we will learn how to do this by adding histograms inside the diagonal cells.

Getting ready

We will use the inbuilt `iris` flowers dataset of R. So, we need not load any other datasets. We can simply type in the given code at the R prompt.

How to do it...

So, let's make an enhanced pairs plot showing the relationship between different measurements of the `iris` flower species and how each measurement's values are spread across the range:

```
panel.hist <- function(x, ...)
  {
    par(usr = c(par("usr")[1:2], 0, 1.5) )
    hist(x, prob=TRUE,add=TRUE,col="black",border="white")
  }

plot(iris[,1:4],
main="Relationships between characteristics of iris flowers",
pch=19,col="blue",cex=0.9,
diag.panel=panel.hist)
```

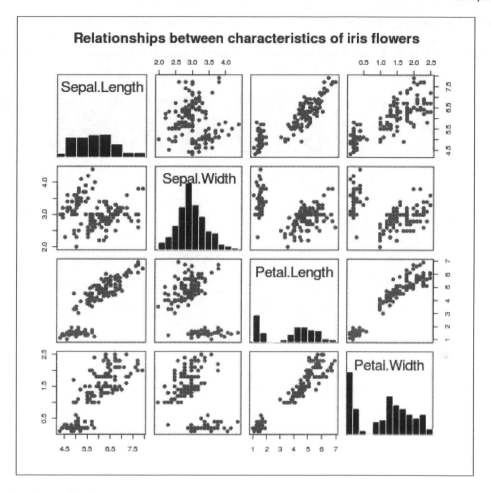

How it works...

We first defined the `panel.hist()` function that handles how the histograms are drawn. It is called by the `plot()` function later when the `diag.panel` argument is set to `panel.hist`.

The `panel.hist()` function only has two simple lines of code. First, we call the `par()` function to set the X and Y limits using the `usr` argument. To reiterate what we learnt in *Chapter 3, Beyond the Basics – Adjusting Key Parameters*, the `usr` arguments take values in the form of a vector, `c(xmin, xmax, ymin, ymax)`, giving the minimum and maximum values on the *x* and *y* axes, respectively. In the code, we keep the *x* axis limits the same as already set up by the `plot()` function call. We need to change the *y* axis limits for each diagonal cell because they are set by `plot()` to be the same as the *x* axis limits. We need the *y* axis limits in terms of the kernel density of each variable, so we set them to `0` and `1.5`.

Then, we make the `hist()` function call with the style arguments of our choice and one key argument, `add` (set to `TRUE`), which makes sure the histograms are added to the existing pairs plot and not drawn as new plots. Any panel function should not start a new plot or it will terminate the pairs plot. So, we can't use the `hist()` function without setting `add` to `TRUE`.

Histograms in the margins of line and scatter plots

In this recipe, we will learn how to draw histograms in the top and right margins of a bivariate scatter plot.

Getting ready

We will use the `airpollution.csv` example dataset for this recipe. So, let's make sure it is loaded:

```
air<-read.csv("airpollution.csv")
```

How to do it...

Let's make a scatter plot showing the relationship between concentrations of respirable particles and nitrogen oxides with histograms of both the variables in the margins:

```
#Set up the layout first
layout(matrix(c(2,0,1,3),2,2,byrow=TRUE), widths=c(3,1),
heights=c(1,3), TRUE)

#Make Scatterplot
par(mar=c(5.1,4.1,0.1,0))
plot(air$Respirable.Particles~air$Nitrogen.Oxides,
pch=19,col="black",
xlim=c(0,600),ylim=c(0,80),
xlab="Nitrogen Oxides Concentrations",
ylab="Respirable Particle Concentrations")

#Plot histogram of X variable in the top row
par(mar=c(0,4.1,3,0))
hist(air$Nitrogen.Oxides,
breaks=seq(0,600,100),ann=FALSE,axes=FALSE,
col="black",border="white")

#Plot histogram of Y variable to the right of the scatterplot
```

```
yhist <- hist(air$Respirable.Particles,
breaks=seq(0,80,10),plot=FALSE)

par(mar=c(5.1,0,0.1,1))
barplot(yhist$density,
horiz=TRUE,space=0,axes=FALSE,
col="black",border="white")
```

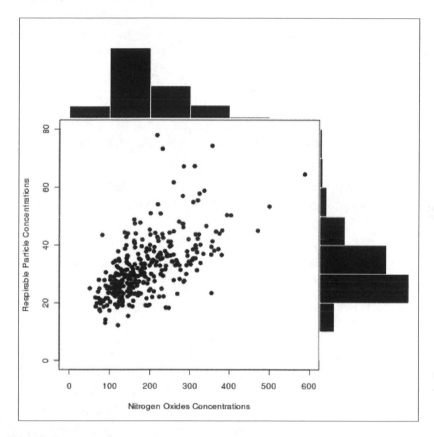

How it works...

The given example is a bit more complex than the recipes we have seen so far. However, if we look at each line of code one-by-one, we can understand it quite easily.

First, we used the `layout()` function to divide the graph into separate regions for the scatter plot and the two histograms. We could also use the `par()` function with the `mfrow` argument instead, but `layout()` gives us finer control over the height and width of each cell of the graph. When we use `par()` with `mfrow` or `mfcol` to create a matrix layout, all cells are automatically created of equal height and width.

The first argument to the `layout()` function is a matrix that specifies the number of rows and columns the graphics device should be divided into and the location of each figure. Run just the matrix command from the code at the R prompt to see the resultant matrix:

```
matrix(c(2,0,1,3),2,2,byrow=TRUE)
     [,1] [,2]
[1,]    2    0
[2,]    1    3
```

The matrix values shown here mean that the first figure should be drawn in the second row and first column (scatter plot), the second figure in the first row and first column (a histogram of the X variable), and the third figure in the second row and second column (a histogram of the Y variable).

The other arguments to `layout()` are `widths` and `heights` that specify the widths and heights of the columns and rows, respectively, as a vector. The last argument is set to `TRUE` so that a unit column width is the same physical measurement on the device as a unit row height.

We have chosen this particular layout so that the scatter plot occupies most of the area of the graph and the histograms are plotted in a smaller area as they are only giving supplementary information.

Once the layout is created, we draw the plots one by one in the order that we set up the layout matrix. So, first we made the scatter plot giving specific x and y axes limits so that we can use the same limits to plot the histograms with the correct breaks.

Then, we made the histogram of nitrogen oxides in the top margin just above the scatter plot. We first used the `par()` function with the `mar` argument to set the margins so as not to leave any margin at the bottom and matching the margins on the left and right to those of the scatter plot. We specified `breaks` exactly as a vector of values between the x and y limits of the scatter plot by using the `seq()` function. The axes and annotations are suppressed by setting the `axes` and `ann` arguments to `FALSE`, thus giving the histogram a clean minimal look.

Next, we added the rotated histogram of respirable particle concentrations to the right of the scatter plot. We had to do this differently from the first histogram because the `hist()` function does not have an inbuilt way to draw the bars horizontally. As we have seen in earlier chapters, the `barplot()` function does have such a capability. So, we first created a histogram object but suppressed its plotting by setting plot to `FALSE`. Then, we passed the density values from that object to the `barplot()` function to plot them horizontally by setting the `horiz` argument to `TRUE`. Just as with the x axis histogram, we set the breaks of the y histogram equal to a sequence matching the Y limits of the scatter plot. Then, we set the margins so that the bottom and top margins match those of the scatter plot and the left margin is `0`. Then, we called the `barplot()` function to draw the horizontal bars. Note that we set the space argument equal to `0`; otherwise, the bars are drawn with gaps between them by default.

8
Box and Whisker Plots

In this chapter, we will cover the following recipes:

- Creating box plots with narrow boxes for a small number of variables
- Grouping over a variable
- Varying box widths by number of observations
- Creating box plots with notches
- Including or excluding outliers
- Creating horizontal box plots
- Changing box styling
- Adjusting the extent of plot whiskers outside the box
- Showing the number of observations
- Splitting a variable at arbitrary values into subsets

Introduction

In this chapter, we will look at box and whisker plots in detail, which are a great form of visualization to summarize large amounts of data by showing Tukey's five-number summary: minimum, lower-hinge, median, upper-hinge, and maximum. Box plots are a good way to spot outliers and compare the key statistics for different variables or groups.

We will learn various stylistic and structural variations on how to adjust box plots in R (using the basic `boxplot()` command). In addition to changing the look of our box plots, we will also learn how to add additional useful information to them. We will start by looking at some basic arguments to change individual aspects of a box plot and slowly move to more advanced recipes that involve the use of multiple function calls and arguments to create more complex types of box plots.

As with the previous chapters, it's best to try out each recipe first with the example shown here and then with your own datasets so that you can fully understand each line of code.

Creating box plots with narrow boxes for a small number of variables

R automatically adjusts the widths of boxes in a box plot according to the number of variables. This works fine when we have a relatively large number of variables (more than 4), but you might find that for a small number of variables, the default boxes are too wide. In this recipe, we will learn how to make the boxes narrower.

Getting ready

We are only using the base graphics functions for this recipe. So, just open up the R prompt and type in the following code. We will use the `airpollution.csv` example dataset for this recipe. So, let's first load it:

```
air<-read.csv("airpollution.csv")
```

How to do it...

We want to make a box plot summarizing the two columns in our dataset: respirable particles and nitrogen oxides. If we simply use the `boxplot` command, we get a box plot with very wide boxes:

```
boxplot(air,las=1)
```

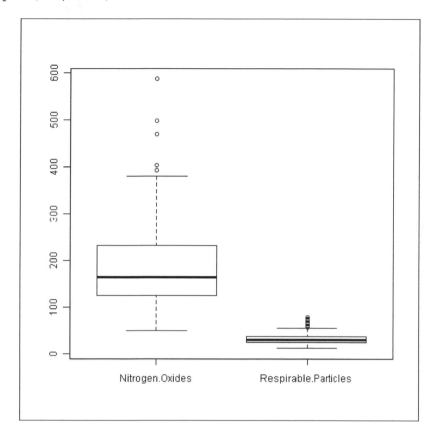

Let's improve the look of the graph by making the boxes narrower:

```
boxplot(air,boxwex=0.2,las=1)
```

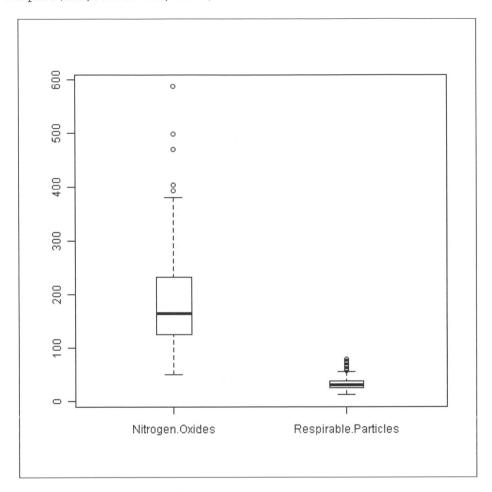

How it works...

So, we changed the width of the boxes by passing the boxwex argument to the boxplot()
command. We set boxwex to a value of 0.2. The value depends on the number of variables
we are plotting, but it should usually be less than one.

Note that we also passed the las argument with a value of 1 to make the *y* axis labels
horizontal. By default, they are parallel to the *y* axis, thus making them difficult to read. As we
want this setting in all our graphs, we can set it globally by calling the par() function:

```
par(las=1)
```

Note that we must not close the graphics device if we want to retain the setting. If we do close the device, we will need to set las to 1 again either using the par() function call or within each boxplot() function call. From now on, it is assumed that we will set las to 1 globally.

There's more

Note that when we specify a width using boxwex, the same value is applied to all the boxes in the plot. There is another argument, width, which can be used to set the relative widths of boxes. The width argument takes values in the form of a vector containing a value for each box. For example, if we want the box for respirable particles twice as wide as nitrogen oxides, we will run the following line of code:

```
boxplot(air,width=c(1,2))
```

See also

Setting arbitrarily different widths for boxes using the width argument is not a good idea unless the difference in widths conveys another important fact about the data. We will see one such example later in the chapter.

Grouping over a variable

In this recipe, we will see how we can summarize data for a variable with respect to another variable in the dataset. We will learn to group over a variable such that a separate box plot is created for each group.

Getting ready

We will only use the base graphics functions for this recipe. So, just open up the R prompt and type in the following code. We will use the metals.csv example dataset for this recipe. So, let's first load it:

```
metals<-read.csv("metals.csv")
```

How to do it...

Let's make a box plot that shows copper (Cu) concentrations grouped over measurement sites:

```
boxplot(Cu~Source,data=metals,
main="Summary of Copper (Cu) concentrations by Site")
```

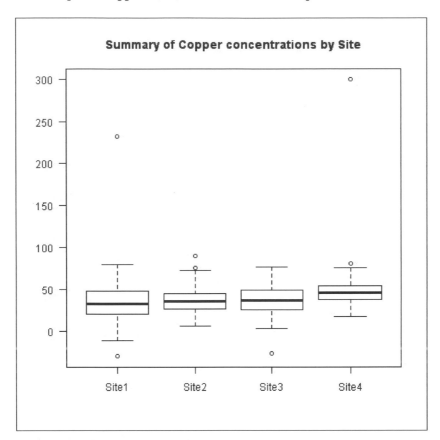

How it works...

The preceding box plot works by using the formula notation, y~group, where y is the variable whose values are depicted as separated box plots for each value of group.

There's more

Grouping over a variable works well only when the group variable has a limited number of values, for example, when it is a category (or factor in terms of an R data type) such as Source in this example. Grouping over another numerical variable with lots of unique values (say, manganese (Mn) concentrations) would result in a graph with too many box plots and not tell us much about the data.

We can also group over more than one category. If we wanted to group over Source and another variable, Expt, the experiment number, we can run:

```
boxplot(Cu~Source*Expt,data=metals,
main="Summary of Copper (Cu) concentrations by Site")
```

See also

We will use grouped box plots as examples in the next few recipes.

Varying box widths by the number of observations

In this recipe, we will learn how to vary box widths in proportion to the number of observations for each variable.

Getting ready

Just like the previous recipe, we will continue to use the metals.csv example dataset for this recipe. So, let's first load it:

```
metals<-read.csv("metals.csv")
```

How to do it...

Let's build a box plot with boxes of width proportional to the number of observations in the dataset:

```
boxplot(Cu ~ Source, data = metals,varwidth=TRUE,
main="Summary of Copper concentrations by Site")
```

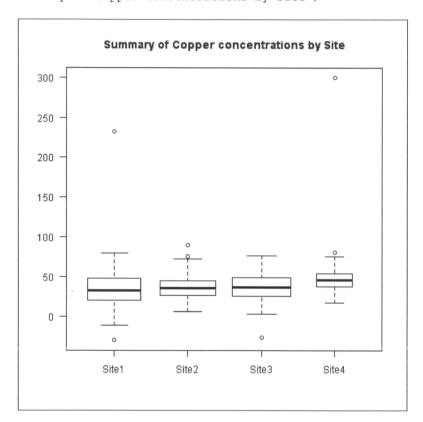

How it works...

In the example, we set the `varwidth` argument to `TRUE`, which makes the width of the boxes proportional to the square roots of the number of observations in the groups.

We can see that the box for **Site4** is the narrowest, as it has the least number of observations in the dataset. Differences in the other boxes' widths might not be so obvious, but this setting is useful when we are dealing with larger datasets. By default, `varwidth` is set to `FALSE`.

Creating box plots with notches

In this recipe, we will learn how to make box plots with notches, which are useful in comparing the medians of different groups.

Getting ready

We will continue to use the `metals.csv` example dataset for this recipe. So, let's first load it:

```
metals<-read.csv("metals.csv")
```

How to do it...

We shall now see how to make a box plot with notches:

```
boxplot(Cu ~ Source, data = metals,
varwidth=TRUE,notch=TRUE,
main="Summary of Copper concentrations by Site")
```

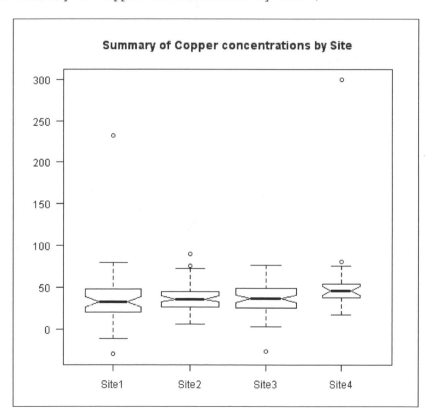

How it works...

In the example, we set the `notch` argument to `TRUE` to create notches on each side of the boxes. If the notches of two plots do not overlap, then the medians are significantly different at the 5-percent level, which suggests that the median concentrations at the four sites as shown are not statistically different from each other.

There's more

We can set the `notch.frac` argument to a value between `0` and `1` to adjust the fraction of the box width that the notches should use. The default value is `0.5` and a value of `1` gives notches using the entire width of the box, effectively producing a box plot without notches.

Including or excluding outliers

In this recipe, we will learn how to remove outliers from a box plot. This is usually not a good idea because highlighting outliers is one of the benefits of using box plots. However, sometimes extreme outliers can distort the scale and obscure the other aspects of a box plot, so it is helpful to exclude them in those cases.

Getting ready

Let's continue using the `metals.csv` example dataset. So, let's first make sure it has been loaded:

```
metals<-read.csv("metals.csv")
```

How to do it...

Once again, we will use the base graphics `boxplot()` function with a specific argument to make our metal concentrations box plot without outliers:

```
boxplot(metals[,-1],outline=FALSE,
main="Summary of metal concentrations by Site \n
(without outliers)")
```

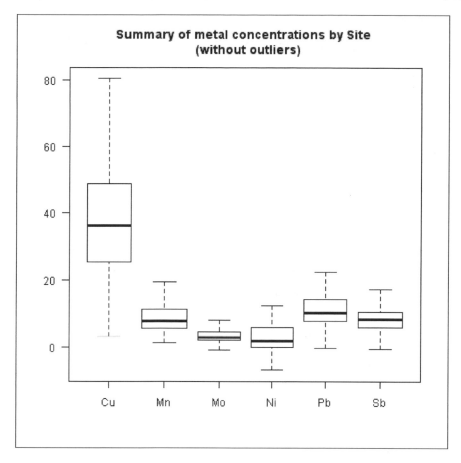

How it works...

We used the `outline` argument in the `boxplot()` function call to suppress the drawing of outliers. By default, `outline` is set to `TRUE`. To exclude outliers, we set it to `FALSE`.

See also

In the *Adjusting the extent of plot whiskers outside the box* recipe, later in the chapter, we will learn how to extend the whiskers of a box plot, which is another way of eliminating outliers by changing the definition of the cutoff value for an outlier.

Creating horizontal box plots

In this recipe, we will learn how to make box plots with horizontal boxes instead of the default vertical ones.

Getting ready

We will continue using the base graphics library functions, so we need not load any additional package. We just need to run the recipe code at the R prompt. We can also save the code as a script to use it later. Here, we will use the `metals.csv` example dataset again:

```
metals<-read.csv("metals.csv")
```

How to do it...

Let's draw the metals concentration box plot with horizontal bars:

```
boxplot(metals[,-1],
horizontal=TRUE,las=1,
main="Summary of metal concentrations by Site")
```

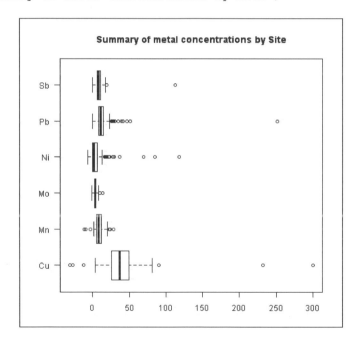

How it works...

We simply had to set the `horizontal` argument in the `boxplot()` command to `TRUE` to make the boxes horizontal. By default, it is set to `FALSE`.

 Note that unlike `barplots`, the argument name is `horizontal` and not just `horiz`.

Changing the box styling

So far, we have used the default styling for our box plots. In this recipe, we will learn how to change the colors, widths, and styles of various elements of a box plot.

Getting ready

We will continue using the base graphics library functions, so we need not load any additional library or package. We just need to run the recipe code at the R prompt. We can also save the code as a script to use it later. Here, we will use the `metals.csv` example dataset again:

```
metals<-read.csv("metals.csv")
```

How to do it...

We can build a box plot with custom colors, widths, and styles in the following way:

```
boxplot(metals[,-1],
border = "white",col = "black",boxwex = 0.3,
medlwd=1, whiskcol="black",staplecol="black",
outcol="red",cex=0.3,outpch=19,
main="Summary of metal concentrations by Site")
grid(nx=NA,ny=NULL,col="gray",lty="dashed")
```

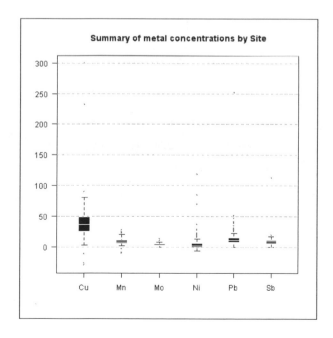

How it works...

We have used a few different arguments in the example to change the styling of the box plot. The first two are `col` and `border`, which set the box color and border color, respectively. Note that the `border` argument also sets the color for the median line, unless it is specified using the `medcol` argument.

In the example, in addition to using `boxwex` to adjust box widths, we used `medlwd` to set the width of the median line. We set the color of the whiskers and staple using `whiskcol` and `staplecol`, respectively. The color and symbol type of the outlier points were set using `outcol` and `outpch`, respectively. The size of the points was set using the `cex` argument.

There's more

We can set the color, size, and styling for each of the components. If you type in `?bxp` at the R prompt, you can see the help section for the `bxp()` function, which is called by `boxplot()` to do the actual drawing. The following table gives a summary:

Argument to boxplot()	Corresponding setting
`boxlty, boxlwd, boxcol, boxfill`	Box outline type, width, color, and fill color
`medlty, medlwd, medpch, medcex, medcol, medbg`	Median line type, line width, point character, point size expansion, color, and background color
`whisklty, whisklwd, whiskcol`	Whisker line type, width, and color
`staplelty, staplelwd, staplewex, staplecol`	Staple line type, width, line width expansion, and color
`outlty, outlwd, outwex, outpch, outcex, outcol, outbg`	Outlier line type, line width, line width expansion, point character, point size expansion, color, and background color

Adjusting the extent of plot whiskers outside the box

Sometimes, we might wish to change the definition of outliers in our dataset by changing the extent of the whiskers. In this recipe, we will learn how to adjust the extent of whiskers in a box plot by passing a simple argument.

Getting ready

We will continue using the base graphics library functions, so we need not load any additional library or package. We just need to run the recipe code at the R prompt. We can also save the code as a script to use it later. Here, we will use the `metals.csv` example dataset again:

```
metals<-read.csv("metals.csv")
```

How to do it...

Let's draw the metal concentrations box plot with the whiskers closer to the box than the default one in the preceding recipe:

```
boxplot(metals[,-1],
range=1,border = "white",col = "black",
boxwex = 0.3,medlwd=1,whiskcol="black",
staplecol="black",outcol="red",cex=0.3,outpch=19,
main="Summary of metal concentrations by Site \n
(range=1) ")
```

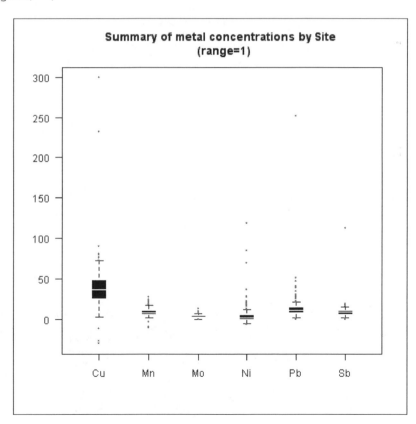

How it works...

We passed the `range` argument with a value of `1` to the `boxplot()` function in order to reduce the extent of the whiskers. The default value of `range` is `1.5`—it only takes positive values. The whiskers extend to the most extreme data point, which is no more than range times the interquartile range from the box.

There's more

If we want to extend the whiskers to the data extremes, we can either set `range` to a high enough value such that range times the interquartile range from the box is more than the most extreme data point. Alternatively, we can simply set range to `0`:

```
boxplot(metals[,-1],
range=0,border = "white",col = "black",
boxwex = 0.3,medlwd=1,whiskcol="black",
staplecol="black",outcol="red",cex=0.3,outpch=19,
main="Summary of metal concentrations by Site \n (range=0)")
```

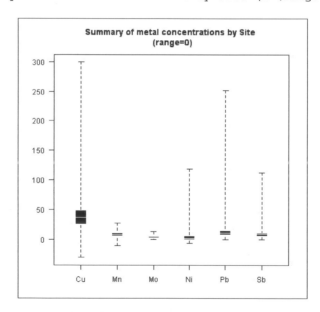

Showing the number of observations

It is often useful to know the number of observations for each variable or group when comparing them on a box plot. We did this earlier with the `varwidth` argument that makes the widths of boxes proportional to the square root of the number of observations. In this recipe, we will learn how to display the number of observations on a box plot.

Getting ready

We will continue using the base graphics library functions, so we need not load any additional library or package. We just need to run the recipe code at the R prompt. We can also save the code as a script to use it later. Here, we will use the `metals.csv` example dataset again:

```
metals<-read.csv("metals.csv")
```

How to do it...

Once again, let's use the metal concentrations box plot and display the number of observations for each metal below its label on the x axis:

```
b<-boxplot(metals[,-1],
xaxt="n",border = "white",col = "black",
boxwex = 0.3,medlwd=1,whiskcol="black",
staplecol="black",outcol="red",cex=0.3,outpch=19,
main="Summary of metal concentrations by Site")

axis(side=1,at=1:length(b$names),
labels=paste(b$names,"\n(n=",b$n,")",sep=""),
mgp=c(3,2,0))
```

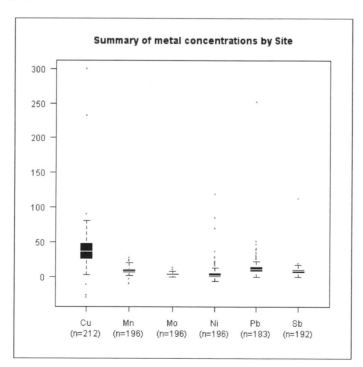

How it works...

In the example, we first made the same stylized box plot as we did two recipes ago, but we suppressed drawing the default x axis by setting `xaxt` to `"n"`. We then used the `axis()` command to create our custom axis with the metal names and number of observations as labels.

We set `side` to `1` to denote the x axis. Note that we saved the object returned by the `boxplot()` function as b, which is a list that contains useful information about the box plot. You can test this by typing in b at the R prompt and hitting the *Enter* key (after you've run the `boxplot` command). We combined the `names` and `n` (number of observations) components of b using `paste()` to construct the `labels` argument. The `at` argument was set to integer values starting from `1` to the number of metals. Finally, we also used the `mgp` argument to set the margin line for the axis labels to `2`, instead of the default `1`, so that the extra line with the number of observations doesn't make the labels overlap with the tick marks (you can see this if you omit `mgp`).

There's more

Another way of displaying the number of observations on a box plot is to use the `boxplot.n()` function from the `gplots` package. First, let's make sure that the `gplots` package is installed and loaded:

```
install.packages("gplots")
library(gplots)

boxplot.n(metals[,-1],
border = "white",col = "black",boxwex = 0.3,
medlwd=1,whiskcol="black",staplecol="black",
outcol="red",cex=0.3,outpch=19,
main="Summary of metal concentrations by Site")
```

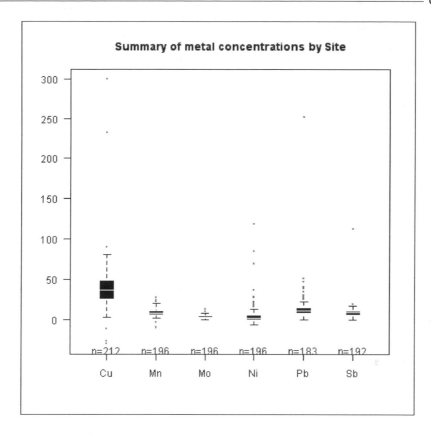

The problem with using this function is that the number labels are cut off by the axis. One way to get around this problem is to place the labels at the top of the plot region by setting the `top` argument to TRUE in the `boxplot.n()` function call.

Splitting a variable at arbitrary values into subsets

In this recipe, we will learn how to split a variable at arbitrary intervals of our choice to compare the box plots of values within each interval.

Getting ready

We will continue using the base graphics library functions, so we need not load any additional library or package. We just need to run the recipe code at the R prompt. We can also save the code as a script to use it later. Here, we will use the `metals.csv` example dataset again:

```
metals<-read.csv("metals.csv")
```

How to do it...

Let's make a box plot of copper (Cu) concentrations split at values 0, 40, and 80:

```
cuts<-c(0,40,80)
Y<-split(x=metals$Cu, f=findInterval(metals$Cu, cuts))

boxplot(Y,xaxt="n",
border = "white",col = "black",boxwex = 0.3,
medlwd=1,whiskcol="black",staplecol="black",
outcol="red",cex=0.3,outpch=19,
main="Summary of Copper concentrations",
xlab="Concentration ranges",las=1)

axis(1,at=1:length(clabels),
labels=c("Below 0","0 to 40","40 to 80","Above 80"),
lwd=0,lwd.ticks=1,col="gray")
```

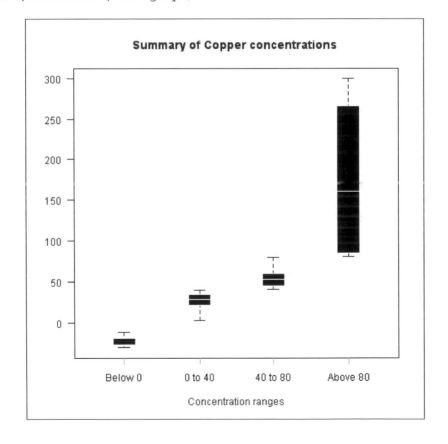

How it works...

We used a combination of a few different R functions to create the example graph shown. First, we defined a vector called `cuts` with values at which we wanted to cut our vector of concentrations. Then, we used the `split()` function to split the copper concentrations vector into a list of concentration vectors at specified intervals (you can verify this by typing in `Y` at the R prompt and hitting the *Enter* key). Note that we used the `findInterval()` function to create a vector of labels (factors) corresponding to the interval each value in `metals$Cu` lies in and set the `f` argument of the `split()` function. Then, we used the `boxplot()` function to create the basic box plot with the new `Y` vector and suppressed the default *x* axis. We then used the `axis()` function to draw the *x* axis with our custom labels.

There's more

Let's turn the previous example into a function to which we can simply pass a variable and the intervals at which we wish to cut it, and it will draw the box plot accordingly:

```
boxplot.cuts<-function(y,cuts,...) {

    Y<-split(metals$Cu, f=findInterval(y, cuts))

    b<-boxplot(Y,xaxt="n",
    border = "white",col = "black",boxwex = 0.3,
    medlwd=1,whiskcol="black",staplecol="black",
    outcol="red",cex=0.3,outpch=19,
    main="Summary of Copper concentrations",
    xlab="Concentration ranges",las=1,...)


    clabels<-paste("Below",cuts[1])

    for(k in 1:(length(cuts)-1)) {
        clabels<-c(clabels, paste(as.character(cuts[k]),
        "to", as.character(cuts[k+1])))
    }

    clabels<-c(clabels,
    paste("Above",as.character(cuts[length(cuts)])))

    axis(1,at=1:length(clabels),
    labels=clabels,lwd=0,lwd.ticks=1,col="gray")

}
```

The . . . notation is used to symbolize extra arguments to be added if required.

Now that we have defined the function, we can simply call it as follows:

```
boxplot.cuts(metals$Cu,c(0,30,60))
```

Another way to plot a subset of data in a box plot is by using the `subset` argument. For example, if we want to plot copper concentrations grouped by `source` above a certain threshold value (say `40`), we can use the following code:

```
boxplot(Cu~Source,data=metals,subset=Cu>40)
```

Note that we included an extra argument . . . to the definition of `boxplot.cuts()` in addition to `y` and `cuts`. This allows us to pass in any extra arguments that we don't explicitly use in the call to `boxplot()` inside the definition of our function. For example, we can pass `ylab` as an argument to `boxplot.cuts()` even though it is not explicitly defined as an argument.

If you find this example too cumbersome (especially with the labels), the following is an alternative definition of `boxplot.cuts()` that uses the `cut()` function and its automatic label creation:

```
boxplot.cuts<-function(y,cuts) {

    f=cut(y, c(min(y[!is.na(y)]),cuts,max(y[!is.na(y)])),
    ordered_results=TRUE);
    Y<-split(y, f=f)

    b<-boxplot(Y,xaxt="n",
    border = "white",col = "black",boxwex = 0.3,
    medlwd=1,whiskcol="black",staplecol="black",
    outcol="red",cex=0.3,outpch=19,
    main="Summary of Copper concentrations",
    xlab="Concentration ranges",las=1)


    clabels = as.character(levels(f))
    axis(1,at=1:length(clabels),
    labels=clabels,lwd=0,lwd.ticks=1,col="gray")


}
```

To create a box plot similar to the example shown earlier, we can run this:

```
boxplot.cuts(metals$Cu,c(0,40,80))
```

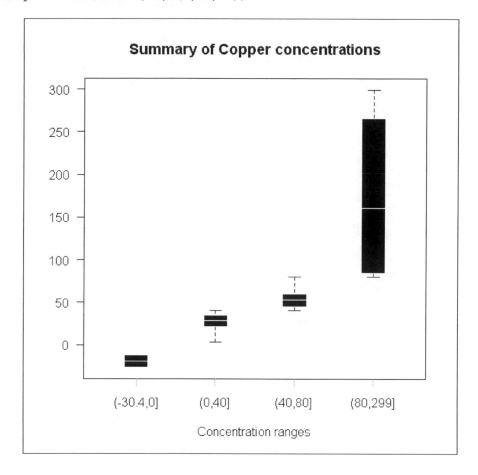

9

Creating Heat Maps and Contour Plots

In this chapter, we will cover the following recipes:

- ▶ Creating heat maps of a single Z variable with scale
- ▶ Creating correlation heat maps
- ▶ Summarizing multivariate data in a single heat map
- ▶ Creating contour plots
- ▶ Creating filled contour plots
- ▶ Creating three-dimensional surface plots
- ▶ Visualizing time series as calendar heat maps

Introduction

In this chapter, we will learn how to make various types of heat maps and contour plots. By heat maps, we mean color-coded grid images, useful for visualizing correlations, trends, and multivariate data. We will learn how contour plots can be used to show topographical information in various two- and three-dimensional ways.

The recipes in this chapter are a bit longer and more advanced than the ones in previous chapters. However, the code is clearly explained step by step so that you can understand how it works.

As with the previous chapters, it is best to try out each recipe first with the example shown here and then with your own datasets so that you can fully understand each line of code.

Creating heat maps of a single Z variable with a scale

In this recipe, we will make a heat map that shows the variation in values of one variable (z) along the *x* and *y* axes as a grid of colors and display a scale alongside.

Getting ready

We will only use the base graphics functions for this recipe. So, just open up the R prompt and type in the following code. We will use the `sales.csv` example dataset for this recipe. So, let's first load it:

```
sales<-read.csv("sales.csv")
```

We will use the `RColorBrewer` package for some good color palettes. So, let's make sure that it's installed and loaded:

```
install.packages("RColorBrewer")
library(RColorBrewer)
```

How to do it...

The `sales` dataset has monthly sales data for four cities. Let's make a heat map with the months along the *x* axis and the cities on the *y* axis:

```
rownames(sales)<-sales[,1]
sales<-sales[,-1]
data_matrix<-data.matrix(sales)

pal=brewer.pal(7,"YlOrRd")

breaks<-seq(3000,12000,1500)

#Create layout with 1 row and 2 columns (for the heatmap and scale);
the heatmap column is 8 times as wide as the scale column

layout(matrix(data=c(1,2), nrow=1, ncol=2), widths=c(8,1),
heights=c(1,1))

#Set margins for the heatmap
par(mar = c(5,10,4,2),oma=c(0.2,0.2,0.2,0.2),mex=0.5)


image(x=1:nrow(data_matrix),y=1:ncol(data_matrix),
```

```
z=data_matrix,axes=FALSE,xlab="Month",
ylab="",col=pal[1:(length(breaks)-1)],
breaks=breaks,main="Sales Heat Map")

axis(1,at=1:nrow(data_matrix),labels=rownames(data_matrix),
col="white",las=1)

axis(2,at=1:ncol(data_matrix),labels=colnames(data_matrix),
col="white",las=1)

abline(h=c(1:ncol(data_matrix))+0.5,
v=c(1:nrow(data_matrix))+0.5, col="white",lwd=2,xpd=FALSE)

breaks2<-breaks[-length(breaks)]

# Color Scale
par(mar = c(5,1,4,7))
# If you get a figure margins error while running the above code,
enlarge the plot device or adjust the margins so that the graph and
scale fit within the device.

image(x-1, y-0:length(breaks2),z-t(matrix(breaks2))*1.001,
col=pal[1:length(breaks)-1],axes=FALSE,breaks=breaks,
xlab="", ylab="",xaxt="n")

axis(4,at=0:(length(breaks2)-1), labels=breaks2, col="white",
las=1)

abline(h=c(1:length(breaks2)),col="white",lwd=2,xpd=F)
```

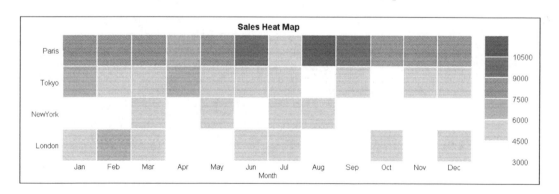

How it works...

We used a lot of steps and different function calls to create the heat map. Let's go through them one by one to understand how it all works.

Basically, we used the `image()` function in the base graphics library to create the heat map and its color scale. There is also a `heatmap()` function and a `heatmap.2()` function in the `gplots` package. However, we used `image()` because it is more flexible for our purpose.

First, we had to format the data in the correct format for `image()`, which requires that the z parameter be in the form of a matrix. The first column of the `sales` dataset contains the month names, which we assigned as `rownames`. Then, we removed the month column from the dataset and cast it as a matrix called `data_matrix`, containing only numerical values.

We defined `breaks` as a sequence of values from `3000` up to `12000` with steps of `1500`. These values are used to map the sales values to the color scale, where each color denotes values within a certain range. We used the `RColorBrewer` palette, `YlOrRd`, which contains seven warm colors.

We created a graph layout with one row and two columns using the `layout()` function. The left column for the heat map is eight times as wide as the right column for the color scale and their heights are equal.

We used the `image()` function to create the heat map. The main argument is z, which we set to `data_matrix`. The x and y arguments take the index of the rows and columns of the matrix, respectively. We set the `breaks` argument to the `breaks` vector we created earlier and set the `col` argument to our palette, but with the number of colors one less than the number of breaks. This is a requirement of the `image()` function.

Note that we suppressed the drawing of the default axes. We used the `axis()` command to draw the x and y axes with the row and column names, respectively, as the labels. The `abline()` function call is used to draw the white lines separating each block of color on the heat map (a bit like gridlines). These lines make the graph look nicer and a bit easier to read.

Finally, we drew the color scale by issuing another `image()` function call. We first created a subset of `breaks`, called `breaks2`, without the last element of `breaks`. We passed a transpose of a matrix of `breaks2` as the z argument to `image()`. Note that we also multiplied it by `1.001`, to create a set of values just above each break so that they are colored appropriately. We used the same `breaks` and `col` arguments as the heat map. We added a y axis on side 4 to mark the break values and also used `abline()` to draw white horizontal lines to separate the breaks.

There's more

The preceding code might seem a bit too complicated at first, but if you go through each statement and function call carefully, you will notice that it is just a big block of code with the same building blocks that we used in earlier recipes in the book. The best way to really understand the recipe and to modify it for your own needs is to change, add, or remove arguments from each function call and see the resulting effects.

See also

In the next few recipes, we will continue using the `image()` function to make some more types of heat maps.

Creating correlation heat maps

In this recipe, we will learn how to make a correlation heat map from a matrix of correlation coefficients.

Getting ready

We will only use the base graphics functions for this recipe. So, just open up the R prompt and type in the following code. We will use the `genes.csv` example dataset for this recipe. So, let's first load it:

```
genes<-read.csv("genes.csv")
```

How to do it...

Let's make a heat map showing the correlation between genes in a matrix:

```
rownames(genes)<-genes[,1]
data_matrix<-data.matrix(genes[,-1])

pal=heat.colors(5)

breaks<-seq(0,1,0.2)

layout(matrix(data=c(1,2), nrow=1, ncol=2), widths=c(8,1),
heights=c(1,1))

par(mar = c(3,7,12,2),oma=c(0.2,0.2,0.2,0.2),mex=0.5)

image(x=1:nrow(data_matrix),y=1:ncol(data_matrix),
```

```
z=data_matrix,xlab="",ylab="",breaks=breaks,
col=pal,axes=FALSE)


text(x=1:nrow(data_matrix)+0.75, y=par("usr")[4] + 1.25,
srt = 45, adj = 1, labels = rownames(data_matrix),
xpd = TRUE)

axis(2,at=1:ncol(data_matrix),labels=colnames(data_matrix),
col="white",las=1)

abline(h=c(1:ncol(data_matrix))+0.5,v=c(1:nrow(data_matrix))+0.5,
col="white",lwd=2,xpd=F)

title("Correlation between genes",line=8,adj=0)

breaks2<-breaks[-length(breaks)]

# Color Scale
par(mar = c(25,1,25,7))
image(x=1, y=0:length(breaks2),z=t(matrix(breaks2))*1.001,
col=pal[1:length(breaks)-1],axes=FALSE,
breaks=breaks,xlab="",ylab="",
xaxt="n")

axis(4,at=0:(length(breaks2)),labels=breaks,col="white",las=1)
abline(h=c(1:length(breaks2)),col="white",lwd=2,xpd=F)
```

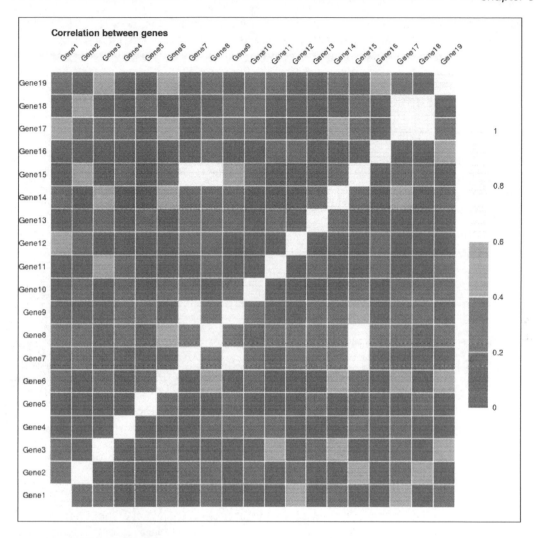

How it works...

Just like in the previous recipe, first we format the data using the first column values as row names and cast the data frame as a matrix. We created a palette of five colors using the `heat.colors()` function and defined a sequence of breaks 0, 0.2, 0.4,...1.0.

Then, we created a layout with one row and two columns (one for the heat map and the other for the color scale). We created the heat map using the `image()` command in a similar way to the previous recipe passing the data matrix as the value of the z argument.

We added custom *x* axis labels using the `text()` function, instead of the `axis()` function to rotate the axis labels. We also placed the labels in the top margin instead of the bottom margin, as usual, to improve the readability of the graph. This way, it resembles a gene correlation matrix of numbers more closely, where the names of the genes are shown on the top and left. To create the rotated labels, we set the `srt` argument to `45`, thus setting the angle of rotation to 45 degrees.

Finally, we added a color scale to the right of the heat map.

There's more

We can use a more contrasting color scale to differentiate between the correlation values. For example, to highlight the diagonal values of `1` more clearly, we can substitute the last color in our palette with white.

 If you get a figure margins error while running the code, enlarge the plot device or adjust the margins so that the graph and scale fit within the device.

Summarizing multivariate data in a single heat map

In the preceding couple of recipes, we looked at representing a matrix of data along two axes on a heat map. In this recipe, we will learn how to summarize multivariate data using a heat map.

Getting ready

We are only using the base graphics functions for this recipe. So, just open up the R prompt and type in the following code. We will use the `nba.csv` example dataset for this recipe. So, let's first load it:

```
nba <- read.csv("nba.csv")
```

This example dataset, which shows some statistics on the top scorers in NBA basketball games has been taken from a blog post on **FlowingData** (see `http://flowingdata.com/2010/01/21/how-to-make-a-heatmap-a-quick-and-easy-solution/` for details). The original data is from the **databaseBasketball.com** website (`http://databasebasketball.com/`). We will use our own code to create a similar heat map showing player statistics.

We will use the `RColorBrewer` library for a nice color palette, so let's load it:

```
library(RColorBrewer)
```

How to do it...

We are going to summarize a number of NBA player statistics in the same heat map using the `image()` function:

```
rownames(nba)<-nba[,1]

data_matrix<-t(scale(data.matrix(nba[,-1])))

pal=brewer.pal(6,"Blues")

statnames<-c("Games Played", "Minutes Played", "Total Points",
"Field Goals Made", "Field Goals Attempted",
"Field Goal Percentage", "Free Throws Made",
"Free Throws Attempted", "Free Throw Percentage",
"Three Pointers Made", "Three Pointers Attempted",
"Three Point Percentage", "Offensive Rebounds",
"Defensive Rebounds", "Total Rebounds", "Assists", "Steals",
"Blocks", "Turnovers", "Fouls")

par(mar = c(3,14,19,2),oma=c(0.2,0.2,0.2,0.2),mex=0.5)

#Heat map
image(x=1:nrow(data_matrix),y=1:ncol(data_matrix),
z=data_matrix,xlab="",ylab="",col=pal,axes=FALSE)

#X axis labels
text(1:nrow(data_matrix), par("usr")[4] + 1,
srt = 45, adj = 0,labels = statnames,
xpd = TRUE, cex=0.85)

#Y axis labels
axis(side=2,at=1:ncol(data_matrix),
labels=colnames(data_matrix),
col="white",las=1, cex.axis=0.85)

#White separating lines
abline(h=c(1:ncol(data_matrix))+0.5,
v=c(1:nrow(data_matrix))+0.5,
```

```
col="white",lwd=1,xpd=F)

#Graph Title
text(par("usr")[1]+5, par("usr")[4] + 12,
"NBA per game performance of top 50corers",
xpd=TRUE,font=2,cex=1.5)
```

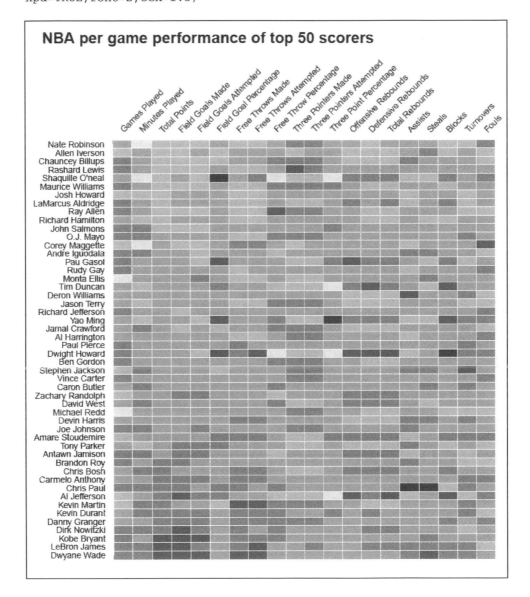

How it works...

Once again, in a way similar to the preceding couple of recipes, we first formatted the dataset with the appropriate row names (in this case, names of players) and cast it as a matrix. We did one additional thing—we scaled the values in the matrix using the `scale()` function, which centers and scales each column so that we can denote the relative values of each column on the same color scale.

We chose a blue color palette from the `RColorBrewer` library. We also created a vector with the descriptive names of the player statistics to use as labels for the *x* axis.

The code for the heat map itself and the axis labels is very similar to the previous recipe. We used the `image()` function with `data_matrix` as z and suppressed the default axes. Then, we used `text()` and `axis()` to add the *x* and *y* axis labels. We also used the `text()` function to add the graph title (instead of the `title()` function) in order to left align it with the *y* axis labels instead of the heat map.

There's more

As shown in the FlowingData blog post, we can order the data in the matrix as per the values in any one column. By default, the data is in the ascending order of total points scored by each player (as can be seen from the light to dark blue progression in the **Total Points** column). To order the players based on their scores from highest to lowest, we need to run the following code after reading the CSV file:

```
nba <- nba[order(nba$PTS),]
```

> See help on the `order()` function by running `?order` or `help(order)` at the R prompt.

Then, we can run the rest of the code to make the following graph:

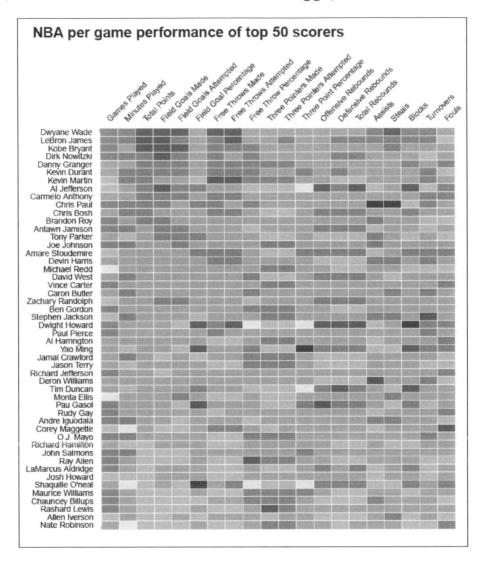

Creating contour plots

In this recipe, we will learn how to make contour plots to visualize topographical data, such as the terrain near a mountain or a volcano.

Getting ready

We are only using the base graphics functions for this recipe. So, just open up the R prompt and type the following code. We will use the inbuilt `volcano` dataset, so we need not load anything.

How to do it...

Let's first make a default contour plot with `volcano`:

```
contour(x=10*1:nrow(volcano), y=10*1:ncol(volcano), z=volcano,
xlab="Metres West",ylab="Metres North",
main="Topography of Maunga Whau Volcano")
```

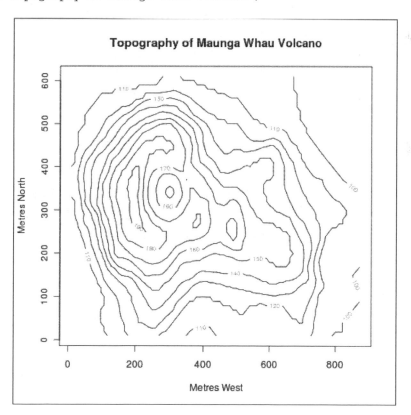

How it works...

We used the contour() base graphics library function to make the graph.

The x and y arguments specify the locations of the grid at which the height values (z) are specified. The volcano dataset contains topographic information on a 10 x 10 m grid, so we set the x and y grid arguments to 10 times the index numbers of rows and columns, respectively.

The contour data, z, is provided by the volcano dataset in a matrix form.

The graph shows the height of the region in the form of contour lines, which outline all areas with the same height. The height for each contour line is shown in gray.

There's more

Now, let's improve the graph by making the *y* axis labels horizontal and adding some colors to the plot area and contour lines:

```
par(las=1)

plot(0,0,xlim=c(0,10*nrow(volcano)),ylim=c(0,10*ncol(volcano)),
type="n",xlab="Metres West",
ylab="Metres North",main="Topography of Maunga Whau Volcano")

u<-par("usr")

rect(u[1],u[3],u[2],u[4],col="lightgreen")

contour(x=10*1:nrow(volcano),y=10*1:ncol(volcano),
volcano,col="red",add=TRUE)
```

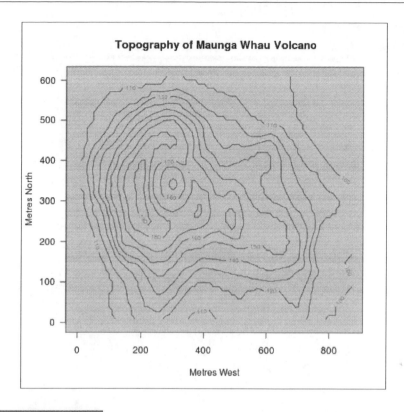

Topography of Maunga Whau Volcano

See also

In the next recipe, we will learn how to make filled contour plots, which use a solid color to make the graph even easier to read.

Creating filled contour plots

In this recipe, we will learn how to make a contour plot with the areas between the contours filled with a solid color.

Getting ready

We will only use the base graphics functions for this recipe. So, just open up the R prompt and type the following code. We will use the inbuilt `volcano` dataset, so we need not load anything.

How to do it...

Let's make a filled contour plot showing the terrain data of the Maunga Whau volcano in R's in-built volcano dataset:

```
filled.contour(x = 10*1:nrow(volcano),y = 10*1:ncol(volcano),
z = volcano, color.palette = terrain.colors,
plot.title = title(main = "The Topography of Maunga Whau",
xlab = "Meters North",ylab = "Meters West"),
plot.axes = {axis(1, seq(100, 800, by = 100))
             axis(2, seq(100, 600, by = 100))},
key.title = title(main="Height\n(meters)"),
key.axes = axis(4, seq(90, 190, by = 10)))
```

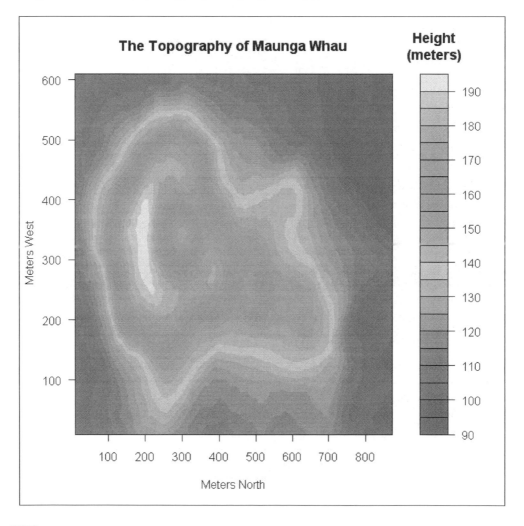

How it works...

If you type in `?filled.contour`, you will see that the preceding example is taken from that help file (see the second example at the end of the help file). The `filled. contour()` function creates a contour plot with the areas between the contour lines filled with solid colors. In this case, we chose the `terrain.colors()` function to use a color palette suitable to show geographical elevations. We set the `color.palette` argument to `terrain.colors` and the `filled.contour()` function automatically calculates the number of color levels.

The basic arguments are the same as those for `contour()`, namely, x and y, that specify the locations of the grid at which the height values (z) are specified. The contour data, z, is provided by the `volcano` dataset in a matrix form.

The `filled.contour()` function is slightly different from other basic graph functions because it automatically creates a layout with the contour plot and key. We can't suppress or customize the styling of the key to a great extent. Also, some of the standard graph parameters have to be passed to other functions. For example, the `xlab` and `ylab` axis labels have to be passed as arguments to the `title()` function, which is passed as the value for the `plot.title` argument. We cannot directly pass `xlab` and `ylab` to `filled.contour()`.

We also have to add our custom axes by setting the `plot.axes` argument to a list of function calls to the `axis()` function. Unlike other functions, we cannot simply set `axes` to `FALSE` and call `axis()` after drawing the graph because of the internal use of `layout()` in `filled. contour()`. If we add axes after calling `filled.contour()`, the x axis will extend beyond the contour plot up to the key.

Finally, we set the title and tick labels of the key using the `key.title` and `key.axes` arguments, respectively. Once again, we had to set these arguments to function calls to `title()` and `axis()`, respectively, instead of directly specifying the values.

There's more

We can adjust the level of detail and smoothness between the contours by increasing their number using the `nlevels` argument:

```
filled.contour(x = 10*1:nrow(volcano),
y = 10*1:ncol(volcano), z = volcano,
color.palette = terrain.colors,
plot.title = title(main = "The Topography of Maunga Whau",
xlab = "Meters North",ylab = "Meters West"),nlevels=100,
plot.axes = {axis(1, seq(100, 800, by = 100))
            axis(2, seq(100, 600, by = 100))},
key.title = title(main="Height\n(meters)"),
key.axes = axis(4, seq(90, 190, by = 10)))
```

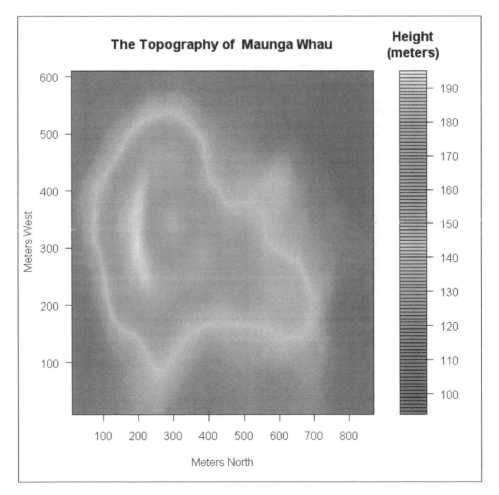

Note that there are a lot more contours now and the plot looks a lot smoother. The default value of `nlevels` is `20`, so we increased it by five times. The key doesn't look very nice because of too many black lines between each tick mark; however, as pointed out earlier, we cannot control that without changing the definition of the `filled.contour()` function itself.

See also

In the next recipe, we will learn how to make a three-dimensional version of a filled contour plot.

Creating three-dimensional surface plots

In this recipe, we will use a special library to make a three-dimensional surface plot for the `volcano` dataset. The resulting plot will also be interactive so that we can rotate the visualization using a mouse to look at it from different angles.

Getting ready

For this recipe, we will use the `rgl` package, so we must first install and load it:

```
install.packages("rgl")
library(rgl)
```

We will only use the inbuilt `volcano` dataset, so we need not load any other dataset.

How to do it...

Let's make a simple three-dimensional surface plot that shows the terrain of the Maunga Whau volcano:

```
z <- 2 * volcano
x <- 10 * (1:nrow(z))
y <- 10 * (1:ncol(z))

zlim <- range(z)
zlen <- zlim[2] - zlim[1] + 1

colorlut <- terrain.colors(zlen)
```

```
col <- colorlut[ z-zlim[1]+1 ]

rgl.open()
rgl.surface(x, y, z, color=col, back="lines")
```

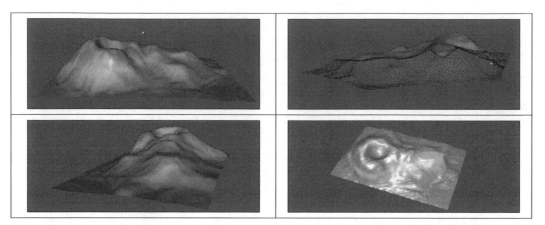

How it works...

RGL is a three-dimensional real-time rendering device driver system for R. We used the `rgl.surface()` function to create the preceding visualization. See the help section (by running `?rgl.surface` at the R prompt) to see the original example at the bottom of the help file, on which the example is based.

We basically used the `volcano` dataset that we used in the previous couple of recipes and created a three-dimensional representation of the volcano's topography instead of the two-dimensional contour representation.

We set up the x, y, and z arguments in a similar way to the contour examples, except that we multiplied the volcano height data in z by 2 to exaggerate the terrain, which helped us appreciate the library's three-dimensional capabilities better.

Then, we defined a matrix of colors for each point in z such that each height value has a unique color from the `terrain.colors()` function. We saved the mapped color data in col (if you type in col at the R prompt and hit the *Return* (or *Enter*) key, you will see that it contains 5307 colors).

Then, we opened a new RGL device with the `rgl.open()` command. This brings up a blank window with a gray background. Finally, we called the `rgl.surface()` function with the x, y, z, and color arguments. We also set the back argument to `"lines"`, which resulted in a wireframed polygon underneath the visualization.

Once `rgl.surface()` has ran, we can rotate the visualization using our mouse in any direction. This lets us look at the volcano from any angle. If we look underneath, we can also see the wireframe. The images show snapshots of the volcano from four different angles.

There's more

The example is a very basic demonstration of the `rgl` package's functionality.

There are a number of other functions and settings we can use to create a lot more complex visualizations customized to our needs. For example, the `back` argument can be set to other values to create a filled, point, or hidden polygon. We can also set the transparency (or opacity) of the visualization using the `alpha` argument. Arguments controlling the appearance of the visualization are sent to the `rgl.material()` function, which sets the material properties.

Read the related help sections (`?rgl`, `?rgl.surface`, `?rgl.material`) to get a more in-depth understanding of this library.

Visualizing time series as calendar heat maps

In this recipe, we will learn how to make intuitive heat maps in a calendar format to summarize time series data.

Getting ready

In this recipe, we will use a custom function called `calendarHeat()` written by Paul Bleicher (released as open source under the GPL license). So, let's first load the source code of the function (available from the downloads area of the book's website):

```
source("calendarHeat.R")
```

We are going to use the `google.csv` example dataset, which contains stock price data for Google (ticker GOOG). Let's load it:

```
stock.data <- read.csv("google.csv")
```

The `calendarHeat()` function also makes use of the `chron` library, which has to be installed and loaded using the following code:

```
install.packages("chron")
library("chron")
```

How to do it...

Let's visualize the adjusted closing price of the Google stock in a calendar heat map:

```
calendarHeat(dates=stock.data$Date,
values=stock.data$Adj.Close,
varname="Google Adjusted Close")
```

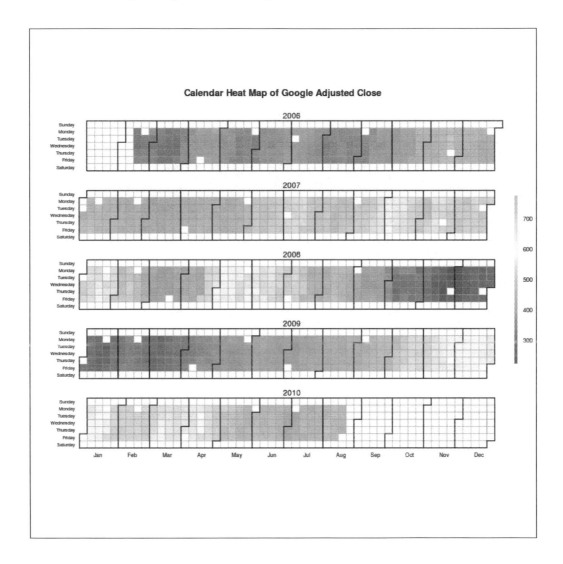

How it works...

We used the `calendarHeat()` function, which uses the `grid`, `lattice`, and `chron` libraries to make the heat map. The main arguments are `dates` and `values`, which we set to the `Date` and `Adj.Close` columns of our dataset, respectively. We also used the `varname` argument to set the title of the heat map.

There are several other arguments that can be passed to `calendarHeat()`. For example, we can specify the format our input dates are in using the `date.form` argument. The default format is YYYY-MM-DD, which matches our original dataset. However, if the dates were in another format, say MM-DD-YY, we can set `date.form` to `"%m-%d-%y"`.

The number of colors in the color scale are controlled by the `ncolors` argument, which has a default value of `99`. The color scheme is specified by the `color` argument, which takes some predefined palette names as values. The default is `r2g` (red to green), and other options are `r2b` (red to blue) and `w2b` (white to blue). We can add more options simply by adding a definition for a new color palette as a vector of colors.

There's more

Another useful package that provides a calendar heat map functionality is the `openair` package, which has been primarily created for air pollution data analysis. Let's make a pollution heat map using this package.

First, we need to install and load it:

```
install.packages("openair")
library(openair)
```

To make our first air pollution calendar heat map, we can simply run the following line of code:

```
calendarPlot(mydata)
```

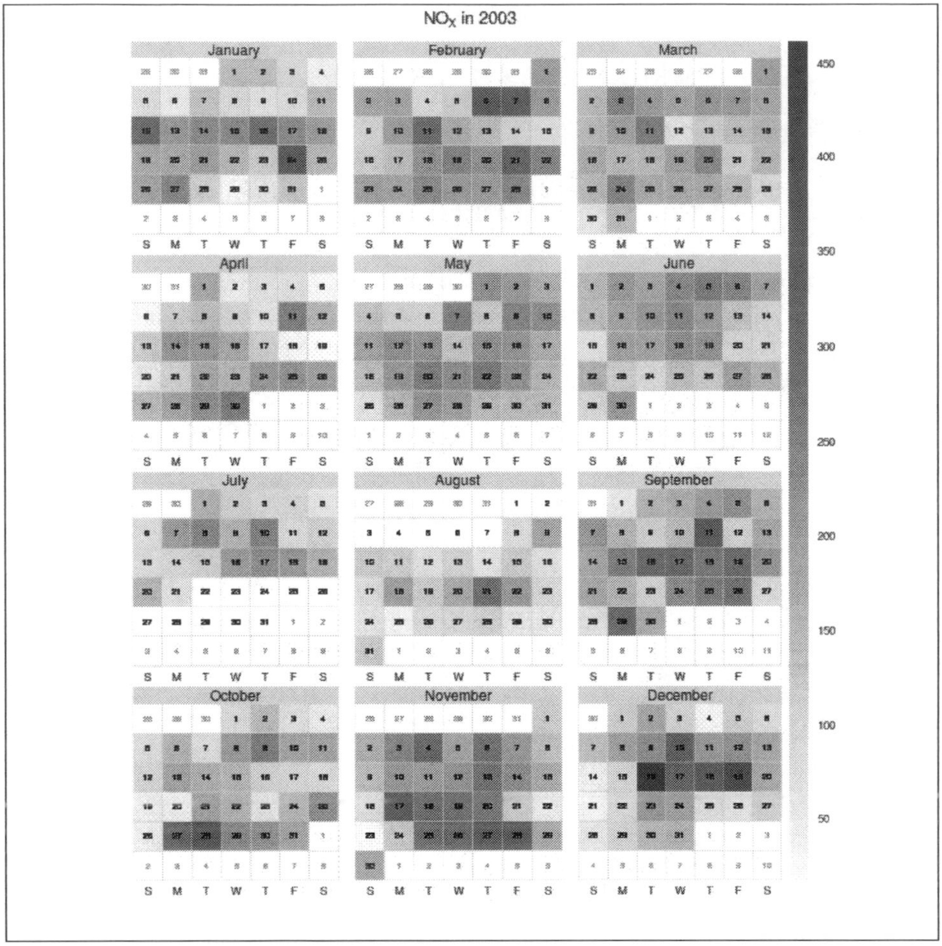

NOx in 2003

The graph shows some **Nitrogen Oxides (NOx)** concentration data from London in 2003 in the form of a heat map overlaid on a regular calendar.

We only had to pass one argument, `mydata`, to the `calendar.plot()` function, which uses the package's default `mydata` dataset. Run `head(mydata)` at the R prompt to see what the data looks like and all the columns in the dataset. The first column contains the GMT date and time values in a long format (YYYY-MM-DD HH:MM:SS). If we want to use the `calendar.plot()` function, as it is for visualizing other types of temporal data, we can do so as long as the `date` column is in the same format and we specify the variable to be plotted using the `pollutant` argument. The default value of `pollutant` is `"nox"`, which is the name of the column that contains the NOx values.

Let's say, we want to plot daily sales data instead. Let's use the `rnorm()` function to create some fake data and add it as a column to the `mydata` dataset:

```
mydata$sales<-rnorm(length(mydata$nox),mean=1000,sd=1500)
```

The code added a `sales` column to `mydata`, with random values following a normal distribution with a mean of `1000` and standard deviation of `1500`. Now, let's use `calendar.plot()` to make a heat map for this sales data:

```
calendarPlot(mydata,pollutant="sales",main="Daily Sales in 2003")
```

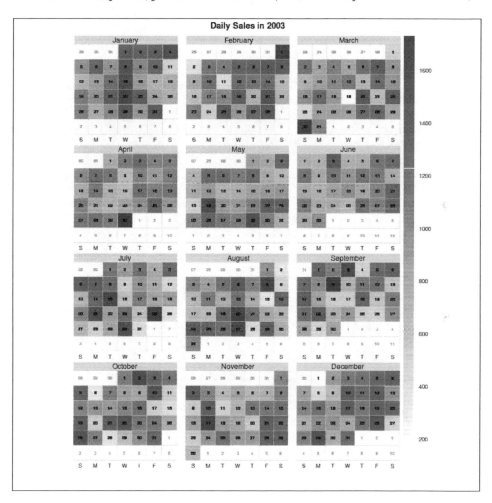

In the example, we set the `pollutant` argument to the newly created `sales` column (note that we have to pass it as a string in quotes). We also set the plot title using the `main` argument. The `calendar.plot()` function uses the `lattice` library to generate the heat maps. Refer to the help file (`?calendar.plot`) to see other arguments you can use.

10
Creating Maps

In this chapter, we will cover the following recipes:

- ▶ Plotting global data by countries on a world map
- ▶ Creating graphs with regional maps
- ▶ Plotting data on Google Maps
- ▶ Creating and reading KML data
- ▶ Working with ESRI shapefiles

Introduction

In this chapter, we will take an in-depth look at visualizing data on geographical maps, building on top of our brief introduction in *Chapter 1, R Graphics*.

Overlaying datasets from different parts of the world on maps is a very good way of summarizing data in its correct geographical context. A lot of data is being made freely available. For example, the World Bank and World Health Organization (WHO) publish lots of socio-economic and health-related data that can be plotted on maps. Google Maps provides a good API that can be directly connected to from R, as we will see in this chapter.

We will also learn how to work with **Geographical Information Systems** (**GIS**) data formats in R.

As with the previous chapters, it is best to try out each recipe first with the example shown here and then with your own datasets so that you can fully understand each line of code.

Plotting global data by countries on a world map

In this recipe, we will learn how to plot country-wise data on a world map.

Getting ready

We will use a few different additional packages for this recipe. We need the `maps` package for the actual drawing of the maps, the `WDI` package to get the World Bank data by countries, and the `RColorBrewer` package for color schemes. So, let's make sure these packages are installed and loaded:

```
install.packages("maps")
library(maps)
install.packages("WDI")
library(WDI)
install.packages("RColorBrewer")
library(RColorBrewer)
```

How to do it...

There are a lot of different data we can pull in using the world bank API provided by the `WDI` package. In this example, let's plot some CO2 emissions data:

```
colours = brewer.pal(7,"PuRd")
wgdp<-WDIsearch("gdp")
w<-WDI(country="all", indicator=wgdp[4,1], start=2005, end=2005)

w[63,1] <- "USA"

x<-map(plot=FALSE)

x$measure<-array(NA,dim=length(x$names))

for(i in 1:length(w$country)) {
    for(j in 1:length(x$names)) {
        if(grepl(w$country[i],x$names[j],ignore.case=T))
            x$measure[j]<-w[i,3]
    }
}

sd <- data.frame(col=colours,
values <- seq(min(x$measure[!is.na(x$measure)]),
```

```
max(x$measure[!is.na(x$measure)]) *1.0001,
length.out=7))

sc<-array("#FFFFFF",dim=length(x$names))

for (i in 1:length(x$measure))
    if(!is.na(x$measure[i]))
        sc[i]=as.character(sd$col[findInterval(x$measure[i],
        sd$values)])

#2-column layout with color scale to the right of the map
layout(matrix(data=c(2,1), nrow=1, ncol=2), widths=c(8,1),
heights=c(8,1))

# Color Scale first
breaks<-sd$values

par(mar = c(20,1,20,7),oma=c(0.2,0.2,0.2,0.2),mex=0.5)

image(x=1, y=0:length(breaks),z=t(matrix(breaks))*1.001,
col=colours[1:length(breaks)-1],axes=FALSE
breaks=breaks,xlab-"",ylab-"",xaxt="n")

axis(side=4,at=0:(length(breaks)-1),
labels=round(breaks),col="white",las=1)

abline(h=c(1:length(breaks)),col="white",lwd=2,xpd=F)

#Map
map(col=sc,fill=TRUE,lty="blank")
```

```
# If you get a figure margins error while running the above code,
enlarge the plot device or adjust the margins so that the graph and
scale fit within the device.
```

```
map(add=TRUE,col="gray",fill=FALSE)
title("CO2 emissions (kg per 2000 US$ of GDP)")
```

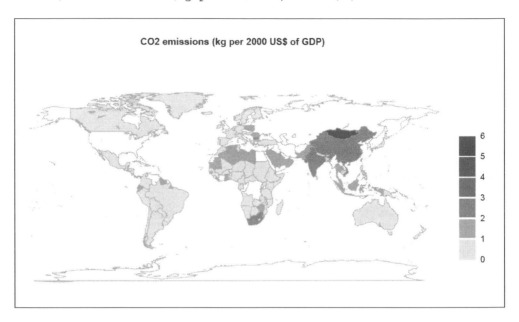

How it works...

We used the `maps` package in combination with the world bank data from the WDI package above to plot CO2 emissions data per 2000 US$ of GDP for various countries across the world.

First, we chose an `RColorBrewer` color scheme and saved it as a vector called `colours`. We then pulled a list of GDP-related variables using the `WDIsearch()` function. If you type in `wgdp` at the R prompt and hit the *Enter* key, you will see a list of codes and descriptions of each of these variables. For the preceding example, we chose the fourth variable (`wgdp[4,1]`), which gives CO2 emissions (kg per 2000 US$ of GDP), and passed it to the `WDI()` function to get data for all countries for the year 2005 by setting the `country` argument to `"all"` and `start` and `end` to `2005`.

Next, we created an `x` map object simply by calling the `map()` function and setting `plot` to `FALSE` so that the map is not drawn yet. We did this so that we can map the data we pulled from WDI to the country polygons contained in the `map` object.

First, we added a new array called measure to x, with NA as the default values and length, matching the number of country names in x. If you type in x$names at the R prompt and hit *Enter*, you will see the whole list of country names. Similarly, w$country contains the names of the countries for which the WDI package has data. Note that the map object has a lot more names because it contains region information in finer detail than just countries. So, we must first match the names of countries in the two datasets.

For the example, we use a simple search function, grepl(), which looks for the WDI country names in the map object x and assigns the corresponding CO2 emissions values from w to x$measure. This is a very approximate solution and misses on countries where the names in the two datasets are not the same. For example, the United States is named USA in the WDI dataset. To match all the countries exactly, we need to manually check the important ones we are interested in. In the example, the United States was corrected manually.

Next, we created a data frame called sd to define a color scheme with intervals based on a sequence from the minimum to the maximum values in x$measure. We use sd to assign a color for each of the values in x$measure by creating a vector called sc. First, we create sc with default values of white so that any missing values are depicted without any color. Then, we used the findInterval() function to assign a color to each value of x$measure.

Finally, we have all the ingredients to make the map. We first used the layout() function to create a 1 x 2 layout just as we did for heat maps in the previous chapter.

We need to plot the color scale first here because, if we plot the map first, the scale cannot be plotted on the same layout and results in a new plot with just the scale. We reversed this plotting order by setting the data argument in layout() to c(2,1) instead of c(1,2).

The color scale is drawn in exactly the same way as in the previous chapter for heat maps, using the image() function. To draw the map itself, we used the map() function. We set the col argument to the sc vector that contains colors corresponding to each polygon on the map. We set fill to TRUE and lty to "blank" so that we get the polygons filled with the specified colors and no blank borders around them. Instead, we add gray borders by calling the map() function with add set to TRUE, col set to gray, and fill set to FALSE. Finally, we added a plot title using the title() function.

There's more

The example shows just one variable for one year visualized on a map. The world bank package gives 73 different metrics related to GDP alone (as can be seen in the wgdp variable). See the help section for the WDI package for more details about other data available (?WDI and ?WDIsearch). If you have any other data by country from another source, you can use that with the map() function in the example as long as the country names can be matched to the names of regions in the map object.

See also

In the next recipe, we will learn how to plot regional data on individual country maps instead of on a world map.

Creating graphs with regional maps

In this recipe, we will learn how to plot data on regional maps within individual countries rather than the whole world map. We will look at examples based on the United States and European countries.

Getting ready

Just as with the previous recipe, we will make use of the maps package to draw the map and the RColorBrewer package to choose color schemes. So, let's make sure that they are loaded:

```
library(maps)
library(RColorBrewer)
```

We will use the inbuilt USArrests example dataset, which contains crime statistics, in arrests per 100,000 residents for assault, murder, and rape in each of the 50 US states in 1973.

How to do it...

Let's plot the arrests rate for murders in US states in 1973. The default graphics device size might not be big enough for the map; thus, if you get an error about figure margins, enlarge the graphics device:

```
x<-map("state",plot=FALSE)

for(i in 1:length(rownames(USArrests))) {
    for(j in 1:length(x$names)) {
        if(grepl(rownames(USArrests)[i],x$names[j],ignore.case=T))
            x$measure[j]<-as.double(USArrests$Murder[i])
    }
}

colours <- brewer.pal(7,"Reds")

sd <- data.frame(col=colours,
values=seq(min(x$measure[!is.na(x$measure)]),
max(x$measure[!is.na(x$measure)])*1.0001,
length.out=7))

breaks<-sd$values

matchcol<-function(y) {
    as.character(sd$col[findInterval(y,sd$values)])
}


layout(matrix(data=c(2,1), nrow=1, ncol=2),
widths=c(8,1), heights=c(8,1))

# Color Scale first
par(mar = c(20,1,20,7),oma=c(0.2,0.2,0.2,0.2),mex=0.5)
image(x=1, y=0:length(breaks),z=t(matrix(breaks))*1.001,
col=colours[1:length(breaks)-1],axes=FALSE,breaks=breaks,
xlab="", ylab="", xaxt="n")
axis(4,at=0:(length(breaks)-1),
labels=round(breaks),col="white",las=1)
abline(h=c(1:length(breaks)),col="white",lwd=2,xpd=F)
```

```
#Map
map("state", boundary = FALSE,col=matchcol(x$measure),
fill=TRUE,lty="blank")

map("state", col="white",add = TRUE)

title("Murder Rates by US State in 1973 \n
(arrests per 100,000 residents)", line=2)
```

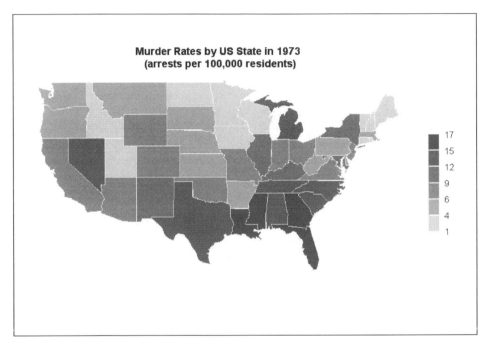

How it works...

The example is similar to the previous recipe in its overall structure, but it differs mainly in the fact that we plotted data for one country's states. We used the USArrests dataset, which is inbuilt in R and contains various crime figures by state for the United States.

Just as in the previous recipe, we first mapped the values of the chosen statistic (murder rates, in this case) to the corresponding region names (in this case, states) in the map object created using the map() function. We chose a red color scheme from RColorBrewer.

Instead of creating a vector of colors for each of the values plotted, we defined a function matchcol() that takes a value as an argument and uses the findInterval() function to return a color value from the data frame, sd, that contains the breaks and corresponding colors from the chosen palette.

We then created a two-column layout and drew the color scale first in the right column. Then, we plotted the map with `fill` set to TRUE and `col` set to a function call to `matchcol()` with x$measure as the argument. We set the boundary to FALSE, to draw white boundaries instead of the default black ones. We did so by calling `map()` again with `col` set to white and add set to TRUE. Finally, we used the `title()` function to add a map title.

There's more

Mapping data by states is just one of the options in the `maps` package for the United States. We can also map data by counties and regions defined as groups of specific states. For example, we can draw a county map of New York using the following line of code:

```
map("county", "new york")
```

Otherwise, we can draw a map with three states with:

```
map("state", region = c("california", "oregon", "nevada"))
```

Now, let's look at another example, this time from a European country:

```
map('italy', fill = TRUE, col = brewer.pal(7,"Set1"))
```

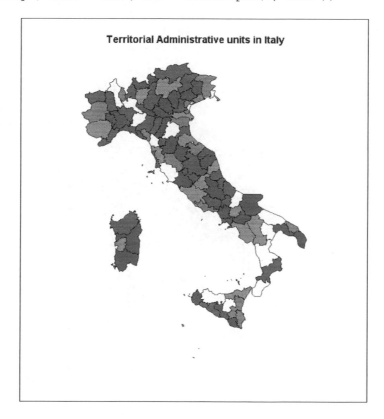

Territorial Administrative units in Italy

The preceding example uses the inbuilt dataset for Italy in the `maps` package. We used the colors just to differentiate the various territorial units from each other; the colors do not represent any numerical quantity. The `maps` package does not have geographical data for other countries. However, there is one good source for worldwide geographical data: the GADM database of Global Administrative Areas. One can freely download data for countries across the world in R's native RData format for noncommercial use from `http://gadm.org`.

The GADM data can be used in combination with the `sp` package to plot regional data on maps. Let's look at an example of rainfall in France. First, let's make sure that the `sp` package is installed and loaded:

```
install.packages("sp")
library(sp)
```

Now, let's create some pseudo rainfall data for the French administrative regions and plot it on a map of France:

```
load(url("http://gadm.org/data/rda/FRA_adm1.RData"))

gadm$rainfall<-rnorm(length(gadm$NAME_1),mean=50,sd=15)

spplot(gadm, "rainfall",
col.regions = rev(terrain.colors(gadm$rainfall)),
main="Rainfall (simulated) in French administrative regions")
```

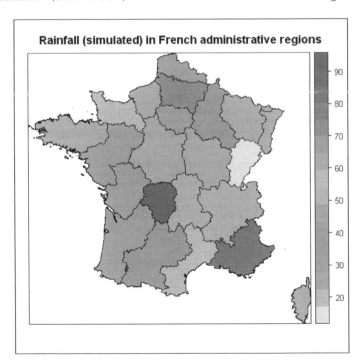

First, we loaded the geographical boundary data for France by calling the load() function with a url of the location of the dataset on the GADM website. In this case, the dataset loaded was FRA_adml.RData. This function call stores the data in an object called gadm (you can verify this by typing in gadm at the R prompt and hitting *Enter*). Next, we appended a vector of pseudo rainfall data to gadm by calling the rnorm() function. Finally, we used the spplot() function from the sp package to plot the data. The first argument to the spplot() function is the gadm object itself and the second argument is the name of the variable we wish to plot on the map. We set the fill color of the regions using col.region; this is slightly different from the map() function because the sp package is based on the lattice library. We used a color scheme based on the terrain.colors() function, but reversed it with rev() so that low to high rainfall is represented by gray through brown to green.

Plotting data on Google maps

In this recipe, we will learn how to plot data on top of Google map images using a special package that connects to Google's Static Maps API.

Getting ready

First, we need to install the RgoogleMaps package and a related package, rgdal:

```
install.packages("rgdal")
library(rgdal)

install.packages("RgoogleMaps")
library(RgoogleMaps)
```

We will use the londonair example dataset for this recipe. This dataset contains annual average concentrations of particulate matter in London's atmosphere measured at 12 different air quality monitoring sites across the city (data source: London air website http://www.londonair.org.uk). So, let's load that too:

```
air<-read.csv("londonair.csv")
```

How to do it...

Let's pull a Google map of the London city and plot the pollution data as points on top of it:

```
london<-GetMap(center=c(51.51,-0.116),
zoom =10, destfile = "London.png",maptype = "mobile")

PlotOnStaticMap(london,lat = air$lat, lon = air$lon,
cex=2,pch=19,col=as.character(air$color))
```

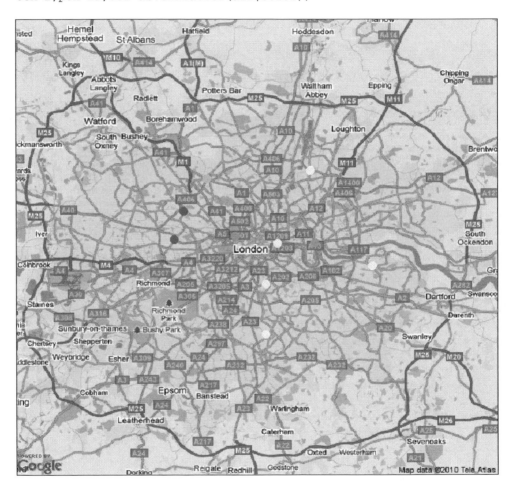

Now, let's make the same graph with a satellite image map instead of the roadmap:

```
london<-GetMap(center=c(51.51,-0.116),zoom =13,
destfile = "London_satellite.png",maptype = "satellite")

PlotOnStaticMap(london,lat = air$lat, lon = air$lon,
cex=2,pch=19,col=as.character(air$color))
```

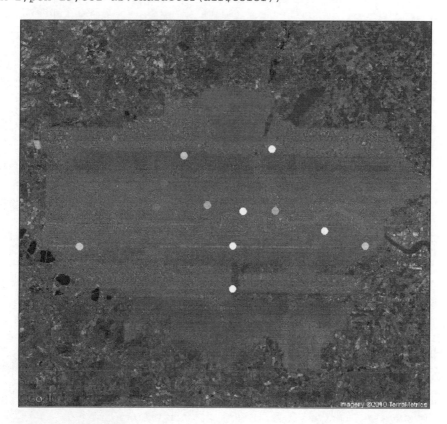

How it works...

In the examples, we first used the GetMap() function from the RgoogleMaps package to pull a map of London from the Google Static Maps API (see http://code.google.com/apis/maps/documentation/staticmaps/ for more details about the API). We then used the PlotOnStaticMap() function to overlay our air pollution data points on the map.

The first and most important argument to the GetMap() function is the center argument, which takes a vector of two values that specify the latitude and longitude of the location to be used as the center of the map. The zoom level is specified by the zoom argument, which has a default value of 12. The higher the value of zoom, the more detailed and zoomed in the view. In the example, we set zoom to 10 so as to capture a wide area of London.

We also specified the `destfile` argument to save the retrieved map as `London.png`. The default value of `destfile` is `MyTile.png`. You can check whether the map is retrieved by looking for the PNG file in your working directory.

Finally, we also set the `maptype` argument, which can take one of a number of different values such as `"roadmap"`, `"mobile"`, `"satellite"`, `"terrain"`, `"hybrid"`, `"mapmaker-roadmap"`, and `"mapmaker-hybrid"`. The default map type is `terrain`. We set `maptype` to `mobile` in the first example and `satellite` in the second example.

If you look at the output of the `GetMap()` function call at the R prompt, you will notice that it shows a URL such as:

```
[1] http://maps.google.com/staticmap?center=51.51,-0.116&zoom=10&size=
640x640&maptype=mobile&format=png32&key=&sensor=true
```

Basically, the `GetMap()` function creates an HTTP GET request URL with parameters based on the arguments supplied. To test this, copy the provided URL and paste it into the address bar of a web browser. You should get the image of the specified map.

We saved the object returned by the `GetMap()` function call as `london`, which we then passed as the first argument to the `PlotOnStaticMap()` function. As the name suggests, this function plots data on top of `map` objects. The air pollution dataset, `londonair`, that we loaded earlier contains monitoring site data including site code, name, latitude, longitude, particle concentration (PM10), and a color based on the concentration value. We passed these values to the `PlotOnStaticMap()` function. We set the `lat` and `lon` arguments to the `lat` and `lon` columns in the air data frame, respectively. We set the `col` argument to the color column in air.

There's more

We can overlay more data points or lines successively on top of a map by setting an additional argument `add` to `TRUE`. By default, `add` is set to `FALSE`, which creates a new map with the specified data points or lines. To draw lines instead of points, we need to set the `FUN` (meaning function) argument to `lines`. By default, `FUN` is set to `points`.

The following is another example pulling in a hybrid map of New York:

```
GetMap(center=c(40.714728,-73.99867), zoom =14,
destfile = "Manhattan.png", maptype = "hybrid");
```

Another maps library that is becoming increasingly popular is Open Street Map (`http://www.openstreetmap.org/`). It's a free and open source editable library, unlike Google's proprietary maps API. The following is an example based on the `GetMap.OSM()` function that uses the Open Street Map server:

```
GetMap.OSM(lonR= c(-74.67102, -74.63943),
latR = c(40.33804,40.3556),scale = 7500,
```

```
destfile = "PrincetonOSM.png")
```

The GetMap.OSM() function takes the ranges of longitude and latitude as two two-valued vectors lonR and latR, respectively. The scale argument is analogous to the zoom argument for the Google API. The larger this value, the more detailed is the resulting map.

See also

In the next recipe, we will learn how to interact with Google's KML language to express geographic data.

Creating and reading KML data

In this recipe, we will learn how to read and write geographic data in Google's **Keyhole Markup Language** (**KML**) format, which can be used to visualize geographic data with Google Earth and Google Maps.

Getting ready

We will use the rgdal package in this recipe. So, let's make sure it's installed and load it:

```
install.packages("rgdal")
library(rgdal)
```

How to do it...

We will use data from the cities shapefile that's installed as part of the rgdal package. First, we will write a KML file and then read it:

```
cities <- readOGR(system.file("vectors",
package = "rgdal")[1],"cities")

writeOGR(cities, "cities.kml", "cities", driver="KML")

df <- readOGR("cities.kml", "cities")
```

How it works...

In the preceding example, we first used the readOGR() function to read the cities shapefile dataset. The first argument is the folder (directory) where the data shapefile is and the second argument is the name of the shapefile (without the .shp extension). We stored the object returned by the readOGR() function as cities, which is of the SpatialPointsDataFrame class.

To create a KML file, we used the `writeOGR()` function. We passed the `cities` object as the first argument. The second argument specifies the name of the output KML file, the third argument specifies the shapefile layer name (without extension), and the fourth argument is the driver (in this case, `KML`).

To read the KML file back into R, we used the `readOGR()` function with only two arguments. The first argument specifies the KML data file to be read and the second argument specifies the name of the layer.

See Also

In the next recipe, we will learn how to work with ESRI shapefiles.

Working with ESRI shapefiles

In this recipe, we will learn how to read and write geographic data in the form of shapefiles (`.shp`), using **Geographical Information Systems** (**GIS**) software created by ESRI and some other similar software.

Getting ready

We are going to use the `maptools` package for this recipe. So, let's install and load it first:

```
install.packages("maptools")
library(maptools)
```

How to do it...

We are going to read an example shapefile provided with the `maptools` package and plot it:

```
sfdata <- readShapeSpatial(system.file("shapes/sids.shp",
package="maptools")[1], proj4string=CRS("+proj=longlat"))

plot(sfdata, col="orange", border="white", axes=TRUE)
```

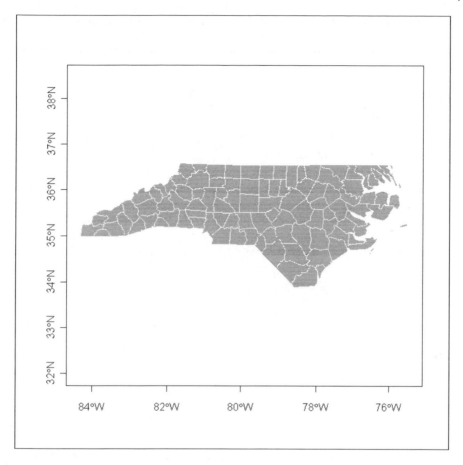

To write out the data as another shapefile, we can do:

```
writeSpatialShape(sfdata, "xxpoly")
```

How it works...

We used the `readShapeSpatial()` function of the `maptools` package to read in a shapefile. This function takes a shapefile name as an argument and reads the data into a `SpatialPolygonsDataFrame` object. The first argument in the example is the path to the `sids.shp` example shapefile, which is provided as part of the `maptools` package installation. The second argument `proj4string` specifies the projection type as `longlat` so that the spatial coordinates are interpreted correctly as longitudes and latitudes.

We saved the object returned by `readShapeSpatial()` as `sfdata` (of data class `SpatialPolygonsDataFrame`), which we then passed to the `plot()` function to create a map from the shapefile data.

Once we've read the data into the appropriate format, we can perform any transformations on the data. To save the transformed dataset back into a shapefile, we use the `writeSpatialShape()` function, which takes the data object as the first argument and the name of the output shapefile (without any file type extension) as the second argument.

There's more

There is another package called `shapefiles` that can be used to read and write shapefiles. To use it, we must first install and load it:

```
install.packages("shapefiles")
library(shapefiles)
```

To read a shapefile using this package, we can use the `read.shapefile()` function:

```
sf<-system.file("shapes/sids.shp", package="maptools")[1]
sf<-substr(sf,1,nchar(sf)-4)
sfdata <- read.shapefile(sf)
```

We first saved the path of the `sids.shp` example file in a variable called `sf`. We had to trim the path string to remove the extension `.shp` because the `read.shapefile()` function takes just the name of the shapefile as its argument. The shapefile data is saved in a list called `sfdata`.

To write out a shapefile using this package, we need to use the `write.shapefile()` function:

```
write.shapefile(sfdata, "newsf")
```

The `write.shapefile()` takes two key arguments: the first is the data object (`sfdata` in the example) and the second is the name of the new shapefile without any file extension.

11
Data Visualization Using Lattice

In this chapter, we will cover the following recipes:

- ▶ Creating bar charts
- ▶ Creating stacked bar charts
- ▶ Creating bar charts to visualize cross-tabulation
- ▶ Creating a conditional histogram
- ▶ Visualizing distributions through a kernel-density plot
- ▶ Creating a normal Q-Q plot
- ▶ Visualizing an empirical Cumulative Distribution Function
- ▶ Creating a boxplot
- ▶ Creating a conditional scatter plot

Introduction

In this chapter, we intend to show you data visualization using the `lattice` package where producing conditional plots is much easier than the basic graphs. The focal point of the chapter will be basic graphs that are most commonly used during data visualization. Starting from a single variable bar chart, we will continue to conditional scatter plots. We will primarily use the `lattice` package to produce the graphs, but we will use other packages when required. If we use any other package, then we will mention the reason for that in the respective sections.

We will supply the dataset for this chapter or generate datasets through very simple random number generation functions in R. For example, `runif()` is used to generate a random number from a uniform distribution, `rnorm()` is used to generate a random variable from a normal distribution, and `rbinom()` is used to generate a binomial random variable. During the data generation process, we will use the code in such a way that all the examples can be reproduced at any time.

We might not use all the arguments of the functions used for each recipe, so it would be good to have a look at the possible arguments on the help documentation page. Before starting the actual recipe, let's set the following:

- ▸ The working directory to a convenient location
- ▸ Load the `lattice` library to your current working session

Now, let's start the actual recipe!

Creating bar charts

Bar charts are the most common data visualization for categorical data. However, we can also produce bar charts for summarized numeric variables over the category of other variables. In this recipe, we will see how to produce a bar chart that summarizes numeric variables over the category of other variables.

Getting ready

To create the bar chart, we will simulate a dataset with three numeric variables and one categorical variable for the purpose of grouping. The three numeric variables will indicate the incubation period of three different diseases—say, disease A, B, and C—in weeks. The categorical variable will indicate four different age groups, for example, 1 indicates age 0-1 year, 2 indicates 1-5 years, 3 indicates 5-10 years, and 4 indicates over 10 years. Here is the code that produces the dataset:

```
# Set a seed value to make the data reproducible
set.seed(12345)
data_barchart <-data.frame(disA=rnorm(n=100,mean=20,sd=3),
                disB=rnorm(n=100,mean=25,sd=4),
                disC=rnorm(n=100,mean=15,sd=1.5),
                age=sample((c(1,2,3,4)),size=100,replace=T))
```

Now, we will produce a summarized dataset because we want to compare the mean incubation period across different age groups for each disease:

```
dis_dat <- round(aggregate(data_barchart[,1:3],list(data_
barchart$age),mean),digits=1)
colnames(dis_dat)<-c("age","disA","disB","disC")
```

How to do it...

The lattice `barchart` command is very similar to the base `barplot` command, but we can use the formula interface to produce the bar chart. To produce the plot using `lattice`, we need to load the `lattice` library. Then, to produce the bar chart to display the mean incubation period for disease A, B, and C for different age groups 1, 2, 3, and 4, we can use the following command:

```
barchart(disA+disB+disC~factor(age),data=dis_dat)
```

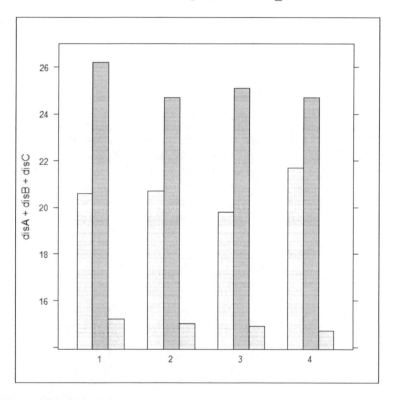

How it works...

The `barchart()` command is used to produce a bar chart using the `lattice` package. The first argument is the formula interface that specifies how many bars need to be produced, and the right-hand side of the formula specifies the grouping of the bars. In this case, we have created a bar chart of the mean incubation period for three different diseases over different age groups. The second argument is the data set. Note that in the first argument, we just need to write the variable names without using any quotation (" "). For multiple variables, we just need to write each of the variable names, separated by a plus (+) sign.

There's more...

The default implementation does not specify the title of the plot, and it also does not specify the *x* axis and *y* axis. More importantly, it does not produce the legend key. Without the legend key, it is difficult to communicate the information contained in the plot. Here is the code that is used to update the initial bar chart:

```
barchart(
  disA+disB+disC~factor(age),
  data=dis_dat,
  auto.key=list(column=3),
  main="Mean incubation period comparison
  \n among different age group",
  xlab="Age group",
  ylab="Mean incubation period (weeks)"
  )
```

In this new code snippet, `auto.key` produces the legend key with three columns. The other arguments produce the chart title specified by `main`, the *x* axis label specified by `xlab`, and the *y* axis label specified by `ylab`. One important thing in this new code is the use of `\n` within the text of the chart title; we use this `\n` control to create a new line when the title is long. This breaks the text into two lines. The following graph shows the bar chart produced from the preceding code snippet. It shows the two line title, legend with three columns, and labels for the x and y axis.

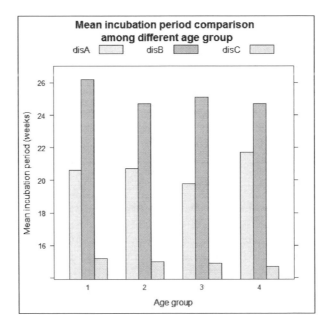

Bar charts such as stacked bar charts and bar charts that visualize cross tabulations will be explored in the subsequent recipes.

Creating stacked bar charts

When we want to visualize more than one summarized numeric variable over the category of another variable, we need to produce a stacked bar chart. In this case, each bar represents summary statistics of each variable. The different variables occupy different heights with various colors in that single bar.

Getting ready

To produce stacked bar charts, we will use the same summarized data that we created in the *Creating bar charts* recipe.

How to do it...

The command that produces the stacked bar chart is exactly the same as the simple bar chart. The only difference is that we need a new argument, which is `stack=TRUE`:

```
barchart(disA+disB+disC~factor(age),data=dis_dat,stack=TRUE)
```

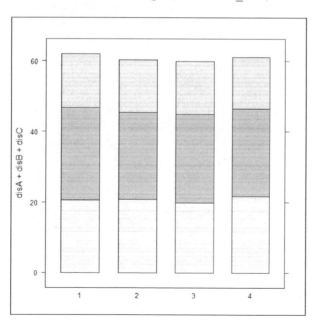

How it works...

The first argument is the formula that specifies the variables to be displayed in the plot. The left-hand side indicates how many components there will be in each of the bars. The right-hand side indicates the grouping information. The `stack=TRUE` argument makes sure that the bar plot will be stacked, which means that each of the variables will occupy a certain height in a single bar with specific colors.

There's more...

The default implementation does not specify the title of the plot, and it also does not specify the x axis, y axis, and more importantly, it does not produce the legend key. Without the legend key, it is difficult to communicate the information contained in the plot. Here is the code that updates the initial bar chart:

```
barchart(
  disA+disB+disC~factor(age),
  data=dis_dat,
  auto.key=list(column=3),
  main="Mean incubation period comparison
\n among different age group",
  xlab="Age group",
  ylab="Mean incubation period (weeks)",stack=TRUE)
```

In this new code snippet, `auto.key` produces the legend key with three columns. The production of the chart title is specified by `main`, x axis label is specified by `xlab`, and y axis label is specified by `ylab`. One important thing in this new code is the use of `\n` within the text of the chart title; we use this `\n` control to create a new line when the title is long. This breaks the text into two lines.

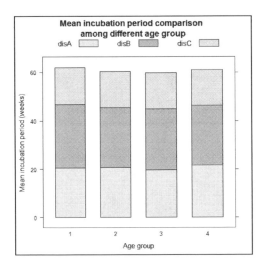

In the next recipe, we will see how we can visualize a cross-tabulated frequency distribution through a bar chart.

Creating bar charts to visualize cross-tabulation

In most real-world research data, we have multiple categorical variables. Though we can summarize these variables using cross-tabulation, if we want to visualize this through the bar chart, we can do so easily. In this recipe, we will see how we can produce a bar chart in order to visualize cross-tabulation.

Getting ready

To produce a bar chart from cross-tabulation, we will add two new variables with the dataset that we used in the first two recipes. The new variable will represent the sex and economic status. Here is the code that prepares the dataset:

```
# Set a seed value to make the data reproducible
set.seed(12345)
cross_tabulation_data <-data.frame(disA=rnorm(n=100,mean=20,sd=3),
                disB=rnorm(n=100,mean=25,sd=4),
                disC=rnorm(n=100,mean=15,sd=1.5),
                age=sample((c(1,2,3,4)),size=100,replace=T),
                sex=sample(c("Male","Female"),size=100,replace=T),
                econ_status=sample(c("Poor","Middle","Rich"),
                size=100,replace=T))
```

Since we want to produce a bar chart for cross-tabulated data, we will summarize the dataset in such a way that it contains the frequency count of each combination of the variables. For this, we will use the `table()` function; here is the code:

```
# producing the cross tabulation data
# with three categorical variables
cross_table <- as.data.frame(table(cross_tabulation_data[,4:6]))
```

How to do it...

We want to visualize the frequency distribution for each combination of the variable age for the sex and economic status; for this, the lattice code structure is as follows:

```
barchart(age~Freq|sex+econ_status,data=cross_table)
```

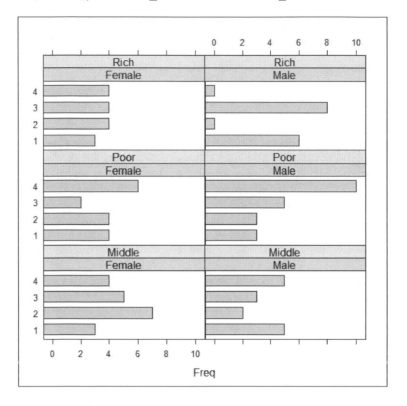

How it works...

In the following bullet points, we will describe how the code produced the preceding figure. We will explain each of the arguments separately:

- The code is `barchart(age~Freq|sex+econ_status,data=cross_table)`
- The first argument specifies what will be on the *x* axis and what will be on the *y* axis
- The next part indicates what the different panel or grouping will be
- The very left-hand side of the `age~Freq` formula specifies that the age will be displayed on the *y* axis, and the *x* axis will display the frequency count

▸ On the other hand, `sex+econ_status` specifies that the final display will be grouped by each unique combination of these two variables

The noticeable feature of this plot is the way to write the formula in the `barchart()` function. If we write the formula differently, then it will produce a different visualization. For example, let's replace `age` with the `econ_status` variable and write the following code:

```
barchart(econ_status~Freq|sex+age,data=cross_table)
```

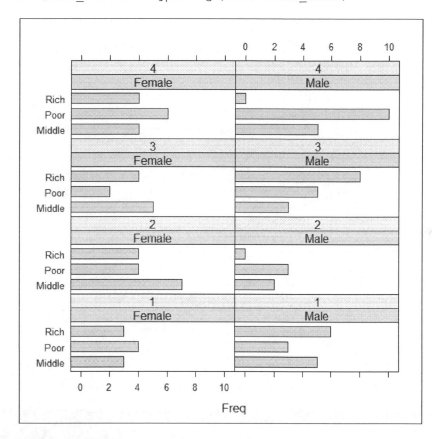

There's more...

If we want to write a label for each axis and provide a title for this chart, we need to specify the respective argument in the plot function. For the title, we need to use the `main` argument; for the *y* axis label, we need to use `ylab`; and for the *x* axis label, we need to use `xlab`, as shown in the following code:

```
barchart(econ_status~Freq|sex+age,data=cross_table,
main="Chart title",xlab="Frequency count",ylab="Economic Status")
```

To change the color of the plot, we can use the `col` argument to specify the desired color as `col="black"`. The following figure shows the bar chart from a cross-tabulated frequency distribution. Particularly, this figure shows a three way frequency distribution of the age, economic status, and the sex of the individuals.

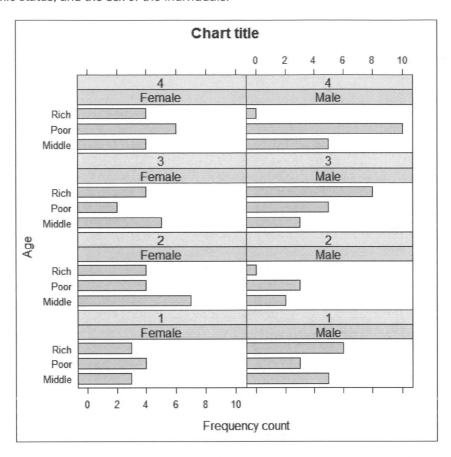

Creating a conditional histogram

A histogram is one of the simplest ways to visualize the univariate distribution. Sometimes, we need to produce a histogram for each group in order to compare the distribution in a subgroup of another categorical variable. In this recipe, we will see how we can create a conditional histogram using the lattice functionality.

Getting ready

To visualize a conditional histogram, we need at least one numeric variable and one categorical variable. We have all this information in the dataset that we have simulated in earlier recipes. Here, we will reproduce the same cross-tabulation raw data with the following code:

```
# Set a seed value to make the data reproducible
set.seed(12345)
cross_tabulation_data <-data.frame(disA=rnorm(n=100,mean=20,sd=3),
            disB=rnorm(n=100,mean=25,sd=4),
            disC=rnorm(n=100,mean=15,sd=1.5),
            age=sample((c(1,2,3,4)),size=100,replace=T),
            sex=sample(c("Male","Female"),size=100,replace=T),
            econ_status=sample(c("Poor","Middle","Rich"),
            size=100,replace=T))
```

How to do it...

We want to produce a histogram for each value of the sex variable; for this, take a look at this simple code with the lattice implementation:

```
histogram(~disA|sex,data=cross_tabulation_data,type="density")
```

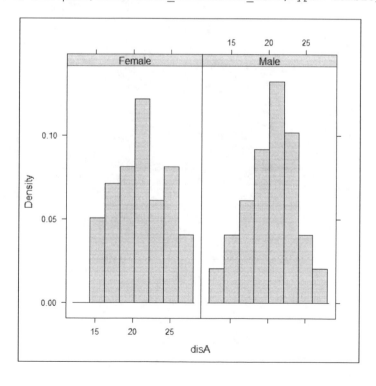

How it works...

In the `histogram` command, the most important part of the formula is the name of the variable just after the ~ symbol. We need to write the name of the variable for which we want to create a histogram just after the ~ symbol. For a conditional histogram, we need to provide the input of that variable after the vertical bar symbol (|). The default value for the *y* axis is the percentage for each of the interval in *x*-axis, but we can change this as per our need. Here, we have used *density* for the *y* axis values, which actually calculated probability density values instead of frequency counts.

There's more...

If we want to apply conditions on multiple categorical variables, then we can do this by simply adding the additional variable name using a plus (+) sign, as shown in the following code:

```
histogram(~disA|sex+econ_status,data=cross_tabulation_
data,type="density")
```

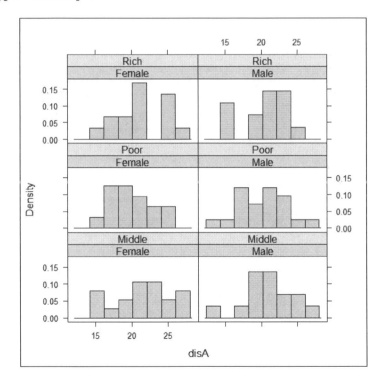

To plot more than one numeric variable, we just need to add the new variable as shown in the following line of code:

```
histogram(~disA+disB|sex,data=cross_tabulation_data,type="density")
```

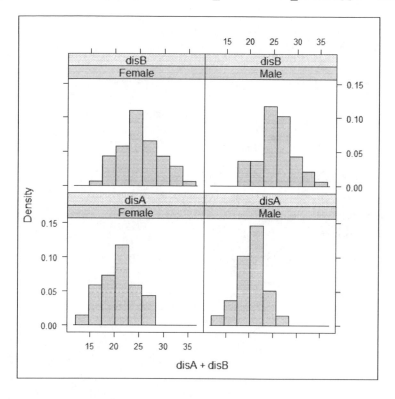

To annotate the histogram, we can use `main`, `xlab`, and `ylab`, as we previously did for bar charts.

See also

▸ The *Visualizing distribution through kernel density plot* recipe

Visualizing distributions through a kernel-density plot

The kernel-density plot is another method of visualizing the distribution of numeric variables. In this recipe, we will see how we can produce a kernel density plot with minor modifications to the code that produces a histogram.

Getting ready

Recall the data from the histogram recipe using the following code:

```
# Set a seed value to make the data reproducible
set.seed(12345)
cross_tabulation_data <-data.frame(disA=rnorm(n=100,mean=20,sd=3),
            disB=rnorm(n=100,mean=25,sd=4),
            disC=rnorm(n=100,mean=15,sd=1.5),
            age=sample((c(1,2,3,4)),size=100,replace=T),
            sex=sample(c("Male","Female"),size=100,replace=T),
            econ_status=sample(c("Poor","Middle","Rich"),
            size=100,replace=T))
```

How to do it...

Use the following code if you want to visualize the kernel density of the `disA` variable for each value of the `sex` variable:

```
densityplot(~disA|sex,data=cross_tabulation_data)
```

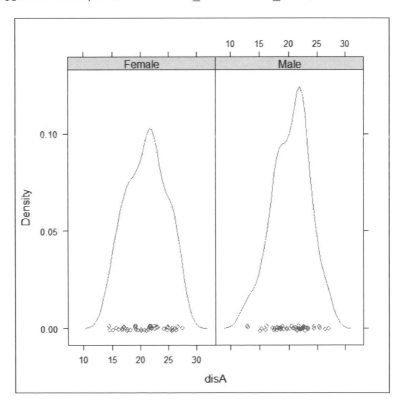

How it works...

The `densityplot` function works the same as `histogram`, but the visualization is different. The numeric variable after the ~ symbol specifies the variable for which we are expecting the density plot. Then, the categorical variable after the vertical bar indicates the grouping information. Grouping refers to the number of density plots that should be produced. Now, if we want a multiple variable density plot, then we will write the formula as `~disA+disB`. In this case, we need to use the legend key to identify the plots for two variables. So, the final code will be as follows:

```
densityplot(~disA+disB|sex,data=cross_tabulation_data,auto.key=T)
```

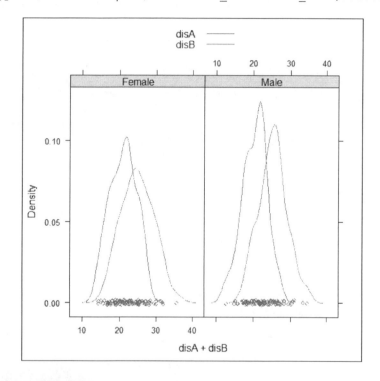

There's more...

To get a multiple density plot with a unique combination of more than one categorical variable, we just need to add a new categorical variable using a plus (+) sign. In the kernel density plot (a way to approximate the PDF of data that is smoother than the histogram), the default kernel function is `gaussian`, but we can easily change this to another function through the `kernel=` argument. We can also specify the other necessary parameters of the kernel function, such as the bandwidth (`bw`). The other argument, such as `main`, `xlab`, `ylab`, and `col`, will be similar to other recipes.

Creating a normal Q-Q plot

Commonly, we compare an empirical distribution with known theoretical distribution. The most popular and most used theoretical distribution is the *normal* distribution. To compare an empirical distribution with a normal distribution, we use a normal Q-Q plot. In this recipe, we will see how we can compare a distribution of a numeric variable with the theoretical normal distribution through a normal Q-Q plot.

Getting ready

The data for this recipe is generated using the following code:

```
# Set a seed value to make the data reproducible
set.seed(12345)
qqdata <-data.frame(disA=rnorm(n=100,mean=20,sd=3),
            disB=rnorm(n=100,mean=25,sd=4),
            disC=rnorm(n=100,mean=15,sd=1.5),
            age=sample((c(1,2,3,4)),size=100,replace=T),
            sex=sample(c("Male","Female"),size=100,replace=T),
            econ_status=sample(c("Poor","Middle","Rich"),
            size=100,replace=T))
```

How to do it...

We can produce the plot with the following code:

```
qqmath(~disA|sex,data=qqdata,f.value=ppoints(50),distribution=qnorm)
```

The preceding code will produce the Q-Q plot for the `disA` variable for each value in the `sex` variable (shown in the following figure):

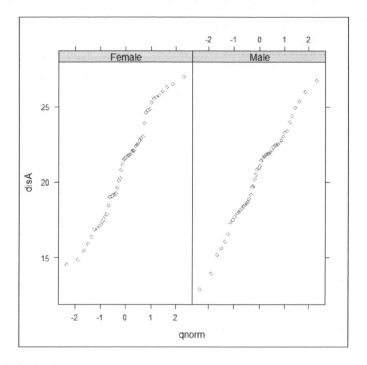

How it works...

The formula argument is the same as any other function in the lattice environment.
A noticeable feature of the `qqmath()` function is the `f.value` argument and
`distribution=`; `f.value` specifies how many quantile points should be used to produce
the plot. The default is the number of quantiles that equal the number of actual data points.
In our case, we have used 50 quantiles, which means that there will be 50 points that
display the distribution in our plot. The `distribution` argument specifies the theoretical
distribution; here, we have used the normal distribution.

There's more...

If we want to produce the same plot for multiple numeric variables, then we can simply add the new variable in the formula as ~disA+disB. For example, to produce the same plot for three variables grouped by the sex variable, we can use the following code:

```
qqmath(~disA+disB+disC|sex,data=qqdata,f.value=ppoints(50))
```

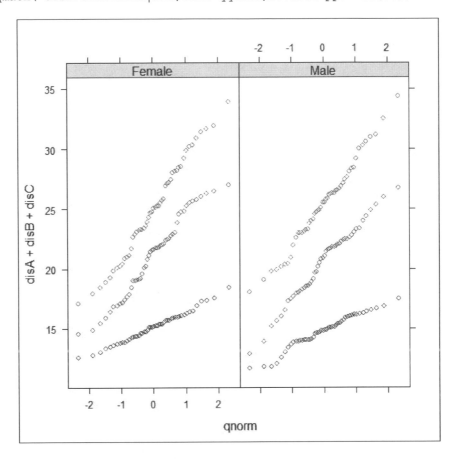

Visualizing an empirical Cumulative Distribution Function

The empirical **Cumulative Distribution Function (CDF)** is the non-parametric maximum-likelihood estimation of the CDF. In this recipe, we will see how the empirical CDF can be produced.

Getting ready

To produce this plot, we need to use the `latticeExtra` library. We will use the simulated dataset as shown in the following code:

```
# Set a seed value to make the data reproducible
set.seed(12345)
qqdata <-data.frame(disA=rnorm(n=100,mean=20,sd=3),
              disB=rnorm(n=100,mean=25,sd=4),
              disC=rnorm(n=100,mean=15,sd=1.5),
              age=sample((c(1,2,3,4)),size=100,replace=T),
              sex=sample(c("Male","Female"),size=100,replace=T),
              econ_status=sample(c("Poor","Middle","Rich"),
              size=100,replace=T))
```

How to do it...

To plot an empirical CDF, we first need to call the `latticeExtra` library (note that this library has a dependency on `RColorBrewer`). Now, to plot the empirical CDF, we can use the following simple code:

```
library(latticeExtra)
ecdfplot(~disA|sex,data=qqdata)
```

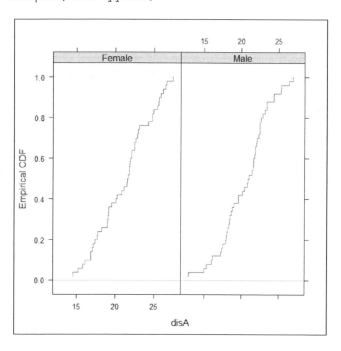

How it works...

The basic structure of the `ecdfplot()` function is a formula that specifies the variable to be plotted and the data argument. If we want to replicate the plot within another variable's group, then we have to specify the name of variable after the vertical bar (|). To plot more than one variable, we can add the variable with a plus sign, for example, `~disA+disB`.

There's more...

In the `ecdfplot()` function, there are other arguments that are also applicable to most of the functions in the `lattice` library. One special feature of this function is the subset argument. If we want to produce the plot with a subset of the data for the specified variable, then we can utilize the subset argument with a conditional statement:

```
ecdfplot(~disA,data=qqdata,subset=disA>15)
```

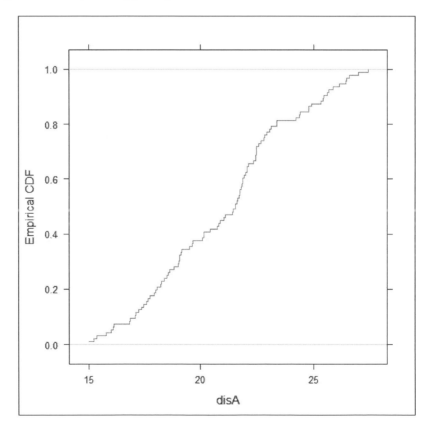

Creating a boxplot

A boxplot is another important graph that summarizes the data along with the distribution. In this recipe, we will see how we can produce a boxplot in order to visualize the data summary with distributions.

Getting ready

To create the boxplot, we simulated the dataset as per the following code snippet:

```
# Set a seed value to make the data reproducible
set.seed(12345)
qqdata <-data.frame(disA=rnorm(n=100,mean=20,sd=3),
                disB=rnorm(n=100,mean=25,sd=4),
                disC=rnorm(n=100,mean=15,sd=1.5),
                age=sample((c(1,2,3,4)),size=100,replace=T),
                sex=sample(c("Male","Female"),size=100,replace=T),
                econ_status=sample(c("Poor","Middle","Rich"),
                size=100,replace=T))
```

How to do it...

The basic command that produces a box plot is as follows:

```
bwplot(~disA,data=qqdata)
```

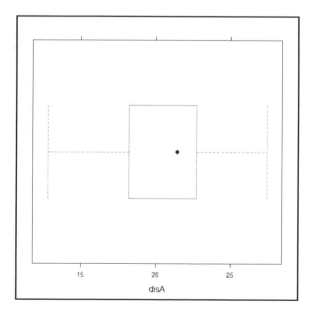

How it works...

The basic command produces the boxplot of a single variable with the horizontal orientation. Now, if we want the box plot in the vertical orientation and want it to repeat for each value of another categorical variable—for example `sex`—then the syntax will be like the following line of code:

```
bwplot(disA~sex,data=qqdata)
```

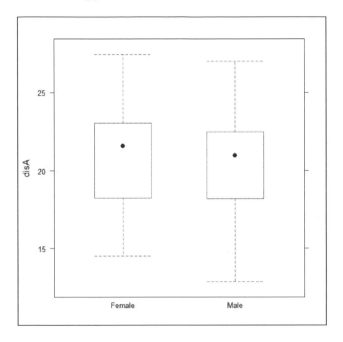

There's more...

To produce multiple boxplots of a numeric variable over the categorical variables, we can simply add the categorical variable to the right-hand side of the formula part:

```
bwplot(disA~sex|econ_status,data=qqdata)
```

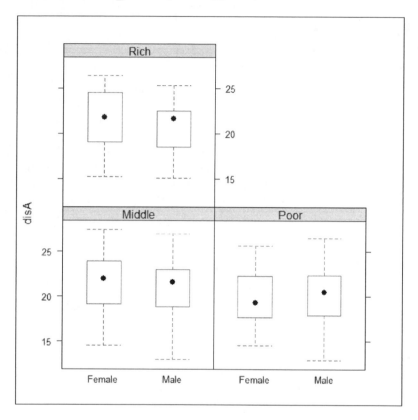

Creating a conditional scatter plot

A scatter plot is the simplest plot that visualizes the relationship pattern between numeric variables. In this recipe, we will see how we can produce a scatter plot of two numeric variables conditional on a categorical variable.

Getting ready

The dataset used for this recipe is as follows:

```
# Set a seed value to make the data reproducible
set.seed(12345)
qqdata <-data.frame(disA=rnorm(n=100,mean=20,sd=3),
            disB=rnorm(n=100,mean=25,sd=4),
            disC=rnorm(n=100,mean=15,sd=1.5),
            age=sample((c(1,2,3,4)),size=100,replace=T),
            sex=sample(c("Male","Female"),size=100,replace=T),
            econ_status=sample(c("Poor","Middle","Rich"),
            size=100,replace=T))
```

How to do it...

The primary code structure that produces the scatter plot using the lattice environment is as follows:

```
xyplot(disA~disB, data=qqdata)
```

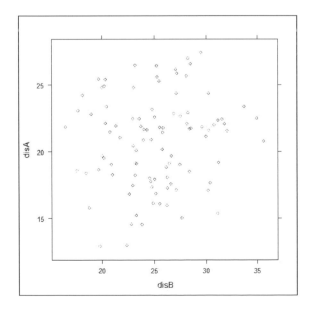

However, in this recipe, we want to produce a conditional scatter plot. We can perform the conditioning in two different ways:

- We can create a scatter plot and color the points based on the value of another variable
- We can create a scatter plot with a separate panel for each unique value of another variable

Here are both the code respectively:

```
# colored scatter plot
xyplot(disA~disB,group=sex,data=qqdata,auto.key=T)
```

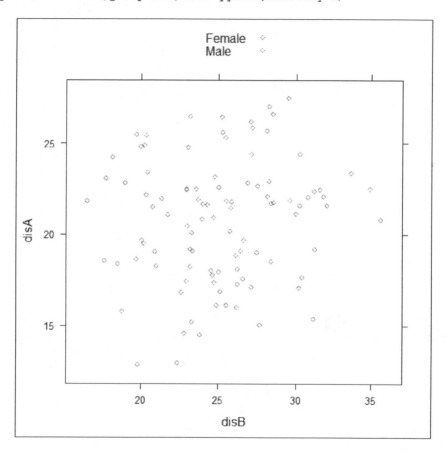

To create the panel scatter plot, we could use the following code, where the scatter plot will be created for each unique value of a categorical variable. In this case, `sex` is the categorical variable:

```
# panel scatter plot
xyplot(disA~disB|sex,data=qqdata)
```

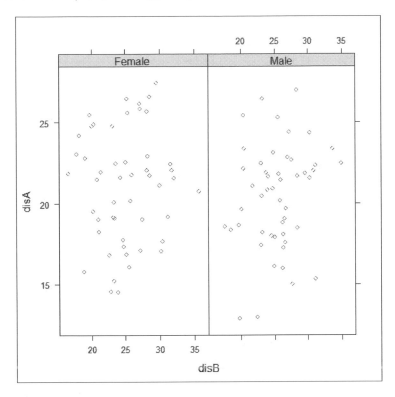

How it works...

The formula part of the `xyplot()` function specifies the variables for each axis that corresponds to a single point for each pair of values. The `group` argument has been used to create the conditional plot with the color for each point. However, if we do not use the group argument and use a vertical bar in the formula, then a panel scatter plot is produced.

There's more...

Like the other plot, we can use the title and label for each axis. We can also specify the limit of values for each axis using the `xlim` and `ylim` arguments.

12
Data Visualization Using ggplot2

In this chapter, we will cover the following recipes:

- ▶ Creating bar charts
- ▶ Creating multiple bar charts
- ▶ Creating a bar chart with error bars
- ▶ Visualizing the density of a numeric variable
- ▶ Creating a box plot
- ▶ Creating a layered plot with a scatter plot and fitted line
- ▶ Creating a line chart
- ▶ Graph annotation with ggplot

Introduction

In this chapter, we will mainly use the `ggplot2` library to visualize data with common graphs, such as bar charts, histograms, boxplots, and scatter plots. The `ggplot2` library has the implementation of Grammar of Graphics, which gives the user the flexibility to produce any kind of graph by introducing layered facilities. At the end of this chapter, we will see how we can easily annotate the graphs using the theme option of the `ggplot2` library.

Throughout this chapter, we will use a single dataset. We will simulate the dataset with some numeric and categorical variables so that we can use the same dataset for each recipe.

There are four numeric variables, namely disA, disB, disC, and disD. Here, disA and disD are correlated in the sense that disD is produced with the same values of disA but with an added random error from the normal distribution with a mean of zero and a standard deviation of three. There are three categorical variables that represent the age category, sex, and economic status. In the following code snippet we will create the dataset as described. First of all we will set a seed value so that we can have the same data from any computer and any number of attempts. Here is the code:

```
# Set a seed value to make the data reproducible
set.seed(12345)
ggplotdata <-data.frame(disA=rnorm(n=100,mean=20,sd=3),
disB=rnorm(n=100,mean=25,sd=4),
disC=rnorm(n=100,mean=15,sd=1.5),
age=factor(sample(c(1,2,3,4),size=100,replace=T),levels=c(1,2,3,4),lab
els=c("< 5yrs","5-10 yrs","10-18 yrs","18 +yrs")),
sex=factor(sample(c(1,2),size=100,replace=T),
levels=c(1,2),labels=c("Male","Female")),
econ_status=factor(sample(c(1,2,3),size=100,replace=T), levels=c(1,2,3
),labels=c("Poor","Middle","Rich")))

ggplotdata$disD <- ggplotdata$disA+rnorm(100,sd=3)
```

We will use this data throughout the chapter. We will explicitly use the ggplot2 library, but if required, we will use other libraries and mention them in the respective recipe section. So, let's start the actual recipes.

Creating bar charts

A bar chart is the simplest chart that displays the frequency of a categorical variable or the summary statistics of a numeric variable over the category of other variables. In this recipe, we will learn how we can produce a bar chart using the ggplot2 library.

Getting ready

Let's call the ggplotdata dataset that was created in the preceding section. We intend to produce a bar chart that will represent the mean of a numeric variable on the *y* axis over the category of the economic status variable on the x-axis. So, we need to prepare the summarized dataset as follows:

```
library(plyr)
bardata <- ddply(ggplotdata, .(econ_status),summarize,meandisA=mean(di
sA),
meandisB=mean(disB),meandisC=mean(disC),meadisD=mean(disD))
```

The description of the most important components of the preceding function is as follows:

- The ddply() function takes the data frame as the input and produces the output in the data frame as well. In the function name, the first d signifies the input data frame and the second d signifies the output data frame.

- In the variable name of the first argument, the dot (.) is being used so that we do not need to write the variable name within quotes.

Now, let's call the ggplot2 library using the following line of code:

```
library(ggplot2)
```

How to do it...

The standard code that produces a bar chart is as follows:

```
ggplot(data= bardata, aes(x=econ_status, y=meandisA)) + geom_
bar(stat="identity")
```

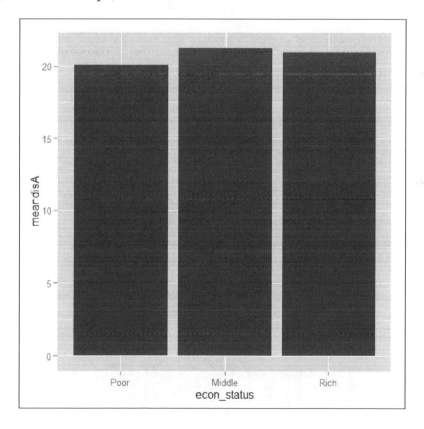

How it works...

Each of the code's arguments is described as follows:

- ▶ `data`: This argument inputs the desired dataset.
- ▶ `aes`: This is to specify the aesthetic of the plot, such as the values of the *x* and *y* axis. Beside specifying only the axes we can use other aesthetics that we will use later can be specified here, such as shape or color).
- ▶ `geom_bar`: This is the actual function that produces the bar chart. There are some other arguments within `geom_bar()`, such as `stats="identity"`, that refer to one-to-one mapping of the data points, that is, the value of y-axis should be displayed as it is, without any transformation.

There's more...

We can change the width of the bar and also change the orientation of the bar using some of the arguments with the primary function. An example of this is shown in the following code:

```
# to change bar width we could use width= argument within geom_bar()
ggplot(data= bardata, aes(x=econ_status, y=meandisA)) + geom_
bar(stat="identity",width=0.5)
# change the layout to horizontal use coord_flip()
# with the main plot
ggplot(data= bardata, aes(x=econ_status, y=meandisA)) + geom_bar(stat=
"identity",width=0.5)+coord_flip()
```

The plot will look like what's shown in the following figure:

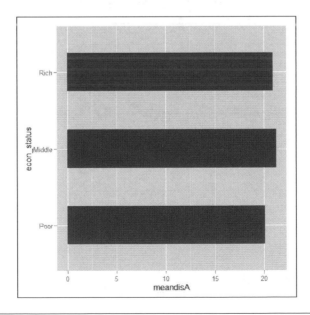

See also

To produce a bar chart for more than one numeric variable, follow the *Creating multiple bar charts* recipe; to produce a bar chart with error bars, refer to the *Creating a bar chart with error bars* recipe.

Creating multiple bar charts

In some situations, we need to produce bar charts for more than one numeric variable over the category of other variables. In this recipe, we will learn how we can produce a bar chart with more than one numeric variable.

Getting ready

To produce multiple bar charts, we will use the same `ggplotdata` source data, but we need some preprocessing to create the input data for the plot. Firstly, we will summarize the source data and calculate the mean for each numeric variable for each unique value of economic status variable:

```
library(plyr)
bardata <- ddply(ggplotdata,.(econ_status),summarize,meandisA=mean(disA),
meandisB=mean(disB),meandisC=mean(disC),meandisD=mean(disD))
```

In `ggplot2`, we need to transform the data in a layout where the variable names will be a value of a certain variable in order to produce multiple bar charts; this is sometimes called tidy data. Tidy data means that each row will contain information related to one variable and one observation. So, we will lay out the data in such a way that each row will contain information on a single variable and single observation. To produce the tidy data, we need to call the `reshape` library using the following code:

```
library(reshape)
bardata_tidy <- melt(bardata,id.vars="econ_status")
head(bardata_tidy)
```

Now, we will use this data to produce multiple bar charts.

How to do it...

The basic code that produces multiple bar charts using `ggplot2` is as follows:

```
ggplot(data= bardata_tidy, aes(x=econ_status, y=value, fill=variable))
+ geom_bar(stat="identity",position="dodge")
```

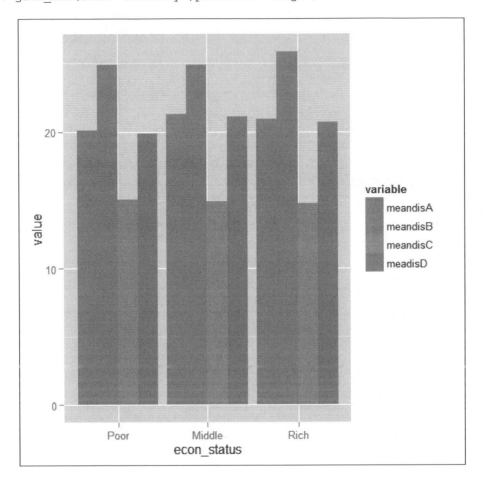

How it works...

The task for each argument can be described as follows:

> ► `data`: This is the input dataset for the plot.

- ▶ `aes`: This specifies the x- and y-axis variables and the third variable that specifies the values for grouping the plots for multiple bars.

- ▶ `geom_bar()`: This is the actual bar chart command. There are some arguments within it that control the bar width, position, and even the mapping information.

- ▶ `position`: This argument specifies the position of each bar—whether it will be side-by-side or one on top of the other like a stacked bar.

There's more...

With the basic plot, we can add other graph annotations, but we are not discussing the graph annotation here. We will have a separate recipe on graph annotations. If we want to change the layout of the bar plot to horizontal, then we can flip the coordinate system as follows:

```
# To make horizontal bar chart
ggplot(data= bardata_tidy, aes(x=econ_status, y=value, fill=variable))
+ geom_bar(stat="identity",position="dodge")+coord_flip()
```

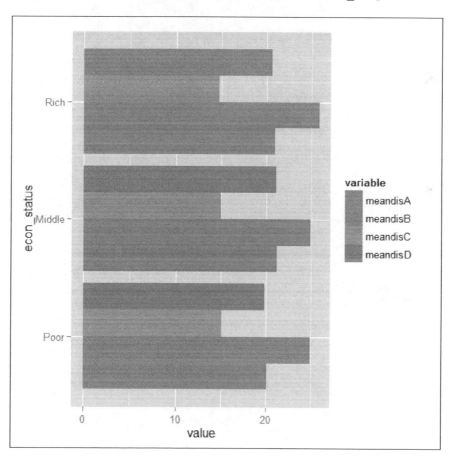

We can also produce a stack bar with the following position argument:

```
ggplot(data= bardata_tidy, aes(x=econ_status, y=value, fill=variable))
+ geom_bar(stat="identity",position="stack")
```

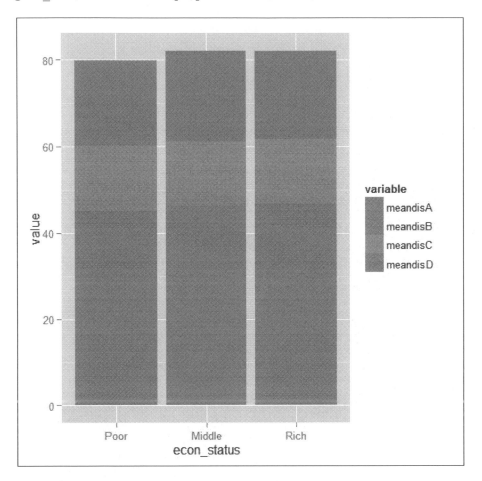

See also

Sometimes, we are interested in seeing the error bar with the usual bar chart. To produce an error bar with a bar chart, refer to the *Creating bar chart with error bars* recipe.

Creating a bar chart with error bars

A bar chart with error bars is another commonly used data visualization technique. In this recipe, we will produce a bar chart with error bars.

Getting ready

To produce a bar chart with error bars, we need to process the dataset in such a way that we have the relevant data at hand. In fact, to produce the error bar, we need to have the standard error of the mean that can be transformed into the lower and upper limit. To make this happen, we will call `ggplotdata` first, and then will do some processing using the following code:

```
# Summarizing the dataset to calculate mean
# calculating margin of error for 95% confidence interval of mean
bardata <- ddply(ggplotdata,.(econ_status),summarize,n=length(d
isA),meandisA=mean(disA),sdA=sd(disA),errMargin= 1.96*sd(disA)/
sqrt(length(disA)))

# transforming the dataset to calculate
# lower and upper limit of confidence interval
bardata <- transform(bardata, lower= meandisA-errMargin,
upper=meandisA+errMargin)
```

Now, we will use `bardata` to produce the bar chart with the error bar representing a 95 percent confidence interval of the mean.

How to do it...

To produce a bar chart with an error bar, firstly, we will create the basic bar chart with the following code and store it in an R object, which is `errbar`:

```
errbar <- ggplot(data= bardata, aes(x=econ_status, y=meandisA)) +
geom_bar(stat="identity")
```

The preceding code will produce the bar chart, but it will not display the output until we call the object separately. Now, we will add the error bar with the basic chart as follows:

```
errbar + geom_errorbar(aes(ymax=upper,ymin=lower),data=bardata)
```

The plot looks like what is shown in the following figure:

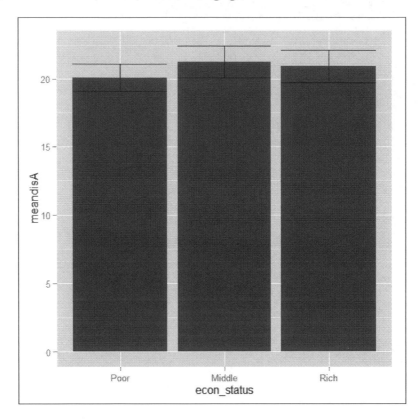

How it works...

The main mechanism of this plot is the data processing itself. We need to create the variables for each part of the bar chart. In this case, our objective was to create a bar chart of the mean of the `disA` variable over the category of economic status. At the same time, we wanted to create the error bar in order to represent a 95 percent confidence interval of each mean. So, we have created variables for the mean and the lower and upper limit of a 95 percent confidence interval.

Once we have the data in hand, we can just produce the bar chart following the basic command. To add the error bar, we need to add a layer to the existing plot using `geom_errorbar()`. Within `geom_errorbar()`, we used the lower and upper limit of the 95 percent confidence interval as the minimum and maximum value of the y-axis.

There's more...

Initially, the bar width looks very thick, and we can easily control this using the `width` argument within the `geom_bar()` function. We can do the following with the basic bar chart:

- To change the bar width: `geom_bar(width=0.5)`
- To change the fill color of each bar: `geom_bar(fill="green")`
- To change the bar outline color: `geom_bar(col=="red")`
- To flip the orientation: `coord_flip()`

Now, it's your turn to try the various options in order to play with the bar charts.

Visualizing the density of a numeric variable

The density plot is mostly used to compare distributions of two numeric variables or a single numeric variable over the category of other variables. In this recipe, we will produce a density plot using the `ggplot2` library.

Getting ready

To display the density, we will recall `ggplotdata` here and will use the `disA` variable to display the density plot.

How to do it...

To create a density plot, the basic code is as follows:

```
ggplot(data=ggplotdata,aes(x=disA))+geom_density()
```

The following figure shows us the visual output of the preceding code:

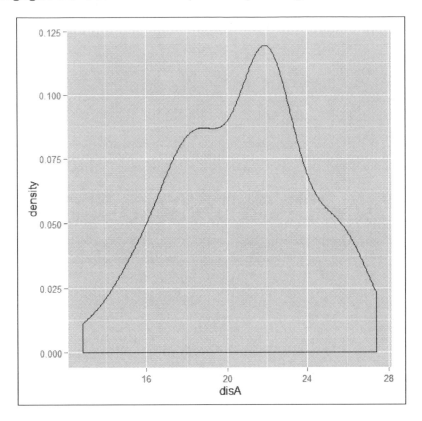

How it works...

The basic command is the same with `ggplot()`, but the main visualization is produced by the `geom_density()` part of the function.

There's more...

With the basic command, we can use another argument to modify the original visualization, such as the color and fill, and we can add other layers to the plot as well.

Creating a box plot

A box plot is another important graph that summarizes the data along with the distribution. In this recipe, we will produce a box plot to visualize the data summary with the distribution using the `ggplot2` implementation.

Getting ready

Recall `ggplotdata` for this recipe; we will use the `disB` numeric variable over the category of the `sex` variable in order to produce a box plot.

How to do it...

The primary code to produce a boxplot is as follows:

```
ggplot(data=ggplotdata,aes(y=disB,x=sex))+geom_boxplot()
```

The following figure shows us the visual output of the preceding code:

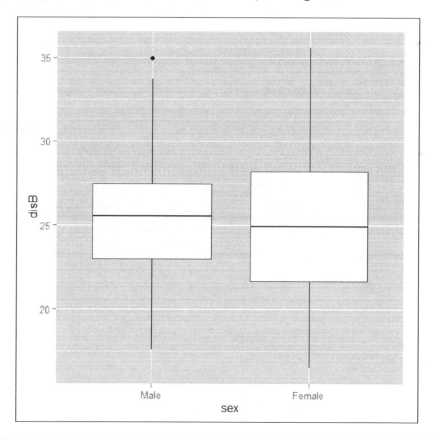

How it works...

The main visualization is produced by the `geom_boxplot()` part of the function. The `ggplot` function takes the argument of the data frame that we want to use, along with the x- and y-axis variable names. The `geom` part maps the data and produces the actual visualization.

Creating a layered plot with a scatter plot and fitted line

To visualize a relation between two numeric variables, we usually create a scatter plot. We also add a fitted line or smooth curve to the scatter plot, which represents the majority of the data points. In this recipe, we will see how we can produce a scatter plot and then add a layer of fitted line along with a linear smooth and curved line. The curved line could be the lowess or local regression, but here, is loess the default.

Getting ready

Once again, we recall `ggplotdata` for this plot. In this case, we will use the two numeric variables, which are `disA` and `disD`.

How to do it...

Perform the following steps:

1. We can easily produce the scatter plot with the `ggplot` function along with the `geom` point options, as follows:

   ```
   Sctrplot <- ggplot(data=ggplotdata,aes(x=disA,y=disD))+geom_
   point()
   ```

2. We will add a layer of fitted linear line to the scatter plot object, as follows:

   ```
   Sctrplot <- Sctrplot + geom_smooth(method="lm",col="red")
   ```

3. Now, we will add another layer to the curved line, as follows:

   ```
   Sctrplot + geom_smooth(col="green")
   ```

The visual output of this plot looks like what is shown in the following figure:

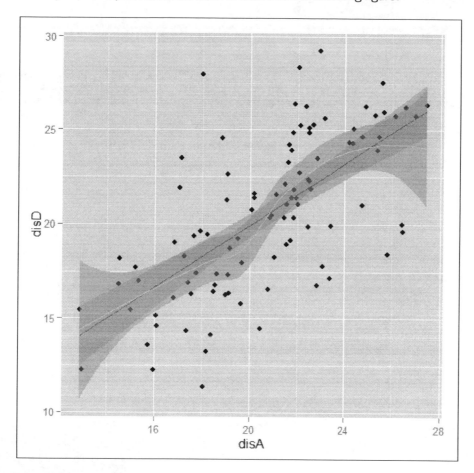

How it works...

Firstly, we created a plot object. Then, we added layers along with different visualizations one by one. The original plot was a scatter plot of two numeric variables. Then we added least square fitted line with the default 95 percent prediction interval. We then added another curved line with the default 95 percent confidence interval. To distinguish the two different lines, we used different colors.

There's more...

If we want to modify the line thickness and point patterns, we can use the arguments inside the corresponding `geom` parts.

Creating a line chart

Line charts are sometimes useful in order to view the pattern of a single variable against its index. Also, in some cases, bivariate connected lines are also useful. In this recipe, we will draw a line chart using `ggplot2` with `geom_line`.

Getting ready

Once again, we recall `ggplotdata` for this plot. In this case, we will use the two numeric variables, which are `disA` and `disD`.

How to do it...

To produce a connected line of a single numeric variable against its observation index, we will use the following code:

```
# connected line
ggplot(data=ggplotdata,aes(x=1:nrow(ggplotdata),y=disA))+geom_line()
```

The line chart produced is shown in the following figure:

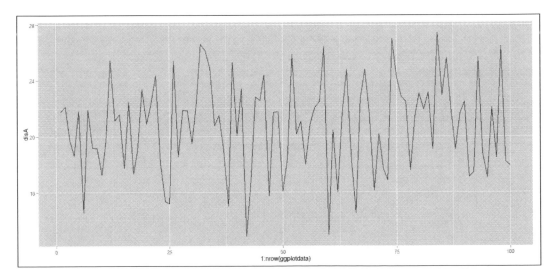

How it works...

The single variable's connected line looks like a time series plot, but the difference is that this plot does not have the time axis. The x argument within aes() specifies the values of the x-axis. In this case, the value of x-axis is just the sequence number starting from 1 to the number of observations in the dataset. So, the aes() function internally produces coordinates in the x-y plane with x with the index value and y, takes the value from the disA variable, and then connects the points in order to produce the line.

To display the data points along with a connected line, we can use the following code:

```
# connected line with points
ggplot(data=ggplotdata,aes(x=1:nrow(ggplotdata),y=disA))+geom_
line()+geom_point()
```

There's more...

So far, we have produced a connected line of a single numeric variable. Now, in order to produce a different line with a different color—where color is based on other factor variables—we can use the col= argument within aes(). Here is how we can do this:

```
# connected line with points separated by factor variable
ggplot(data=ggplotdata,aes(x=1:nrow(ggplotdata),y=disA,col=sex))+ge
om_line()+geom_point()
```

The plot will look like what is shown in the following figure:

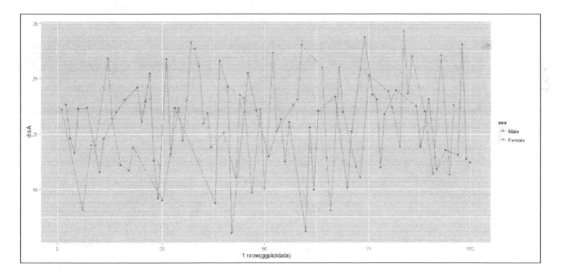

To produce a time series plot, the only thing that needs to be taken care of is that the x-axis should be a `date` variable. Here is a test case of a time series plot with the same data, but now, the x-axis is represented as a date:

```
ggplot(data=ggplotdata,aes(x=as.Date(1:nrow(ggplotdata),origin =
"2013-12-31"),y=disA,col=sex))+geom_line()+geom_point()
```

In this code snippet, the `as.Date(1:nrow(ggplotdata),origin = "2013-12-31")` part creates a sequence of dates starting with December 31, 2013 as the origin. So the first row of the data frame represents January 1, 2014, the second row represents January 2, 2014, and so on. The plot will be as follows:

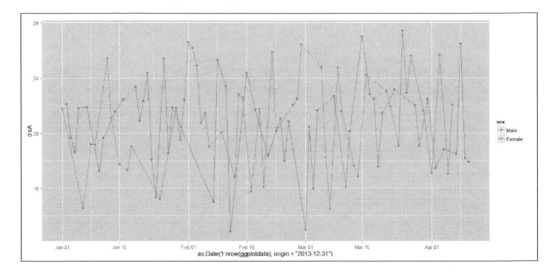

Graph annotation with ggplot

To produce a publication-quality data visualization, we often need to annotate the graph with various texts, symbols, or even shapes. In this recipe, we will learn how we can easily annotate an existing graph.

Getting ready

In this recipe, we will use the `disA` and `disD` variables from `ggplotdata`. Let's call `ggplotdata` for this recipe. We also need to call the `grid` and `gridExtra` libraries for this recipe.

How to do it...

In this recipe, we will execute the following annotation on an existing scatter plot. So, the whole procedure will be as follows:

1. Create a scatter plot.

2. Add customized text within the plot.

3. Highlight a certain region to indicate extreme values.

4. Draw a line segment with an arrow within the scatter plot to indicate a single extreme observation.

Now, we will implement each of the steps one by one:

```
library(grid)
library(gridExtra)
# creating scatter plot and print it
annotation_obj <- ggplot(data=ggplotdata,aes(x=disA,y=disD))+geom_
point()
annotation_obj

# Adding custom text at (18,29) position
annotation_obj1 <- annotation_obj + annotate(geom="text",x=18,y=29,lab
el="Extreme value",size=3)
annotation_obj1

# Highlight certain regions with a box
annotation_obj2 <- annotation_obj1+
annotate("rect", xmin = 24, xmax = 27,ymin=17,ymax=22,alpha = .2)
annotation_obj2

# Drawing line segment with arrow
annotation_obj3 <- annotation_obj2+
annotate("segment",x = 16,xend=17.5,y=25,yend=27.5,colour="red", arrow
= arrow(length = unit(0.5, "cm")),size=2)
annotation_obj3
```

The preceding four steps are displayed in the following single graph:

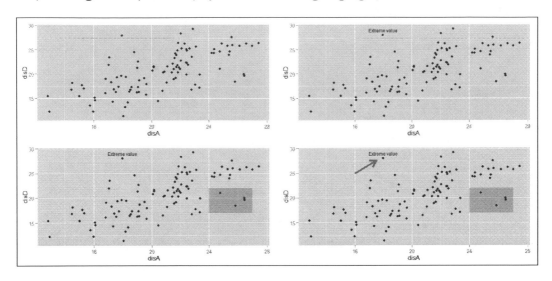

How it works...

The `annotate()` function takes input of a `geom` such as `"segment"` and `"text"`, and then it takes another input regarding position of that geom that is where to draw or where to place.. In this particular recipe, we used three `geom` instances, such as `text` to write customized text within the plot, `rect` to highlight a certain region in the plot, and `segment` to draw an arrow. The `alpha` argument represents the transparency of the region and `size` argument to represent the size of the text and line width of the line segment.

13
Inspecting Large Datasets

In this chapter, we will cover the following recipes:

- ▶ Multivariate continuous data visualization
- ▶ Multivariate visualization of categorical data
- ▶ Visualizing mixed data
- ▶ Zooming and filtering

Introduction

Exploratory data analysis is one of the most popular techniques to view patterns in data and the pattern of association among variables. In this chapter, we will learn how we can visualize multivariate data in a single plot where both continuous and categorical data can be graphed. The continuous variable can take any values, including decimal points; this can be the age of a person, height, or any numeric value, whereas categorical variables usually take a limited number of values, representing a nominal group. The examples of categorical variables include sex, occupation, and so on. In this chapter, we will use the `tabplot` library to produce the plot and view various options of this library.

We will create a dataset by modifying a default dataset in R, which is stored in the `mtcars` dataset. We will keep the same variables but with high amount of observation. The following are the variables that are present in the `mtcars` dataset:

- ▶ `mpg`: Miles/(US) gallon
- ▶ `cyl`: The number of cylinders
- ▶ `disp`: Displacement (cu.in)

- ▸ `hp`: The gross horsepower
- ▸ `drat`: The rear axle ratio
- ▸ `wt`: Weight (lb/1000)
- ▸ `qsec`: Quarter mile time
- ▸ `vs`: Versus
- ▸ `am`: Transmission (`0`= automatic, `1`= manual)
- ▸ `gear`: The number of forward gears
- ▸ `carb`: The number of carburetors

In this dataset, we will consider the `cyl`, `vs`, `am`, `gear`, and `carb` variables as categorical variables and the others as continuous variables. Now, we will modify this dataset to make the number of observations `1000` through empirical simulation by generating quantiles, as follows:

```
# calling mtcars dataset and store it in the dat object
dat <- mtcars

# set seed to make the data reproducible. Here reproducible
# means the code will create same dataset in each and every
# run in any computer
set.seed(12345)

# Generate 1000 random uniform number
# The random uniform number will be
# used as probability argument in quantile function
probs <- runif(1000)

# Generate each of the variables separately
mpg <- quantile(dat$mpg,prob=probs)
cyl <- as.integer(quantile(dat$cyl,prob=probs))
disp <- as.integer(quantile(dat$disp,prob=probs))
hp <- as.integer(quantile(dat$hp,prob=probs))
drat <- quantile(dat$drat,prob=probs)
wt <- quantile(dat$wt,prob=probs)
qsec <- quantile(dat$qsec,prob=probs)
vs <- as.integer(quantile(dat$vs,prob=probs))
am <- as.integer(quantile(dat$am,prob=probs))
gear <- as.integer(quantile(dat$gear,prob=probs))
carb <- as.integer(quantile(dat$carb,prob=probs))

# Make a new dataframe containing all the variables
# Some of the variables we converted to factor
```

```
# to represents as categorical variable
modified_mtcars <- data.frame(mpg,cyl=factor(cyl),
                      disp,hp,drat,wt,qsec,vs=factor(vs),
                      am=factor(am),gear=factor(gear),
                      carb=factor(carb))
row.names(modified_mtcars) <- NULL
```

Now, let's look at the actual recipe to see the pattern of this data.

Multivariate continuous data visualization

In this recipe, we will visualize multivariate data with all continuous variables. The plot will look like a table of a bar plot but the important feature of this plot is that we can easily understand the relationship among variables.

Getting ready

Let's call the modified mtcars dataset that we created in the introduction section. Then, we will take only the continuous variables for this recipe:

```
# Taking subset with only continuous variables
con_dat <- modified_mtcars[c("mpg","disp","drat","wt","qsec")]
```

To produce multivariable visualization, we need to call the tabplot library. If this is not preinstalled, then users can install it using the following command and then load it:

```
# To install tabplot library
install.packages("tabplot")

# Loading the library
library(tabplot)
```

How to do it...

The primary command structure for this visualization is as follows:

```
tableplot(con_dat)
```

The resultant plot is very much similar to a bar plot, but it contains all the variables at once. This enables us to quickly examine the patterns of relation among variables, anomalies, or even unusual observations.

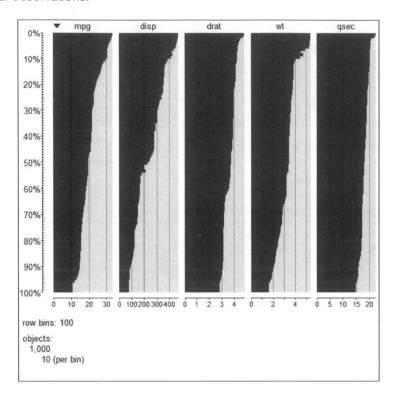

How it works...

By default, the `tableplot` function produces the visualization for each of the columns in the input dataset. Each column is divided into 100 bins (the default) and produces a horizontal bar plot. The dataset is sorted on the first column (the default). If there is any missing value in any column, then it automatically puts a category for that missing value and is represented by the color red.

There's more...

By default, the `tableplot` function produces the plot for all variables available in the input data, but we can change this using the argument within the function. The following is a list of arguments and their role within the `tableplot` function:

- ▸ nBin: This is to specify number of bins for the *y* axis. By default, it splits into 100 bins but we can control it using this argument. This is similar to the `nclass` argument within this function.

- ▸ select: If we are interested in plotting only a subset of variables, then we can specify the variable names using this argument, for example, select=c(mpg,wt). Note that in order to write a variable name, we do not need to include quotation marks ("").

- ▸ sortCol: The default sort order is based on the first variable in the input dataset, but we can change it using this argument, for example, sortCol=wt.

See also

To produce similar visualizations for categorical variables, refer to the *Multivariate visualization of categorical data* recipe.

Multivariate categorical data visualization

In this recipe, we will learn how we can visualize more than one categorical variable into a single plot and see what it looks like. The command structure will be similar, but this will be applicable for factor variables.

Getting ready

Let's call the modified mtcars dataset once again. After loading the modified mtcars dataset we will select a subset of that data by taking only the factor variables:

```
cat_dat <- modified_mtcars[c("cyl","vs","am","gear","carb")]
```

Now, we will use this data to produce a plot.

How to do it...

The command structure is the same as with the continuous data but the input variables are factors in this case:

```
tableplot(cat_dat,sortCol=carb)
```

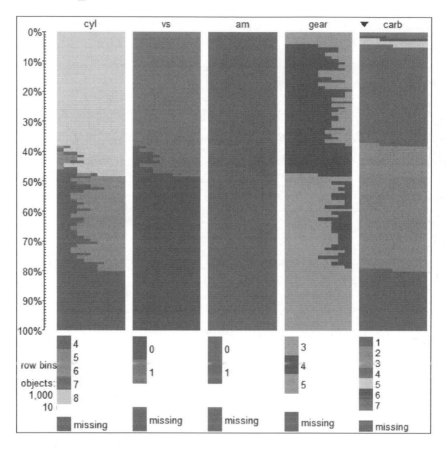

How it works...

Though the function to produce the plot is the same for both categorical and continuous data, for the categorical data, the tableplot function produces each bar with a different color, corresponding to each category in the variable. The noticeable feature is that we have to supply the factor variable for this plot. If we do not input the factor variable, then it automatically treats the input as a continuous variable during the plotting process.

There's more...

With the main plot, we can use different color palettes using the `pal` argument.

Visualizing mixed data

In this recipe, we will see the visualization of mixed data where both continuous and factor variables are present.

Getting ready

For this plot, we will use our modified `mtcars` data that we created earlier.

How to do it...

The command is similar as with continuous and categorical data; here is the code to create the plot:

```
tableplot(modified_mtcars)
```

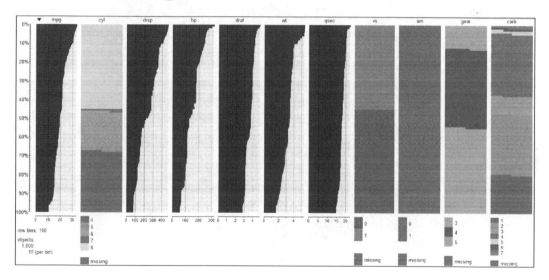

Zooming and filtering

Sometimes, we need to zoom in to see the special pattern in the dataset. In this recipe, we will see how we can zoom in to the plot with the use of a simple argument in the existing function.

Getting ready

Let's recall the same data with continuous variables only (`con_dat`). We want to create the plot with 20 to 50 percent of the data based on sorted variables.

How to do it...

The code to produce the plot by zooming into the `mpg` variable with 20 to 50 percent of the observation is as follows:

```
tableplot(con_dat,from=20,to=50,sortCol=mpg)
```

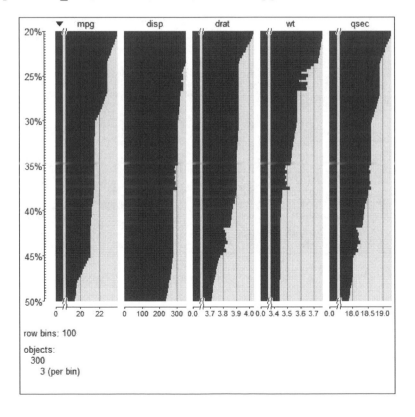

How it works...

The `from` and `to` arguments specify which part of the data needs to be used during plotting. These two arguments work on the variable that is mentioned in the `sortCol` argument. If `sortCol` is not specified, then the tableplot function takes the default sort column that is usually the first variable in the dataset by default.

There's more...

There is another argument for continuous variables, which is scales. With this argument, we can specify the mathematical transformation that is required to be performed with the continuous variables. For example, if we want to plot all the log-transformed continuous variables, then the code will look like the following code snippet. However, if we want to perform log transformation on some of the variables, then we need to perform that transformation separately:

```
tableplot(con_dat,from=20,to=50,sortCol=mpg,scales="log")
```

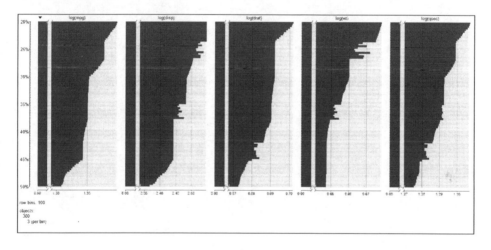

To filter the observation, we can use the `subset` argument. The `subset` argument is used to specify which observation we should use during plotting.

14
Three-dimensional Visualizations

In this chapter, we will cover the following recipes:

- ▶ Three-dimensional scatter plots
- ▶ Three-dimensional scatter plots with regression plane
- ▶ Three-dimensional bar charts
- ▶ Three-dimensional density plots

Introduction

In basic data visualization, we usually think about a two-dimensional plot, but in some situations, it is important to produce three-dimensional visualizations in order to see the relationship between variables. In this chapter, we will focus on three-dimensional visualizations using the R libraries in order to create three-dimensional plots. We will mainly cover the basic visualizations such as scatter plots, bar charts, kernel density plots, surface plots, and contour plots.

In this chapter, we will use the `airquality` dataset from the `datasets` library. This contains 153 observations with the following variables:

- ▶ `Ozone`: Ozone (the mean ozone in parts per billion (ppb) from 1300–1500 hours at Roosevelt Island)
- ▶ `Solar.R`: Solar R (the solar radiation in Langleys (lang) in the 4000–7700 Angstroms frequency band from 0800–1200 hours at Central Park)
- ▶ `Wind`: The wind (the average wind speed in miles per hour (mph) at 0700 and 1000 hours at LaGuardia Airport)

- ▸ `Temp`: The temperature (the maximum daily temperature in degrees Fahrenheit at LaGuardia Airport)
- ▸ `Month`: The month (1–12)
- ▸ `Day`: The day of the month (1–31)

For more details about the dataset, consult the help documentation of this dataset by writing `?airquality` in the R console. Now, let's enter the actual recipe to see the pattern of this data.

Three-dimensional scatter plots

A scatter plot is one of the simplest plots that help us view the relationship between two numeric variables. In this recipe, we will see how we can produce the scatter plot from three variables with a 3D plot. A 3D plot is good way to visualize the pattern of relation among three variables at a time. Sometimes, it could happen that a 3D plot is not depicting the relation pattern in a good shape; in this case, we might rotate the plot to find out the correct pattern. However, in this recipe, we will create a simple 3D scatter plot using three continuous variables.

Getting ready

To produce a three-dimensional scatter plot, we need to load the `scatterplot3d` library. If it is not already installed, then we can install it using the following command:

```
# To install scatterplot3d library
install.packages("scatterplot3d")

# Loading the library
library(scatterplot3d)
```

We will use the `airquality` dataset for this recipe.

How to do it...

The primary command to produce a three-dimensional scatter plot is as follows:

```
# Attach the dataset in the current environment
# so that we can call using the variable names
attach(airquality)

# Basic scatter plot in 3D space
scatterplot3d(Ozone,Solar.R,Wind)
```

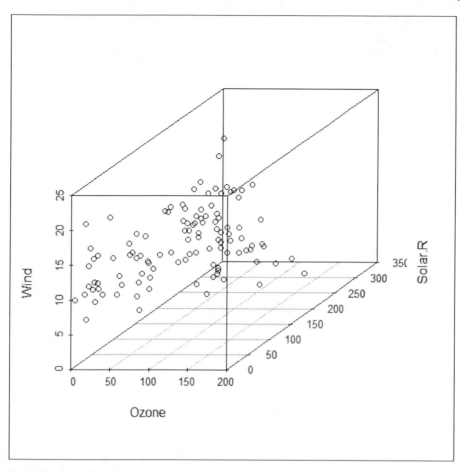

How it works...

The `scatterplot3d` function seeks three numeric variables as input in order to produce the plot in a three-dimensional space. If we do not specify a third variable, then it still produces a 3D scatter plot. If we specify only two variables, then two axes are represented by two variables, and the third axis is represented by a sequential number; the sequential number here acts as third variable.

There's more...

After creating the basic plot, we can add more information, such as a vertical drop line, by specifying the `type="h"` argument. Also, as we mentioned, if we do not specify the third variable, then it still produces the plot. An example of this situation is as follows:

```
# adding horizontal drop line
scatterplot3d(Ozone,Solar.R,Wind,type="h")
```

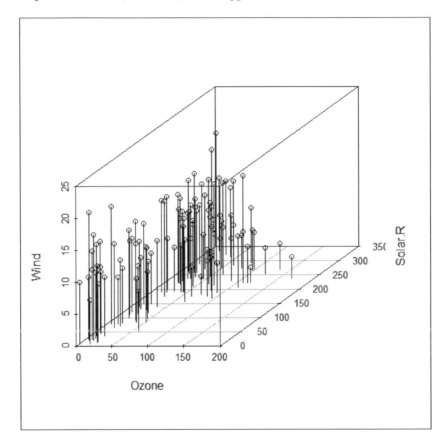

The code to create a three-dimensional scatter plot is as follows but this time we will only use two variable in the input. The third variable is not specified but still it will create a 3D scatter plot assuming the third variable is a sequential number:

```
scatterplot3d(Ozone,Solar.R)
```

See also...

► The *Three dimensional scatter plot with regression plane* recipe

Three-dimensional scatter plots with a regression plane

In this recipe, we will see how we can visualize a three-dimensional scatter plot with a fitted regression plane.

Getting ready

Let's recall the `airquality` data from the datasets library. In this particular recipe, we will use `Ozone` as a dependent variable and `Solar.R` and `Temp` as independent variables in order to fit the regression model, and then we visualized it.

How to do it...

To produce this plot, we will perform the following steps:

1. Attach the dataset using the `attach()` function.
2. Create a basic three-dimensional scatter plot and store it in an R object.
3. Fit the linear regression model, relating `Ozone` as a dependent variable and `Solar.R` and `Temp` as independent variables and store it as an R object. This regression model estimated the linear regression coefficient of the independent variables in relation to the dependent variable.
4. Plot the fitted regression object with the initial scatter plot.

Here is the R code that performs the preceding steps:

```
attach(airquality)
s3dplot<- scatterplot3d(Temp,Solar.R,Ozone)
model <- lm(Ozone~Solar.R+Temp)
s3dplot$plane3d(model)
```

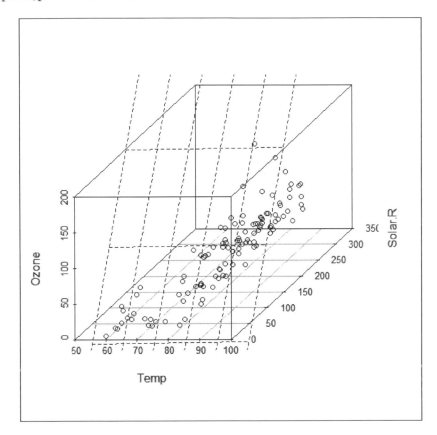

How it works...

The `scatterplot3d` function produces the basic scatter plot for the three input numeric variables. The fitted line (the plane, in this case) is then embedded with the scatter plot using the `plane3d` function.

There's more...

We can now add a horizontal drop line with the existing plot using the `type="h"` argument. There are other arguments to write the customized axis labels and plot title, such as `xlab`, `ylab`, and `main`.

Three-dimensional bar charts

In this recipe, we will create a three-dimensional bar chart. The three-dimensional bar chart will follow the same command as that of a scatter plot, but we will utilize the drop-line functionality to produce this 3D visualization.

Getting ready

Let's call the `airquality` dataset. In this particular recipe, we will use the `Day`, `Month`, and `Temp` variables. The `Day` and `Month` variables will represent two axes, whereas `Temp` will represent the third axis that gives the value of the temperature.

How to do it...

The command used here is similar to the scatter plot with the drop line added, but this time, we will hide the point and just represent each bar based on the value of the third variable. Here is the code:

```
scatterplot3d(Day,Month,Temp,type="h",lwd=5,pch=" ",color="grey10")
```

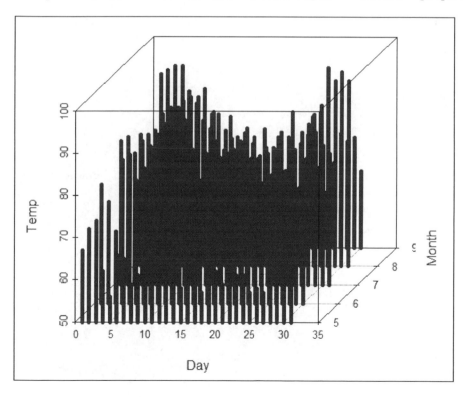

How it works...

The code that we used to produce the 3D bar chart is almost the same as the code that we used to produce a scatter plot. The noticeable feature of this code is that we have omitted the points using the `pch=" "` argument. Also, we increased the line width of the drop line so that it looks like a bar chart.

Three-dimensional density plots

In this recipe, we will see how we can produce a three-dimensional visualization of a bivariate density plot. The two variables will represent two axes, and the estimated density will represent the third axis, which allows us to produce a three-dimensional visualization in turn.

Getting ready

For this recipe, we will use the `airquality` data from the `datasets` library. Particularly, we will use the `Ozone` and `Temp` variables:

```
attach(airquality)
```

We are required to call the MASS library in order to use the `kde2d()` bivariate kernel density estimation function:

```
library(MASS)
```

How to do it...

We are aiming to estimate the bivariate kernel density estimate and then visualize it. The estimation command is as follows:

```
# To fill the NA values in the variables and create new variable
# Create new ozone variable
Ozone_new <- Ozone

#Fill the NA with median
Ozone_new[is.na(Ozone_new)]<-median(Ozone,na.rm=T)

#Create new Temp variable
Temp_new <- Temp

#Fill the NA with median
Temp_new[is.na(Temp_new)]<- median(Temp,na.rm=T)
```

```
#Bivariate kernel density estimation with automatic bandwidth
density3d <- kde2d(Ozone_new, Temp_new)

#Visualize the density in 3D space
persp(density3d)
```

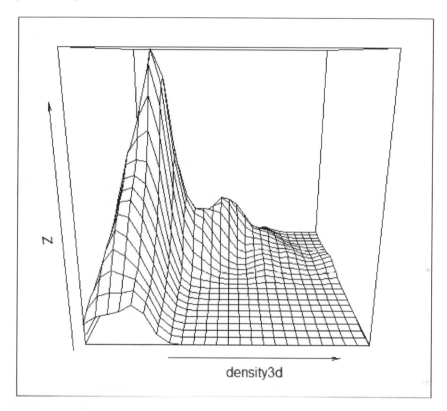

density3d

How it works...

The steps involved in producing 3D density plot are as follows:

1. Density estimation using the `kde2d()` function. Within this function, the required arguments are the two x and y variables for which we want to estimate the density. Then, the bandwidth h can be specified or it can be estimated automatically. We have used the default settings to estimate the bandwidth value.

2. Using the `persp()` function to visualize the density in a 3D space.

3. The z axis represents the estimated probability density of the bivariate density function.

15
Finalizing Graphs for Publications and Presentations

In this chapter, we will cover the following recipes:

- ▶ Exporting graphs to high-resolution image formats – PNG, JPEG, BMP, and TIFF
- ▶ Exporting graphs to vector formats – SVG, PDF, and PS
- ▶ Adding mathematical and scientific notations (typesetting)
- ▶ Adding text descriptions to graphs
- ▶ Using graph templates
- ▶ Choosing font families and styles under Windows, OS X, and Linux
- ▶ Choosing fonts for PostScripts and PDFs

Introduction

In the previous chapters of this book, we learned how to make graphs of different types and styles using various functions and arguments. In this chapter, we will learn some tricks and tips to add some polish to our graphs so that they can be used for publication and presentation.

We will look at the different image file formats we can save our graphs in and learn how to export our graphs at high resolutions. Most publications require authors to submit high resolution figures along with their manuscripts. We will also look in more detail at vector formats such as PDF, SVG, and PS, which are preferred by most publications as these are resolution-independent formats.

We will also learn how to add mathematical and scientific notations to graphs. These are indispensable in any scientific data visualization. We will also see how to add text descriptions inside graphs, which can be very handy as slides for presentation. Graph templates are a way to save time by creating functions, which cut down repetitive code so that, once we are happy with the basic structure of a graph, we can experiment with various predefined themes to choose the most appropriate color combinations and styles.

Finally, we will also look at how to choose fonts under different operating systems and graphic devices. We will also learn how to add new font mappings and to choose additional font families for vector file formats.

As with the previous chapters, it is best to try out each recipe first with the example shown here and then with your own datasets so that you can fully understand each line of code. If you are preparing any graph for publication or presentation, it is also good practice to print out the saved graphs and verify that the printed output looks correct and clear.

Exporting graphs in high-resolution image formats – PNG, JPEG, BMP, and TIFF

In this recipe, we will learn how to save graphs in high-resolution image formats for use in presentations and publications.

Getting ready

We will only use the base graphics functions for this recipe. So, just run the R code at the R prompt. You might wish to save the code as an R script so that you can use it again later.

How to do it...

Let's re-create a simple scatter plot example from *Chapter 1*, *R Graphics*, and save it as a PNG file 600 px high and 600 px wide with a resolution of 200 dots per inch (dpi):

```
png("cars.png",res=200,height=600,width=600)

plot(cars$dist~cars$speed,
main="Relationship between car distance and speed",
xlab="Speed (miles per hour)",ylab="Distance travelled (miles)",
xlim=c(0,30),ylim=c(0,140),
xaxs="i",yaxs="i",col="red",pch=19)

dev.off()
```

The resulting `cars.png` file looks like the following figure:

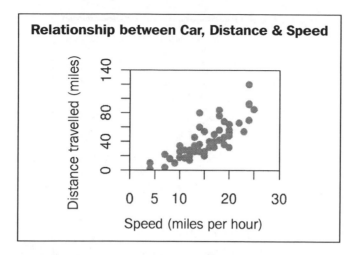

The pictured graph has a high resolution but the layout and formatting has been lost. So, let's create a high-resolution PNG while preserving the formatting:

```
png("cars.png",res=200,height=600,width=600)

par(mar=c(4,4,3,1),omi=c(0.1,0.1,0.1,0.1),mgp=c(3,0.5,0),
las=1,mex=0.5,cex.main=0.6,cex.lab=0.5,cex.axis=0.5)

plot(cars$dist~cars$speed,
main="Relationship between car distance and speed",
xlab="Speed (miles per hour)",ylab="Distance travelled (miles)",
xlim=c(0,30),ylim=c(0,140),
xaxs="i",yaxs="i",
col="red",pch=19,cex=0.5)

dev.off()
```

The resulting PNG file looks like the following figure:

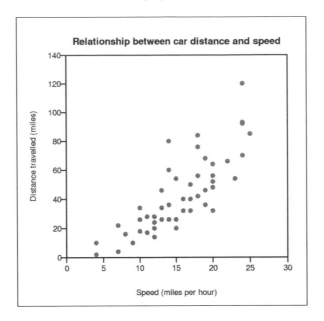

How it works...

To save our graph as a high-resolution PNG (200 dpi), we set the `res` argument of the `png()` function to a value of `200`. The default value of `res` is `72`. We also set both the `height` and `width` arguments to `600`.

In the first example, we can see that simply specifying the resolution and dimensions of the PNG file is not enough. The resultant image loses its original formatting and layout. In addition to specifying the resolution and size, we also need to re-adjust the margins and sizes of various graph elements, including the data points, axes, plot titles, and axis labels. We set these parameters using the `par()` function and its arguments as we learned in *Chapter 1, R Graphics*, and *Chapter 3, Beyond the Basics – Adjusting Key Parameters*.

To save the graphs as even higher resolution images, we will again need to adjust the relative margins and sizes of the graph components.

There's more

To save a graph in other formats such as JPEG, BMP, and TIFF, we can use the `res` argument in the `jpeg()`, `bmp()`, and `tiff()` functions, respectively.

In the next recipe, we will learn how to save graphs in vector formats.

Exporting graphs in vector formats – SVG, PDF, and PS

In this recipe, we will learn how to save graphs in vector formats such as PDF, SVG, and PostScript (PS), which are resolution-independent.

Getting ready

Once again we will use the basic graph functions. So, just make sure that you have started R and type in the code at the R prompt.

How to do it...

Let's use the same scatter plot example from the previous recipe and save it in different vector formats, starting with PDF:

```
pdf("cars.pdf")

plot(cars$dist~cars$speed,
main="Relationship between car distance and speed",
xlab="Speed (miles per hour)",ylab="Distance travelled (miles)",
xlim=c(0,30),ylim=c(0,140),
xaxs="i",yaxs="i",
col="red",pch=19,cex=0.5)

dev.off()
```

Similarly, we can save the graph as SVG or PS using the `svg()` and `postscript()` functions, respectively:

```
svg("3067_10_03.svg")
#plot command here
dev.off()

postscript("3067_10_03.ps")
#plot command here
dev.off()
```

How it works...

The vector format export commands are similar to the image format commands we saw in the previous recipe. First, we open a new device by calling the `pdf()`, `svg()`, or `postscript()` functions with the output filename as its only argument, then issue the plot command, and finally close the device with `dev.off()`.

Windows users will have to use the `CairoSVG()` command in order to export files to the SVG format. First, import the `Cairo` package:

```
install.packages("Cairo")
library(Cairo)
```

Then, use the following commands:

```
CairoSVG("3067_10_03.svg")
#plot command here
dev.off()
```

As vector formats are resolution-independent, you can zoom in or out of them without losing any clarity of the graph. Size does not affect the resolution. So, unlike the image formats in the previous recipe, we did not have to re-adjust the graph margins and component sizes to save the graph as PDF, SVG, or PS.

There's more

We can save more than one graph in a single PDF file by setting the `onefile` argument to `TRUE` (the default value). This is a useful output for presentations. All we have to do is issue the `pdf()` command with the output file name, then issue all the plot commands in the desired order, and close the device with `dev.off()`. For example, let's make three variations of the cars plot with three different colors for the data points and save them into one file:

```
pdf("multiple.pdf")

for(i in 1:3)
  plot(cars,pch=19,col=i)

dev.off()
```

Another important setting when saving graphs in vector formats is the color model. Most publications require authors to use the **CMYK** (**Cyan Magenta Yellow Key**) color model in their graphs, instead of the default **RGB** (**Red Green Blue**) model. We can save our graphs as PDFs or postscripts with the CMYK color model simply by setting the `colormodel` argument to `cmyk`:

```
pdf("multiple.pdf",colormodel="cmyk")

for(i in 1:3)
  plot(cars,pch=19,col=i)

dev.off()
```

By default, `colormodel` is set to `rgb`. The other possible value is `gray` for grayscale.

Adding mathematical and scientific notations (typesetting)

Producing graphs for scientific journals is rarely ever done without adding some special scientific and mathematical notations, such as subscripts, superscripts, symbols, and other notations. In this recipe, we will learn how to add these to annotations to our graphs.

Getting ready

We will only use base graphics functions for this recipe. So, just open up the R prompt and type in the following code. We will use the `airpollution.csv` example dataset for this recipe. So, let's first load it:

```
air<-read.csv("airpollution.csv")
```

How to do it...

Let's make a scatter plot of concentrations of particulate matter versus nitrogen oxides and add titles with subscripts as in PM10 and NOX and units mg m-3:

```
plot(air,las=1,
main=expression(paste("Relationship between ",PM[10]," and ",NO[X])),
xlab=expression(paste(NO[X]," concentrations (",mu*g^-3,")")),
ylab=expression(paste(PM[10]," concentrations (",mu*g^-3,")")))
```

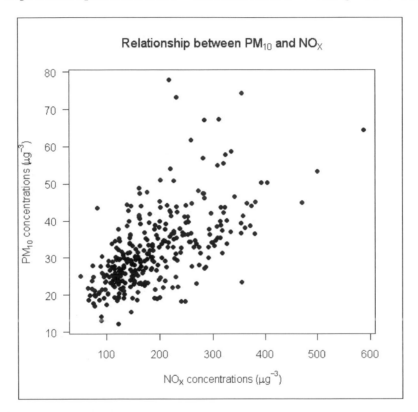

How it works...

In the example, we added three new elements of special formatting and notation: subscripts, superscripts, and a Greek symbol (m), using the `expression()` function.

The `expression()` function accepts arguments in a predefined syntax and translates them into the desired format or symbol. For example, any characters enclosed within square brackets [] are converted to subscripts, such as the X in NOX and 10 in PM10. Similary, any characters following the ^ sign are converted to superscripts, such as the -3 power value in mg m-3. The letters, `mu`, are converted to symbol m, denoting micro.

In the example, we used a combination of regular text and expressions by using the expression() function with the paste() function.

There's more

There are a lot more options and functions we can use inside expression() to create much more advanced notations than subscripts and superscripts. For example, integral(), frac(), sqrt(), and sum() can be used to create mathematical signs for integrals, fractions, square roots, and sums, respectively.

To see and learn all the possible options and symbols, run the following command at the R prompt:

```
demo(plotmath)
```

You will see the following symbols displayed on the plot device. You will need to press the *Return* or *Enter* key to progress through each set of symbols:

Arithmetic Operators		Radicals	
x + y	x + y	sqrt(x)	$\sqrt{x}$
x - y	x − y	sqrt(x, y)	$\sqrt[y]{x}$
x * y	xy	**Relations**	
x/y	x/y	x == y	x = y
x %+-% y	x±y	x != y	x ≠ y
x%/%y	x ÷ y	x < y	x < y
x %*% y	x×y	x <= y	x ≤ y
x %.% y	x·y	x > y	x > y
-x	−x	x >= y	x ≥ y
+x	+x	x %~~% y	x ≈ y
Sub/Superscripts		x %=~% y	x ≅ y
x[i]	x_i	x %==% y	x ≡ y
x^2	x^2	x %prop% y	x ∝ y
Juxtaposition		**Typeface**	
x * y	xy	plain(x)	x
paste(x, y, z)	xyz	italic(x)	*x*
Lists		bold(x)	**x**
list(x, y, z)	x, y, z	bolditalic(x)	***x***
		underline(x)	x̲

Ellipsis		Arrows	
list(x[1], ..., x[n])	$x_1, \ldots, x_n$	x %<->% y	$x \leftrightarrow y$
x[1] + ... + x[n]	$x_1 + \cdots + x_n$	x %->% y	$x \rightarrow y$
list(x[1], cdots, x[n])	$x_1, \cdots, x_n$	x %<-% y	$x \leftarrow y$
x[1] + ldots + x[n]	$x_1 + \ldots + x_n$	x %up% y	$x \uparrow y$
Set Relations		x %down% y	$x \downarrow y$
x %subset% y	$x \subset y$	x %<=>% y	$x \Leftrightarrow y$
x %subseteq% y	$x \subseteq y$	x %=>% y	$x \Rightarrow y$
x %supset% y	$x \supset y$	x %<=% y	$x \Leftarrow y$
x %supseteq% y	$x \supseteq y$	x %dblup% y	$x \Uparrow y$
x %notsubset% y	$x \not\subset y$	x %dbldown% y	$x \Downarrow y$
x %in% y	$x \in y$	**Symbolic Names**	
x %notin% y	$x \notin y$	Alpha - Omega	$A - \Omega$
Accents		alpha - omega	$\alpha - \omega$
hat(x)	$\hat{x}$	phi1 + sigma1	$\varphi + \varsigma$
tilde(x)	$\tilde{x}$	Upsilon1	Υ
ring(x)	$\overset{\circ}{x}$	infinity	∞
bar(xy)	$\overline{xy}$	32 * degree	$32°$
widehat(xy)	$\widehat{xy}$	60 * minute	$60'$
widetilde(xy)	$\widetilde{xy}$	30 * second	$30''$

Style	
displaystyle(x)	x
textstyle(x)	x
scriptstyle(x)	x
scriptscriptstyle(x)	x
Spacing	
x ~ ~y	$x \ \ y$

x + phantom(0) + y	$x + \quad + y$
x + over(1, phantom(0))	$x + \dfrac{1}{\ }$
Fractions	
frac(x, y)	$\dfrac{x}{y}$
over(x, y)	$\dfrac{x}{y}$
atop(x, y)	$\genfrac{}{}{0pt}{}{x}{y}$

Big Operators	
sum(x[i], i = 1, n)	$\sum\limits_{1}^{n} x_i$
prod(plain(P)(X == x), x)	$\prod\limits_{x} P(X = x)$
integral(f(x) * dx, a, b)	$\int\limits_{a}^{b} f(x)dx$
union(A[i], i == 1, n)	$\bigcup\limits_{i=1}^{n} A_i$
intersect(A[i], i == 1, n)	$\bigcap\limits_{i=1}^{n} A_i$
lim(f(x), x %->% 0)	$\lim\limits_{x \to 0} f(x)$
min(g(x), x >= 0)	$\min\limits_{x \geq 0} g(x)$
inf(S)	$\inf S$
sup(S)	$\sup S$

Grouping	
(x + y) * z	$(x+y)z$
x^y + z	$x^y + z$
x^(y + z)	$x^{(y+z)}$
x^{y + z}	x^{y+z}
group("(", list(a, b), "]")	$(a, b]$
bgroup("(", atop(x, y), ")")	$\binom{x}{y}$
group(lceil, x, rceil)	$\lceil x \rceil$
group(lfloor, x, rfloor)	$\lfloor x \rfloor$
group("|", x, "|")	$\|x\|$

Adding text descriptions to graphs

Sometimes, we might wish to add descriptions to a graph, say if we are producing a PDF for a presentation or as a handout with notes. In this recipe, we will learn how to add text descriptions in the margins of a graph, instead of having to add them separately in another program.

Getting ready

We are only using the base graphics functions for this recipe. So, just open up the R prompt and type in the following code. You might wish to save the code as an R script for later use.

How to do it...

Let's plot a random normal distribution and add a little bit of description after the graph:

```
par(mar=c(12,4,3,2))
plot(rnorm(1000),main="Random Normal Distribution")

desc<-expression(paste("The normal distribution has density ",
f(x) == frac(1,sqrt(2*pi)*sigma) ~ plain(e)^frac(-(x-mu)^2,2*sigma^2)))

mtext(desc,side=1,line=4,padj=1,adj=0)

mtext(expression(paste("where ", mu, " is the mean of the distribution
and ",sigma," the standard deviation.")),
side=1,line=7,padj=1,adj=0)
```

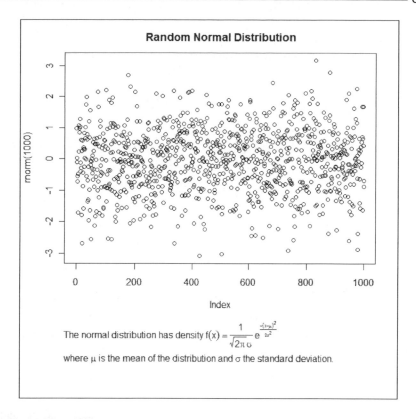

Random Normal Distribution

The normal distribution has density $f(x) = \dfrac{1}{\sqrt{2\pi}\,\sigma}\,e^{\frac{-(x-\mu)^2}{2\sigma^2}}$

where μ is the mean of the distribution and σ the standard deviation.

How it works...

In the example, we set the bottom margin of the plot to a high value and used the `mtext()` function to add a small description below the graph.

We created an expression called `desc` with the `expression()` function we saw in the previous recipe and used `mtext()` to place it in the fourth line of the bottom margin. To make the text top-left aligned, we set `padj` to 1 and `adj` to 0. We used `mtext()` again to place the other half of the description on the seventh line of the margin. We had to split the description into two halves and use `mtext()` twice because we couldn't automatically line-wrap an expression. We will soon see another example with a text-only description, where we can wrap it in just one `mtext()` function call.

There's more

Let's look at another example, where we add the description before the graph but just below the title. This time the description will just be plain text and will not contain any expressions. We will use the `dailysales.csv` example dataset and make a line graph of daily sales data:

```
dailysales<-read.csv("dailysales.csv")
```

```
par(mar=c(5,5,12,2))

plot(units~as.Date(date,"%d/%m/%y"),data=dailysales,type="l",
las=1,ylab="Units Sold",xlab="Date")

desc<-"The graph below shows sales data for Product A in the month of
January 2010. There were a lot of ups and downs in the number of units
sold. The average number of units sold was around 5000. The highest
sales were recorded on the 27th January, nearly 7000 units sold."

mtext(paste(strwrap(desc,width=80),collapse="\
n"),side=3,line=3,padj=0,adj=0)

title("Daily Sales Trends",line=10,adj=0,font=2)
```

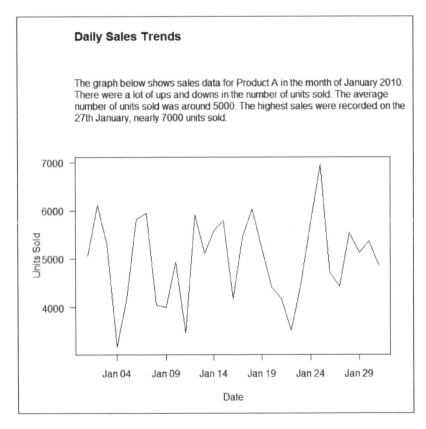

In the example, we set the margins such that the top margin is 12 lines wide. We created a string called `desc` with the description for the graph. We then used `mtext()` to place the string in the third line of the margin. We couldn't simply pass `desc` to `mtext()` because it wouldn't fit within the width of the plot area and would get chopped off after the first sentence. So, we used the `strwrap()` function to wrap the string with a width of 80 characters. We used the `paste()` function to join the split strings created by `strwrap()`, with line breaks added by setting the `collapse` argument to `"\n"`. Finally, we used the `title()` function to add a graph title on top.

Using graph templates

We might often find ourselves using similar code repetitively to plot similar kinds of data or different versions of the same dataset. Once we have analyzed our data and are looking to produce a finished graph, it can be useful to quickly try out different color combinations and other aesthetic settings without having to write too much repetitive code. In this recipe, we will learn how to create graph templates and use them to quickly try out various *looks* for a graph.

Getting ready

We will only use the base graphics functions for this recipe. So, just open up the R prompt and type in the following code. We will use the `themes.csv` file that contains theme parameters for this recipe. So, let's first load it:

```
themes<-read.csv("themes.csv")
```

How to do it...

We will make a simple scatter plot showing a random normal distribution and apply different color combination themes to it with a single command:

```
themeplot<-function(x,theme,...) {
    i<-which(themes$theme==theme)
    par(bg=as.character(themes[i,]$bg_color),las=1)

    plot(x,type="n",...)

    u<-par("usr")
    plotcol=as.character(themes[i,]$plot_color)
    rect(u[1],u[3],u[2],u[4],col=plotcol,border=plotcol)

    points(x,col=as.character(themes[i,]$symbol_color),...)
    box()
}
```

Using this function, we can create a scatter plot using different themes such as the following:

```
themeplot(rnorm(1000),theme="white",pch=21,main="White")
```

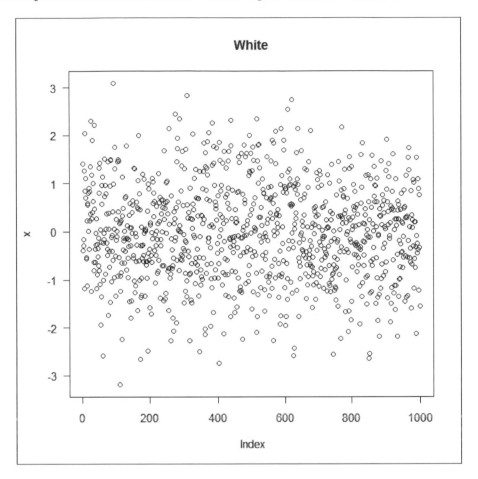

```
themeplot(rnorm(1000),theme="lightgray",pch=21,main="Light Gray")
```

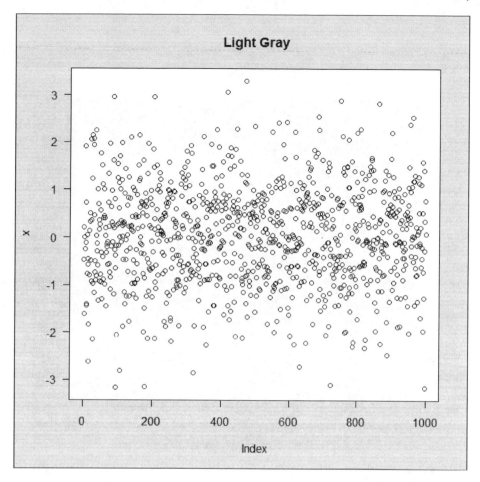

```
themeplot(rnorm(1000),theme="dark",pch=21,main="Dark")
```

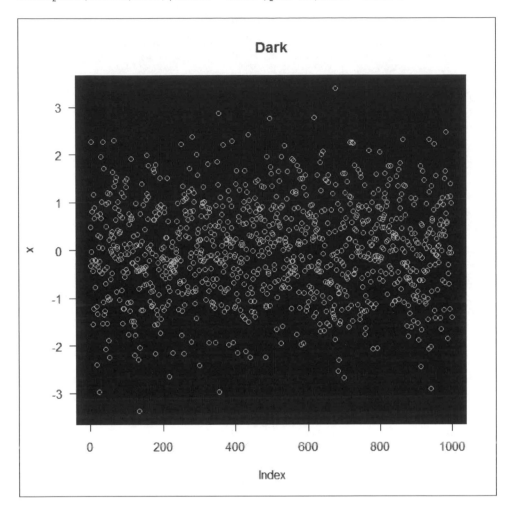

```
themeplot(rnorm(1000),theme="pink",pch=21,main="Pink")
```

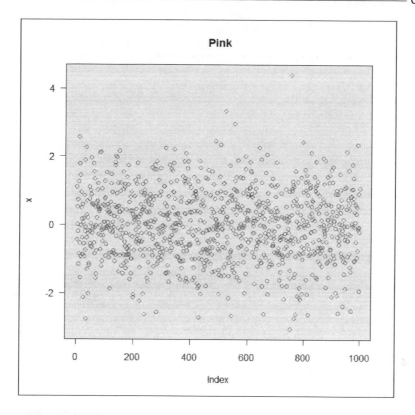

How it works...

In the preceding example, we created a function called `themeplot()` that used predefined color combinations from the `themes.csv` file to create different themed graphs.

We first read the `themes.csv` file into a data frame called themes that contains four columns:

- ▶ `theme`: This is the name of the theme
- ▶ `bg_color`: This is the figure background color
- ▶ `plot_color`: This is the color of the plot region
- ▶ `symbol_color`: This is the color of the plotting symbol

We then created the `themeplot()` function that accepted the plotting variable x and `theme` as arguments. The trailing " . . . " means that additional arguments can be passed; these are passed on to the specified functions within the `themeplot()` function definition. The `themeplot()` function uses the `which()` function to find the row index of the specified theme and then uses the corresponding column values to set the figure background color in `par()`, the plot region color in `rect()`, and the symbol color in `points()`.

Once the function is defined, all we have to do to try out different color combinations is pass the `theme` argument to `themeplot()`. If we wish to modify the color combinations or add new themes, we can simply edit the `themes.csv` file and re-read it. We can also adjust the function definition so that we can pass the color values separately to override the theme specifications.

There's more

In this example, we chose some very simple color parameters to demonstrate the usefulness of themes. However, we can easily add more columns to the themes definitions, such as symbol types, sizes, line types and colors, fonts, grid line styles, legend styles, and so on. It is best to work with your own dataset, define themes as you go along, and have a better idea of what your specific requirements are. Once you have decided on the structure of the graph you can define various themes to quickly experiment and choose from.

Choosing font families and styles under Windows, Mac OS X, and Linux

In this recipe, we will see how to choose font families and styles under the three most popular operating systems, namely, Windows, Mac OS X, and Linux.

Getting ready

We will only use the base graphics functions for this recipe. So, just open up the R prompt and type in the following code. You might wish to save the code as an R script for later use.

How to do it...

Let's look at all the basic default fonts available under Windows:

```
par(mar=c(1,1,5,1))
plot(1:200,type="n",main="Fonts under Windows",axes=FALSE,xlab="",yla
b="")

text(0,180,"Arial \n(family=\"sans\", font=1)",
family="sans",font=1,adj=0)
text(0,140,"Arial Bold \n(family=\"sans\", font=2)",
family="sans",font=2,adj=0)
text(0,100,"Arial Italic \n(family=\"sans\", font=3)",
family="sans",font=3,adj=0)
text(0,60,"Arial Bold Italic \n(family=\"sans\", font=4)",
family="sans",font=4,adj=0)
```

```
text(70,180,"Times \n(family=\"serif\", font=1)",
family="serif",font=1,adj=0)
text(70,140,"Times Bold \n(family-\"serif\", font-2)",
family="serif",font=2,adj=0)
text(70,100,"Times Italic \n(family=\"serif\", font=3)",
family="serif",font=3,adj=0)
text(70,60,"Times Bold Italic \n(family=\"serif\", font=4)",
family="serif",font=4,adj=0)

text(130,180,"Courier New\n(family=\"mono\", font=1)",
family="mono",font=1,adj=0)
text(130,140,"Courier New Bold \n(family=\"mono\", font=2)",
family="mono",font=2,adj=0)
text(130,100,"Courier New Italic \n(family=\"mono\", font=3)",
family="mono",font=3,adj=0)
text(130,60,"Courier New Bold Italic \n(family=\"mono\",
font=4)",
family="mono",font=4,adj=0)
```

Fonts under Windows

Arial
(family="sans", font=1)

Times
(family="serif", font=1)

Courier New
 (family="mono", font=1)

**Arial Bold
(family="sans", font=2)**

**Times Bold
(family="serif", font=2)**

**Courier New Bold
(family="mono", font=2)**

*Arial Italic
(family="sans", font=3)*

*Times Italic
(family="serif", font=3)*

*Courier New Italic
 (family="mono", font=3)*

***Arial Bold Italic
(family="sans", font=4)***

***Times Bold Italic
(family="serif", font=4)***

***Courier New Bold Italic
 (family="mono", font=4)***

How it works...

In this example, we demonstrated all the combinations of the basic font faces and families available in R under Windows. Fonts are specified in R by choosing a font family and a font face. There are three main font families: sans, serif, and mono, which are mapped on to specific fonts under different operating systems. As shown in the example, under Windows, sans maps to Arial, serif to Times New Roman, and mono to Courier New. The font family is specified by the `family` argument, which can be passed to the `text()` function (as in the example) or in `par()` (thus applied to all text in the plot), `mtext()`, and `title()`.

The font face can take four basic values denoted by the numbers 1 to 4, which stand for regular, bold, italic, and bold italic, respectively. The default value of font is 1. Note that font only applies to text inside the plot area. To set the font face for axis annotations, labels and the plot title, we need to use `font.axis`, `font.lab`, and `font.main`, respectively.

In this example, we created a plot area with the x and y coordinates running from 0 to 200 each, but suppressed drawing of any axes or annotations. Then, we used the `text()` function to draw text labels showing the twelve combinations of the three font families and four font faces.

There's more

As you might have noticed, we did not specify the names of the font families in the `text()` command. Instead, we used the keywords, `sans`, `serif`, and `mono`, to refer to the corresponding default fonts under Windows. We can check these font family mappings by running the `windowsFonts()` command at the R prompt, which lists the names of the fonts for each of the font families. We can also add new mappings using this function. For example, to add the Georgia font, we need to run:

```
windowsFonts(GE = windowsFont("Georgia"))
```

Then, we can just set family to `"GE"` to use the Georgia font:

```
text(150,80,"Georgia",family="GE")
```

Just as under Windows, there are default font families under Mac OS X and Linux. The serif and mono fonts are the same as in Windows. However, the sans font is usually Helvetica. To check the default font mappings and add new font families, we need to use the `X11Fonts()` and `quartzFonts()` functions under Linux and OS X, respectively.

See also

In the next recipe, we will see how to use additional font families available for vector formats such as PDF and PS.

Choosing fonts for PostScripts and PDFs

The `pdf` and `postscript` graphic devices in R have special functions that handle the translation of an R graphics font family name to a PostScript or PDF file. In this recipe, we will see how to choose the fonts for these vector formats.

Getting ready

We will only use the base graphics functions for this recipe. So, just open up the R prompt and type in the following code. You might wish to save the code as an R script for later use.

How to do it...

Let's create a PDF of an `rnorm()` graph with the title and axis annotations in the Avant Garde font:

```
pdf("fonts.pdf",family="AvantGarde")
plot(rnorm(100),main="Random Normal Distribution")
dev.off()
```

To save the same graph as a postscript file, we use the following code:

```
postscript("fonts.ps",family="AvantGarde")
plot(rnorm(100),main="Random Normal Distribution")
dev.off()
```

How it works...

As shown in the examples, the font family for a PDF or PostScript output is set exactly the same way as in the previous recipe, by using the `family` argument. In the examples, we passed the `family` argument to the `pdf()` and `postscript()` functions as they open the relevant graphics devices.

Note that we used a font family that was not available in the basic R graphics device. We can also use the default values `sans`, `serif`, and `mono`, which are mapped to Helvetica, Times New Roman, and Courier New, respectively. The `pdf` and `postscript` devices have inbuilt mappings to a lot of font families. To see all the available fonts, we can use the `pdfFonts()` command. Running `pdfFonts()` at the R prompt lists all the names of the font families and related attributes (metrics, encoding, and class). To list just the names of all font families, we can run the following line of code:

```
names(pdfFonts())
```

This line of code gives the following output at the R prompt:

```
 [1]  "serif"            "sans"                 "mono"
 [4]  "AvantGarde"       "Bookman"              "Courier"
 [7]  "Helvetica"        "Helvetica-Narrow"     "NewCenturySchoolbook"
[10]  "Palatino"         "Times"                "URWGothic"
[13]  "URWBookman"       "NimbusMon"            "NimbusSan"
[16]  "URWHelvetica"     "NimbusSanCond"        "CenturySch"
[19]  "URWPalladio"      "NimbusRom"            "URWTimes"
[22]  "Japan1"           "Japan1HeiMin"         "Japan1GothicBBB"
[25]  "Japan1Ryumin"     "Korea1"               "Korea1deb"
[28]  "CNS1"             "GB1"
```

We can check the default mapping to sans by running `pdfFonts()$sans` at the R prompt.

There's more

The `postscript` device has two extra fonts: Computer Modern and Computer Modern Italic (you can check this by running `names(postscriptFonts())` at the R prompt). Just like the commands for specific operating systems, we can use `pdfFonts()` and `postscriptFonts()` to add new font mappings for the `pdf` and `postscript` devices, respectively. Refer to the help section to see some examples of such mappings (`?postscriptFonts()` and `?pdfFonts()`).

Index

Symbol

3D plot 310

A

abline() function
  about 212
  used, for adding marker lines 126-128
  used, for adding vertical markers 138-140
aggregate() function 141
annotate() function 298
annotations
  fonts, setting 70-72
arrows() function 98, 161
as.Date() function 25, 133
as.matrix() function 40
axes, histograms
  adjusting 176-178
axis annotations
  about 65
  adjusting 80, 81
  colors, setting 66, 67
axis() command 202, 212
axis labels
  about 65
  colors, setting 67

B

barchart() command 255
bar charts
  borders, adjusting 153-155
  colors, adjusting 153-155
  creating 26-28, 254-257
  creating, ggplot2 library used 280-283
  creating, to visualize
      cross-tabulation 259-262
  creating, with error bars 287-289
  creating, with horizontal bar
      orientation 151-153
  creating, with multiple factor
      variable 146, 147
  creating, with vertical bar
      orientation 151-153
  creating, with vertical error bars 160-162
  labels, placing inside bars 159, 160
  space, adjusting 153, 154
  stacked bar charts, creating 257, 258
  values, displaying 156-158
  widths, adjusting 153, 154
  working 27, 28
bar colors, histograms
  adjusting 176-178
barplot() function 26, 184
bars
  colors, setting 58-62
base graphics
  about 7
  default package, using for 8, 9
borders, histograms
  adjusting 176-178
boxplot() command 33
boxplot() function 9, 35
box plots
  creating 33, 273-275
  creating, ggplot2 library used 291, 292
  creating, with narrow boxes 186-189
  creating, with notches 193, 194
  grouping, over variable 189-191
  number of observations, displaying 200-203
  styling 197, 198

variable, splitting at arbitrary
intervals 203-206
whiskers, adjusting 198-200
working 34, 35
box styles
selecting 77-79
box widths
varying 191, 192

C

calendar heat maps
time series data, visualizing 229-233
calendar.plot() function 232
closely packed data points
distinguishing, jitter() function used 99-101
CMYK (Cyan Magenta Yellow Key)
color model 325
color combinations
selecting 68-70
colors
of axis annotations, setting 66, 67
of axis labels, setting 67
of bars, setting 59-61
of legends, setting 67
of lines, setting 59-61
of plot titles, setting 67
of points, setting 58-61
Comprehensive R Archive Network. *See* **CRAN**
conditional histogram
creating 262-265
conditional scatter plot
creating 276-278
contour() function 9
contour plots
creating 221-223
correlation heat maps
creating 213-216
correlation matrix
creating, pairs plots used 94-96
CRAN
references 18
URL 18
cross-tabulation
visualizing, bar charts produced for 259-262

customized legends
adding, for multiple-line graphs 118-120

D

data
plotting, on Google maps 245-249
databaseBasketball
URL 216
data points
density, displaying on axes 111-113
grouping, within scatter plots 86-89
labeling 92-94
data visualization
lattice package, using 253
date variable
plotting, on x axis 134, 135
ddply()function 281
default package
used, for base graphics 8, 9
dendrograms
URL 40
density, data points
displaying, on axes 111-113
density() function 32
density line
overlaying, over histograms 179, 180
density plot
creating 29-32
creating, ggplot2 library used 289, 290
dev.off() command 56
dimensions
setting 83, 84
distributions
visualizing, kernel-density plot used 265-267
dotchart() function 26, 164
dot charts
modifying, with grouped variables 162-164
dots per inch (dpi) 56

E

empirical CDF (Cumulative
Distribution Function)
visualizing 270-272
errbar() function 99

Thank you for buying
R Graphs Cookbook
Second Edition

About Packt Publishing

Packt, pronounced 'packed', published its first book "*Mastering phpMyAdmin for Effective MySQL Management*" in April 2004 and subsequently continued to specialize in publishing highly focused books on specific technologies and solutions.

Our books and publications share the experiences of your fellow IT professionals in adapting and customizing today's systems, applications, and frameworks. Our solution based books give you the knowledge and power to customize the software and technologies you're using to get the job done. Packt books are more specific and less general than the IT books you have seen in the past. Our unique business model allows us to bring you more focused information, giving you more of what you need to know, and less of what you don't.

Packt is a modern, yet unique publishing company, which focuses on producing quality, cutting-edge books for communities of developers, administrators, and newbies alike. For more information, please visit our website: www.packtpub.com.

About Packt Open Source

In 2010, Packt launched two new brands, Packt Open Source and Packt Enterprise, in order to continue its focus on specialization. This book is part of the Packt Open Source brand, home to books published on software built around Open Source licenses, and offering information to anybody from advanced developers to budding web designers. The Open Source brand also runs Packt's Open Source Royalty Scheme, by which Packt gives a royalty to each Open Source project about whose software a book is sold.

Writing for Packt

We welcome all inquiries from people who are interested in authoring. Book proposals should be sent to author@packtpub.com. If your book idea is still at an early stage and you would like to discuss it first before writing a formal book proposal, contact us; one of our commissioning editors will get in touch with you.

We're not just looking for published authors; if you have strong technical skills but no writing experience, our experienced editors can help you develop a writing career, or simply get some additional reward for your expertise.

Practical Data Science Cookbook

ISBN: 978-1-78398-024-6   Paperback: 396 pages

89 hands-on recipes to help you complete real-world data science projects in R and Python

1. Learn about the data science pipeline and use it to acquire, clean, analyze, and visualize data.

2. Understand critical concepts in data science in the context of multiple projects.

3. Expand your numerical programming skills through step-by-step code examples and learn more about the robust features of R and Python.

Data Manipulation with R

ISBN: 978-1-78328-109-1   Paperback: 102 pages

Perform group-wise data manipulation and deal with large datasets using R efficiently and effectively

1. Perform factor manipulation and string processing.

2. Learn group-wise data manipulation using plyr.

3. Handle large datasets, interact with database software, and manipulate data using sqldf.

Please check **www.PacktPub.com** for information on our titles

Made in the USA
Lexington, KY
10 December 2016